D0821196

BEHAVIORAL ECONOMICS: A HISTORY

This book presents a history of behavioral economics. The recurring theme is that behavioral economics reflects and contributes to a fundamental reorientation of the epistemological foundations on which economics had been based since the days of Smith, Ricardo, and Mill. With behavioral economics, the discipline has shifted from grounding its theories in generalized characterizations to building theories from behavioral assumptions directly amenable to empirical validation and refutation. Central in this reorientation is the adoption of a normative-descriptive framework at the expense of economists' traditional positive-normative distinction. The book proceeds chronologically and takes the reader from von Neumann and Morgenstern's axioms of rational behavior, through the incorporation of rational decision theory in psychology from the 1950s through the 1970s and to the creation and rise of behavioral economics in the 1980s and the 1990s at the Sloan and Russell Sage Foundations.

Floris Heukelom is Assistant Professor of Economics, Radboud University Nijmegen. He specializes in the use of the experiment in twentieth-century economics and psychology. He has published in *Science in Context*, the *Journal of the History of the Behavioral Sciences*, *History of Political Economy*, and the *Journal of Economic Methodology*, among others.

HISTORICAL PERSPECTIVES ON MODERN ECONOMICS

General Editor: Craufurd D. Goodwin, Duke University

This series contains original works that challenge and enlighten historians of economics. For the profession as a whole, it promotes better understanding of the origin and content of modern economics

Continued after the Index

Behavioral Economics: A History

FLORIS HEUKELOM

Radboud University Nijmegen, Netherlands

CAMBRIDGE
UNIVERSITY PRESS

CAMBRIDGE
UNIVERSITY PRESS

32 Avenue of the Americas, New York, NY 10013-2473, USA

Cambridge University Press is part of the University of Cambridge.

It furthers the University's mission by disseminating knowledge in the pursuit of
education, learning, and research at the highest international levels of excellence.

www.cambridge.org
Information on this title: www.cambridge.org/9781107039346

© Floris Heukelom 2014

First published 2014

Printed in the United States of America

A catalog record for this publication is available from the British Library.

Library of Congress Cataloging in Publication Data
Heukelom, Floris, 1978–
Behavioral economics : a history / Floris Heukelom, Radboud University,
Nijmegen, Netherlands.
pages cm. – (Historical perspectives on modern economics)
Includes bibliographical references and index.
ISBN 978-1-107-03934-6 (hardback)
1. Economics – Psychological aspects.   I. Title.
HB74.P8H48   2014
330.01'9 – dc23   2013027829

ISBN 978-1-107-03934-6 Hardback

*To Marielle,
Kiki, & Pepijn*

Contents

Acknowledgments

From vigilant supervisors of the PhD thesis (2008) that lies at the basis of the present book, John Davis and Harro Maas became professional colleagues. This book owes much, if not everything, to them, and I feel proud to now count them among my friends. It is similarly difficult to overestimate the support of Jan Peil, Esther-Mirjam Sent, and Radboud University Nijmegen. By offering me a permanent position they provided the predictability of a stable job that allowed me to complete this project.

It seems impossible to thank all the individual members of the intellectual community of History of Economics in particular in which this book and its content were conceived, tested, challenged, and many times rewritten, so perhaps I may be forgiven for only thanking explicitly those who commented on the manuscript at various stages (in addition to the four above): Roger Backhouse, Mark Blaug[†], Marcel Boumans, Beatrice Cherrier, Annie Cot, Till Düppe, Ross Emmett, Philippe Fontaine, Craufurd Goodwin, Wade Hands, Klaas Landsman, Robert Leonard, Tiago Mata, Steve Medema, Phil Mirowski, Malcolm Rutherford, Andrej Svorencik, Roy Weintraub, and Carlo Zappia.

Furthermore, this book would not have been possible without the help of archivists at the various archives consulted. In particular, I would like to thank Rockefeller Archive Center's Amy Fitch, who not only keenly noted I might be interested in those unorganized boxes of Sloan/Sage behavioral economics material that had come in two days prior to my visit, but who also made me aware of a RAC grant-in-aid, with which I was subsequently able to study the files in those boxes more carefully.

A number of protagonists of my story were kind to answer queries by email, or in longer face-to-face interviews, including William Baumol, Robyn Dawes, Gerd Gigerenzer, Lyle Jones, Daniel Kahneman, David Krantz, George Loewenstein, James March, Robert Pachella, Stephen

Richards, Timothy Taylor, Richard Thaler, Barbara Tversky, and Eric Wanner. Dave Krantz may not have realized how much his enthusiasm to openly discuss mathematical psychology's early history at the University of Michigan and his permission to draw on his correspondence with Amos Tversky advanced my understanding of this period and topic. Similarly, I cannot but admire and deeply thank Eric Wanner's willingness to extensively discuss the history of the Sloan/Sage behavioral economics project, and to make available its archival records.

As the editors of Cambridge University Press, Craufurd Goodwin, Scott Parris, and Kristin Purdy courageously accepted my idea to publish a book on the history of behavioral economics and devised a reviewing process that turned my manuscript into a book. I would like to sincerely thank the three anonymous reviewers for the innumerable helpful suggestions and comments they offered, but at least as importantly also because of the triangulation of perspectives they offered, which in a way made me read my own manuscript.

The material in this book relies on a number of articles I have previously published. Chapter 3 is an extended and amended version of "Measurement and Decision Making at the University of Michigan in the 1950s and 1960s." *Journal of the History of the Behavioral Sciences* (2010), 46(2): 187–205. Parts of Chapter 4 draw on parts of "Three Explanations for the Kahneman-Tversky Programme of the 1970s." *The European Journal of the History of Economic Thought* (2012), 19(5): 797–828. Chapter 5 combines and extends "What to Conclude from Psychological Experiments: The Contrasting Cases of Experimental and Behavioral Economics." *History of Political Economy* (2011), 43(4): 649–682; as well as "A Sense of Mission – The Alfred P. Sloan and Russell Sage Foundations Behavioral Economics Program, 1984–1992." *Science in Context* (2012), 25(2): 263–283. Chapter 6 draws on "Building and Defining Behavioral Economics." *Research in History of Economic Thought and Methodology* (2011), 29: 1–29.

While writing this book I fell in love with Marielle and became the proud father of Kiki and Pepijn. It is to them I dedicate this book.

Introduction

In economics, the market has been understood to steer behavior toward a competitive equilibrium in which all economic actors behave optimally and in which welfare of society is maximized. Yet many economists have also seen shortcomings to this ideal picture of the market in the forms of limited information, too few buyers or sellers, adverse selection, moral hazards, and other caveats. What psychologists Daniel Kahneman and Amos Tversky brought to economics in the 1980s was the idea that imperfections in the market may, in addition, be caused by fallible human behavior. This resulted in a new branch of economics called behavioral economics, and it won Kahneman the Nobel Memorial Prize in Economics in 2002 (Tversky died in 1996). This book presents a history of behavioral economics.

The common rationale of behavioral economics in the 1980s through the 2000s was in one version or another that "[b]ehavioral economics increases the explanatory power of economics by providing it with more realistic psychological foundations" (Camerer and Loewenstein, 2004, p. 3). This definition conceals a complicated relationship between economics and psychology that goes back at least to the eighteenth century. In addition, it suggests that economics and psychology are stable, universal entities. But the label of behavioral economics itself also seems odd. If economics deals with the behavior of individuals in the economy, "behavioral economics" seems a confusing pleonasm. If, on the other hand, one argues that economics by definition deals with structures and institutions superseding and being independent of theories of human behavior, "behavioral economics" seems oxymoronic. In any case, it calls for some explanation.

In the late eighteenth and early nineteenth centuries of Adam Smith and David Ricardo, the purpose of an economy was understood to be the production of *Wealth of Nations* (the title of Smith's famous book of 1776).

Philosophically, this wealth of nations was argued to be roughly equal to the utility of utilitarianism, as first advanced by Jeremy Bentham around the same time. The objective of the nation's rulers, then, was (or should have been) to increase the wealth or utility of the nation. By exploring the functioning of the economy, (political) economists' objective was to set out how rulers could do so.

Expositions by economists of the working of the economy were based on what were called, principles, doctrines, or premises. These principles partly characterized the economic system, such as Ricardo's famous "true doctrine of rent," which characterized rent as only a remuneration for land and not for capital in the form of fences or buildings that may have been erected on the land. Other principles or doctrines, however, characterized the behavior of individuals in the economy. Examples included the pursuit of wealth and an aversion to labor.

It will be no surprise that questions were raised about how these principles of human behavior in the economy were established and about how they related to other philosophical or scientific investigations of human behavior. The answer by the revolutionary triad of William Stanley Jevons, Carl Menger, and Leon Walras in the 1870s was to redefine Bentham's concept of utility from a measure of the wealth of a nation into a measurement of the mental state of a hedonistic economic subject. Thus, utility was no longer a relatively vague and general concept for the wealth of a nation as a whole, but was an empirical measurement of pleasure derived by individuals. Jevons in particular advanced psychophysics as the means to provide the scientific basis for this reinterpretation of utility. Only ten years earlier, in the 1860s, the new field of psychophysics had risen from work by Gustav Fechner, Ernst Weber, and Wilhelm Wundt and had aimed to base all claims regarding human behavior and the human mind in empirical, and preferably experimental research (as opposed to philosophical speculation). The so-called marginalist revolution of Jevons, Menger, and Walras thus grounded economics explicitly in psychology.

That, however, was merely the start of discussions. One fundamental problem was that it was very difficult to measure this psychophysical utility individuals derive from their economic behavior. What was possible for psychophysicists' carefully controlled experiments with weights and balances, proved impossible in economics. A solution to these methodological difficulties that seemed fruitful for a while was the indifference curve analysis advanced by Francis Ysidro Edgeworth from the 1880s onward. The indifference curve is the idea that between two available goods there are combinations of different quantities of the two goods between which the individual is indifferent. For instance, the individual may be indifferent about (a) two glasses of beer and one glass of wine and (b) one glass of beer and two glasses of wine. The curve that connects all combinations of glasses of beer and glasses of wine between which the individual is indifferent is called the indifference curve. In the end, however, it proved equally difficult to find a proper method to construct indifference curves from the data of the economy and economic behavior at hand, so that by the mid-1930s indifference curves were also finally disbanded as incapable of providing a solid scientific foundation for economics.

As sixty years earlier, psychology seemed to offer a solution, this time in the form of behaviorism. Behaviorism was a scientific program developed by John Broadus Watson, Burrhus Frederick Skinner and others, which reigned in U.S. psychology in the 1920s and 1930s. Behaviorism argued that all human behavior is only a response to external stimuli (present and past) and, hence, that all behavior can be explained by relating observed behavior to stimuli that the individual is and has been exposed to. In consequence, all references to internal states of mind were redundant.

Inspired by behaviorism, Paul Samuelson argued from the late 1930s onward that also in economics only observed behavior by individuals should be used as a basis for scientific reasoning. Samuelson's new theory of "revealed preference" assumed that in economic equilibrium, individuals choose what they prefer and, hence, that the preferences inside their minds could be inferred (i.e., revealed) by the economic choices they make. Thus, revealed preference argued that all references to internal (i.e., psychological) states of mind were unnecessary and that economics had nothing to do with the discipline of psychology insofar as it investigated or relied on internal states of mind. This theory of revealed preference would be the most influential account of human behavior in economics during the following decades.

In all this, use of the concepts of "behavior" or "behavioral" in histories predating the Second World War is, of course, an anachronism. Behavior as a concept encapsulating all acts of the human being – and, more controversially, of the animal being – originates in the United States of the early twentieth century. Subsequently, this new concept of behavior provided the basis for the label of the new development in psychology baptized behaviorism. It was around World War II that behavior's adverbial conjugation *behavioral* was introduced in relation to "science" and "economics." As early as 1943, Clark Hull from Yale University spoke about "the behavioral (social) sciences" in his *Principles of Behavior* (Senn, 1966; Berelson, 1968, Pooley, forthcoming). Yet, it was only after James Miller created the Committee on the Behavioral Sciences at the psychology department of the University of Chicago in 1949 and the Ford Foundation's Behavioral Science Program was created in 1951 that the term became widely used, albeit from the start in different ways by its different users.

The use of *behavioral economics*, then, was initially popularized at the University of Michigan's Institute of Social Research in the late 1940s, where George Katona understood behavioral economics as investigating economic behavior, that is, as the subclass of behavior produced in the course of the agent's activities in the economy. Other users of the adverb *behavioral* included Ward Edwards, also at the University of Michigan, who, starting in the late 1950s, employed it as the name of his branch of operations research called behavioral decision research, and Herbert Simon, who in the 1950s and 1960s advanced what he labeled behavioral economics as an alternative to the dominant neoclassical school in economics. Later the label of behavioral economics was picked up by economists who sought to reform the dominant neoclassical view of the day along the lines set out by Simon. But much more visibly, *behavioral economics* was appropriated by Daniel Kahneman, Richard Thaler, and Eric Wanner in the newly created behavioral economics program at the Alfred P. Sloan foundation in 1984.

In addition, the brief introduction thus far already suggests that economics and psychology are not the stable and well-circumscribed entities that the rationale of behavioral economics wants them to be. For instance, Samuelson's revealed preference embraced psychologists' new theory of behaviorism but at the same time denounced psychology as explaining inner states of mind. More generally, Dorothy Ross (2003), among others, has reminded us that the disciplines recognized in the twentieth century as different scientific projects, based on the methods used, questions asked, and theories advanced, emerged from older branches of knowledge by a process of negotiation and separation between overlapping areas of interest.

But even in the twentieth century, the boundaries between economics, psychology, and the other social and human sciences have not been stable and well defined. For instance, judged by received training, noneconomists who have won the Nobel Memorial Prize in Economics besides Kahneman, include political scientist Simon, and a whole range of physicists and engineers, including in-between cases such as Vernon Smith, who received a BA in electrical engineering and an MA and a PhD in economics. Or consider Colin Camerer, currently one of the leading behavioral economists, who holds a PhD in behavioral decision research. The same is true for psychology. Foremost postwar mathematical psychologists, such as R. Duncan Luce, Patrick Suppes, and David Krantz, received degrees in engineering or mathematics before migrating to psychology. In addition, these postwar scientists were labeled economists or psychologists flexibly and depending on the occasion. Conditional on the situation, Simon called himself a political scientist, an economist, a psychologist, and a mathematician. Mathematician Jimmie Savage has been claimed to be an important economist by economists and to be an important psychologist by psychologists.

Even on the level of individual publications, the standard divisions are problematic. John von Neumann and Oskar Morgenstern's *Theory of Games and Economic Behavior* (2004 [1944]) has been described as a major contribution to their field by economists, psychologists, biologists, and mathematicians. Mathematical psychologists Krantz, Luce, Tversky, and Suppes conceived their three-volume *Foundations of Measurement* (1971, 1989, 1991) to extend the work of economist Gérard Debreu. However, at the same time, they described it as a contribution to the empirical sciences in general, that is, to physics, economics, psychology, and others, and thus as a contribution to the "methodology" of science. Although it has been fundamentally ingrained in twentieth-century science, the distinction between the different disciplines that scientists have employed has been anything but stable or clearly defined.

A second reason for the problematic nature of the division between psychology and economics is that if there is one constant in economics and psychology it has been the attempt to cross the alleged boundary between the two disciplines and to make this boundary disappear. For instance, attempts to unify the behavioral and social sciences in the United States have been a constant theme in the National Science Foundation's recurring reports from committees on Basic Research in the Behavioral and Social Sciences. Or consider the case of behavioral psychology. In the late 1950s, Ward Edwards created behavioral decision research, a new field in psychology that applied economic theories to psychological problems. Three decades later, Kahneman and Tversky introduced an adjusted Edwards program into economics. Another example is Simon. He tried to use the insights he gained originally in political science to alter economic theorizing, which eventually led him to produce a new theory in psychology. And the well-known 1952 Santa Monica conference on "The Design of Experiments in Decision Processes," organized by mathematician Robert Thrall and psychologist Clyde Coombs is often cited as a major event in the history of game theory in economics, in the history of mathematical psychology, and in the history of experimental economics. As much as the division between economics and psychology has been a recurring preoccupation of economists in particular, so has the crossing and dissolving of the boundary been a constant.

Yet, despite the convoluted history of economics and psychology, and of the constant attempts to cross and dissolve the economics-psychology boundary, we should not throw economics and psychology aside as accidental labels of overlapping or indistinguishable scientific projects. Despite all the nuances that may be cited, economics and psychology are useful categories subsuming contrasting scientific traditions. A main line of argument running through this book is that to understand the history of behavioral economics, the difference between the epistemologies of economics and psychology, in particular, is crucial.

Economists from Adam Smith until at least those in the 1960s predominantly constructed their theories on what were alternatively called principles, characterizations, premises, or assumptions of economic behavior. We could call this an epistemology of generalized characterizations. These generalized characterizations were part of an interpretation of economics that sharply distinguished positive claims of the economy from normative value judgments regarding the economist's preferred economic policy. By contrast, the discipline of psychology that commenced in the 1860s with the work of Fechner, Wundt, and others was firmly grounded in an epistemology of directly refutable empirical claims. This epistemology provided the guidelines for conducting scientific, that is, descriptive psychology, within a widely employed normative-descriptive distinction. The psychologist would set up the experiment and determine the, say, brightness of two lightbulbs. Therefore, the brightness of the lamp bulbs formed the objectively given, that is the normative stimuli. Subsequently, the experimental subject's individual sensation of the relative brightness constituted the descriptive output of the experiment. The focal point of the behavioral economics that Kahneman and Thaler created in the 1980s was the replacement of economists' epistemology of generalized characterizations with the epistemology of directly refutable empirical claims of the psychologists. This was expressed by behavioral economists as an urge to trade economists' positive-normative distinction for psychologists' normative-descriptive dichotomy.

To understand how behavioral economists from the early 1980s onward sought to shift the main epistemological orientation in economics from generalized characterizations to directly refutable empirical claims, we first need to appreciate the difference between the economic and the experimental psychological way of dealing with individual behavior as they carried over from nineteenth-century Europe to twentieth-century United States. These two different views became particularly clear when they clashed, as they did in psychologist Thurstone's attempt to experimentally test economists' indifference curve and in economists Friedman and Wallis's rebuttal of Thurstone's psychological experiments. Second, we need to go back to von Neumann and Morgenstern's *Theory of Games and Economics Behavior* (2004 [1944])[1] and its approach of basing social theory on behavioral axioms. In particular, we need to understand how von Neumann and Morgenstern's subtle view of the nature of the behavioral axioms upon which their theory of games was constructed related to the psychological and economic conceptions of human behavior. The brief introduction of these backgrounds constitutes the first chapter.

After the publication of the *Theory of Games and Economic Behavior* followed a period of some ten years during which economists, psychologists, and mathematicians discussed the interpretation of the behavioral axioms and the possible application of the axioms in their respective fields of research. Chapter 2 reconstructs the discussions between a number of main protagonists, and discusses in some detail the Savage–Maurice Allais dispute, which, in retrospect, constitutes the most relevant debate of this period. Subsequently, the second chapter shows which two interpretations along disciplinary lines the different discussions settled around in the mid-1950s and what the main distinction between the psychological and economic interpretations was.

The different incorporations of the von Neumann-Morgenstern axioms by psychologists and economists sowed the seeds for the criticisms of psychologists Daniel Kahneman, Amos Tversky, Paul Slovic, Sarah Lichtenstein, and, later, the behavioral economists. But it cannot be emphasized enough how different the psychological approach was from the economic approach. The third chapter shows how mathematical psychology and behavioral decision research of the 1950s and 1960s considered the axioms, and theories of decision making generally, to constitute two sides of the same coin. The axioms provided the foundations for a theory of measurement – as all measurement in the end is a decision by

---

[1] The first edition was published in 1944. References here are to the 2004 reprint of the second edition (1947).

human beings about which of two values is brighter, higher, larger, and so on – and a psychological theory of rational decision making by human beings.

This psychological program ran into problems when it turned out that behavior by human beings in experiments often systematically deviates from the normative theory. It invalidated not only the axioms as descriptions of rational behavior but also the measurement theory that lay at the basis of investigating experimentally decisions by individuals. This was the problem Tversky struggled with in the late 1960s. The fourth chapter discusses Tversky's work of the late 1960s and, based on an exposition of Kahneman's research of the 1960s, shows which solution Kahneman's research suggested for the problem with which Tversky was struggling. This fruitful integration formed the basis of their collaborative research of the 1970s, which is subsequently set out. Chapter 4 concludes by offering three explanations for Kahneman and Tversky's impact on psychologists and economists.

Yet Kahneman and Tversky's appealing theoretical stance and engaging rhetoric was received in different ways among economists. Chapter 5 argues that two main economic responses may be distinguished. Experimental economists working in the tradition of Vernon Smith accepted the experimental evidence of the psychologists, but took it as only emphasizing further the importance of the mechanism of the market in steering initially fallible behavior of economic agents to a competitive equilibrium. By contrast, a number of finance-oriented economists, led by Richard Thaler, accepted the Kahneman-Tversky program and started applying it to economic questions and to economic theory. Their main vehicle was psychologists' normative-descriptive distinction of human decision making that originated in experimental psychology and in the work of mathematician Savage. Although not completely incompatible, experimental economics and behavioral economics nevertheless constitute two very different ideas of what economics is and of how it relates to psychology. The latter group received a vital boost from the behavioral economics program started in 1984 at the Alfred P. Sloan Foundation and later at the Russell Sage Foundation under the directorship of Eric Wanner.

The sixth and final chapter shows that the conceptual and epistemological redefinition of economics Thaler took over from psychologists Kahneman and Tversky determined the boundaries within which behavioral economics would develop. Subsequently, Chapter 6 describes the most salient developments within behavioral economics of the 1990s and 2000s. More specifically, it discusses the development of behavioral economics by means of the research on intertemporal choice and the dual systems approach, the endogeneity of preferences research, and the new welfare economics of libertarian paternalism. Finally, the Epilogue reflects on the main lines running through the book.

1

Understanding Human Behavior

1. Introduction

The epistemology of generalized characterizations in economics goes back at least to the nineteenth century. A first objective of this chapter, therefore, is to briefly revisit John Stuart Mill's (1806–1873) famous definition of economics (Mill, 1844) and its arguments in favor of an economics that reasons from characterizations that aim to capture the essential aspects of the economic world without being directly amenable to empirical validation or refutation.

The most important explanation for the gradual demise of this Millian epistemology in the twentieth century is the rise of what may loosely be summarized as logical positivism. Initiated by members of the Vienna Circle such as Rudolf Carnap, Moritz Schlick, and Otto Neurath in the 1920s, logical positivism defended a scientific worldview in which any scientific statement either was an empirical claim that could be proved right or wrong by single empirical observations or was a definition. As such, generalized characterizations were ruled unscientific by logical positivism.

Nevertheless, some economists sought to uphold the Millian approach by disguising it in logical positivist terms. A second aim of this chapter is to advance Allen Wallis (1912–1988) and Milton Friedman's (1912–2006) rebuttal of psychologist Louis Leon Thurstone's (1887–1955) laboratory experiment of economic indifference curves as an illustrative case in point (Wallis and Friedman, 1942; Thurstone, 1931). In addition, this episode illustrates the very different ways of investigating human behavior by psychologist Thurstone and economists Wallis and Friedman, and illuminates Friedman's representative view of the relation between economics and psychology.

A final objective is to show that Wallis and Friedman's Millian epistemology is surprisingly similar to the approach taken by a book that, at first sight, seems little related: John von Neumann (1903–1957) and Oskar Morgenstern's (1902–1977) *Theory of Games and Economic Behavior* (2004 [1944]).[1] Central to any appreciation of the Hungarian and Austrian émigrés' axiomatic approach is their idea of generalizing the characteristics of rational behavior, which, at one and the same time, were grounded in empirical reality, not directly subject to empirical verification or refutation, and were understood as rules for rational decision making. This position reflected not only von Neumann's view of the nature of mathematics, but also resonated with the economic position as adhered to by Mill (1844) and by Wallis and Friedman (1942).

2. Mill and the Nature of Economic Reasoning

John Stuart Mill's influential essay "On the Definition of Political Economy; and on the Method of Investigation Proper to It" (1844), presented a complex but coherent view of economics' relation to human behavior. Economists, Mill argued, assume a few general principles of human behavior relevant for the functioning of the economy. Examples include the pursuit of wealth and an aversion to labor. Moreover, "[t]he desires of man, and the nature of the conduct to which they prompt him, are within the reach of our [economists'] observation. . . . The materials of this knowledge every one can principally collect within himself" (Mill, 1844, p. 105). Economists then reasoned from these "assumed premises" to construct their theories of production, wealth distribution, and so on, Mill argued. Although the assumed premises and their derived theories "might be totally without foundation in fact" and "are not pretended to be universally in accordance with [facts]" (Mill, 1844, p. 102), they nevertheless needed to be verified to reduce

---

[1] The *Theory of Games and Economic Behavior* formed the start of game theory in its different expressions and applications (Leonard, 2010; Weintraub, 1992; Dimand and Dimand, 1997, 2005; Machina, 1989). In addition, it transformed the older expected utility theory and provided demand theory in economics with a new foundation (Amadae, 2003; Fishburn, 1964, 1981). Game theory, decision theory, and expected utility theory have been subjected to a wide range of philosophical criticism (Hausman, 1992; Nozick, 1993; Green and Shapiro, 1994; Friedman, 1996). In general, the tumultuous Second World War and Cold War periods, of which the creation and use of game theory forms an integral part, have been the subject of extensive historical investigation (Amadae, 2003; Klein, forthcoming; Leonard, 2010; Mirowski, 2002; Capshew, 1999; Fontaine and Backhouse, 2010; Forman, 1987; Hughes, 1998; Hughes and Hughes, 2000; Thomas, 2007; Erickson, 2010).

"to the lowest point that uncertainty . . . as arising from the complexity of every particular case" (Mill, 1844, p. 107).

At the same time, Mill argued it was not possible to conduct experiments in economics as it was in the physical sciences, because "[w]e cannot try forms of government and systems of national policy on a diminutive scale in our laboratories." It should be emphasized that to Mill, this impossibility of doing experiments in economics had no repercussions for economics as being an empirical science. The assumed premises and derived theories had to be in accordance with "the limited number of experiments which take place . . . of their own accord" (Mill, 1844, p. 103) in the daily course of the economy and the knowledge of the economy each economist could collect within him- or herself. According to Mill, economics was very much an empirical science; it was just that experiments were not feasible for practical reasons (Hands, 2001; Maas, 2005a, 2005b).

As such, Mill argued, the discipline of economics had an epistemology similar to that of mathematics:

[Political economy] must necessarily reason, from assumptions, not from facts. It is built upon hypotheses, strictly analogous to those which, under the name of definitions, are the foundation of the other abstract sciences. Geometry presupposes an arbitrary definition of a line, "that which has length but not breath." Just in the same manner does Political Economy presuppose an arbitrary definition of man, as a being who invariably does that by which he may obtain the greatest amount of necessaries, conveniences, and luxuries, with the smallest quantity of labour and physical self-denial with which they can be obtained in the existing state of knowledge. . . . No mathematician ever thought that his definition of a line corresponded to an actual line. As little did any political economist ever imagine that real men had no object of desire but wealth, or none which would not give way to the slightest motive of a pecuniary kind. But they were justified in assuming this, for the purpose of their argument; because they had to do only with those parts of human conduct which have pecuniary advantage for their direct and principal object; and because, as no two individual cases are exactly alike, no *general* maxims could ever be laid down unless *some* of the circumstances of the particular case were left out of consideration. (Mill, 1844, pp. 101–103)

This understanding of the nature of economics and mathematics was incompatible with the dominant logical positivist sway of the twentieth century. Many economists sought to apply the logical positivist approach to economics, among them, for instance, most econometricians (Morgan, 1990; Boumans, 2005) and, in a different way, Paul Samuelson (Weintraub, 1991; Wong, 1978). Others, consciously or not, continued to prefer the Millian over the logical positivist approach.

3. Thurstone versus Wallis and Friedman

Wallis and Friedman's (1942) refutation of Thurstone's (1931) laboratory experiment of the indifference curve is a well-known and representative example of how some economists tried to maintain the Millian epistemology by reformulating it in twentieth-century, logical positivist terms. Moreover, the two publications are illustrative of the different ways in which psychologists and economists understood the same economic theory and its underlying premises.

In the late 1920s, psychologist Thurstone and economist Henry Schultz (1893–1938) were among the most distinguished members of their respective scientific communities (Gigerenzer, 1987b; Hands and Mirowski, 1998; Mirowski and Hands, 1998). They were also both at the University of Chicago and were close friends (Thurstone, 1931). From their conversations sprang one of the most intriguing episodes in twentieth-century interactions between economists and psychologists. None of their conversations was recorded, and neither left substantial archival traces. Yet, it is not difficult to reconstruct some of the topics the two men discussed. Schultz likely told Thurstone about his attempts at measuring demand curves, which, among others, used indifference curves to connect observed demand to demand for related (combinations of) goods (Schultz, 1928a, 1928b, 1938). No doubt he told Thurstone about the practical difficulties of gathering and processing the data, and of thus proving the assumptions of demand theory (Hands and Mirowski, 1998). In his expositions, Schultz would have referred implicitly or explicitly to the assumption that the individual in his or her economic choice behavior prefers more to less.

Schultz's exposition of his own work and of economic theory in general probably interested Thurstone for at least two reasons. First, Thurstone would have been intrigued by Schultz and his fellow economists basing their theories on assumptions about individual choice behavior without apparently feeling the need to test these assumptions experimentally. In all likelihood, this was all the more surprising to Thurstone because an appropriate experiment did not seem all too difficult to construct. A second reason why Thurstone would have been intrigued is that without being aware of it, he would have realized that the new experimental methodology he offered to his fellow experimental psychologists a few years earlier could, in fact, be applied directly to the assumptions of individual behavior that Schultz was describing (Thurstone 1927a, 1927b, 1927c; Thurstone and Chave, 1929).

Thurstone had proposed to ground experimental psychology in the "discriminal process," by which the human mind compares and decides between two stimuli. This led Thurstone to his "law of comparative judgment." What is important is not so much the exact details of Thurstone's law of comparative judgment but the assumption on which it was based:

> Let us suppose that we are confronted with a series of stimuli or specimens such as a series of gray values, cylindrical weights, handwriting specimens, children's drawings, or any other series of stimuli that are subject to comparison.... It may be gray values, or weights, or excellence, or any other quantitative or qualitative attribute about which we can think "more" or "less" for each specimen. (Thurstone, 1927b, p. 273)

During the conversations with his friend Schultz, Thurstone must have realized that "any other series of stimuli that are subject to comparison" could perhaps also include the goods used in Schultz's economic theories. In fact, "more" and "less" were exactly the terms in which economists appeared to think about goods.

Thurstone has been described as a versatile psychologist who engaged in many different areas of psychology and who liked a challenge (Gigerenzer, 1987a, 1987b), a picture that is quickly confirmed by looking at the number and variety of his publications. Thus, it is no surprise that following his conversations with Schultz, Thurstone decided to test Schultz's economic theory experimentally in his own psychological laboratory. In the resulting article, Thurstone emphasized that "[t]he formulation of this problem is due to numerous conversations . . . with my friend Professor Henry Schultz" (Thurstone, 1931, p. 139).[2] In addition, Thurstone clearly saw a great potential for cooperation between economists and psychologists on this subject: "The problem in its economic setting is old, but the restatement of it in experimental form and its formulation as a psychophysical problem are probably new.... [I]t is clear that here is a fertile field for investigation in a very old problem that overlaps economic theory and psychophysical experimentation" (Thurstone, 1931, p. 139).

Thurstone started his analysis with the formulation of "five fundamental postulates" he considered necessary to allow for a theoretical and experimental analysis of economic decisions between different goods:

---

[2] Lyle V. Jones, who worked with Thurstone both as a postdoctoral fellow and then as a faculty colleague, recalls Thurstone saying that "[he] and Schultz discussed common research interests regularly as they met for lunch at the faculty club at the University of Chicago." Jones adds, "My impression is that they shared strong mutual respect" (Jones, e-mail to author, January 31, 2011).

(1) satisfaction increases with possession of the good; (2) there is a lower limit of the good, beneath which the individual cannot or will not barter; (3) "[m]otivation is defined quantitatively as the anticipated increment in satisfaction per unit increase in the community" (p. 141); (4) motivation is finite; and (5) "motivation is inversely proportional to the amount already possessed" (p. 142). A different label for these fundamental postulates was "rational equations," in the sense of a commonly known or accepted set of observations about human behavior put into scientific, that is, rational language. Thurstone focused his analysis on the indifference curve, or indifference function as he sometimes put it. Thus, Thurstone stated that based on the "rational equations... for the indifference curve," it was possible to "ascertain whether [the indifference curve] can be verified experimentally" (Thurstone, 1931, p. 151). To link this experiment to his earlier work, Thurstone furthermore emphasized that the individual's choice between different bundles of goods is an "act of judgment."

Thurstone's experiment had a straightforward setup and involved only one subject (i.e., individual). In retrospect, it may seem unnecessarily restrictive to use only one subject, but it was not at odds with experimental practice at the time and did not conflict with the aim of the experiment to investigate whether it was possible to verify the existence of the indifference curve for an individual (Danziger, 1990, 1997). The subject, who Thurstone assured "was entirely naïve as regards the psychophysical problem involved and had no knowledge what ever of the nature of the curves that we expected to find" (Thurstone, 1931, p. 154), had to make a hypothetical comparative judgment of his preferences for different bundles of hats and shoes, shoes and coats, and coats and hats. The implicit reference point was zero hats, shoes, or coats. That is, the subject was asked to state his preferences for different bundles of goods assuming he had none of each initially.

More specifically, Thurstone took one constant bundle – eight hats and eight shoes in the case of Figure 1.1 – and asked the subject for a large number of other combinations whether the subject preferred that combination to the bundle of eight hats and eight shoes. In Figure 1.1, the black circles represent the bundles for which the subject said to prefer that bundle to eight hats and eight shoes; the open circles represent cases in which he or she did not. Thurstone then drew what he considered the most plausible indifference curve, adding that because the subject may make mistakes or may be inconsistent for other reasons, the constructed indifference curve is not a perfect fit. The same procedure was followed for hats and coats and for coats and shoes.

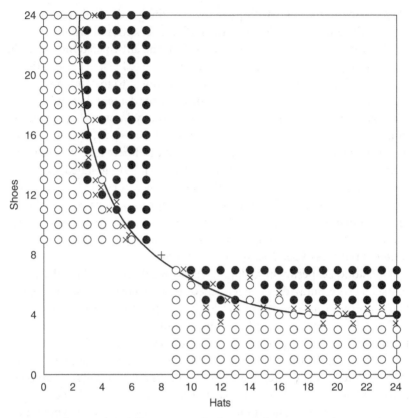

Figure 1.1. Thurstone's indifference curve for hats and shoes. *Source:* Thurstone (1931, p. 153).

In subsequent years, Thurstone's psychological experiment of the indifference curve was mentioned by a number of economists, briefly and critically without exception (Lenfant, 2012).[3] Half a century later, Thurstone's article was rediscovered when, in the 1980s, economists began to look in earnest at experiments on individual decision behavior (Moscati, 2007a).

[3] In the early 1950s, Lyle V. Jones tried to obtain funds for research extending on Thurstone (1931) from the University of Chicago's committee for seed grants for new faculty members. The proposal "was rejected by the committee chairman Milton Friedman, probably fairly and properly, on the grounds that I was an amateur who was fiddling around with issues in economics about which I was ill prepared" (Jones, e-mail to author, January 31, 2011). Wallis and Friedman's (1942) criticism of Thurstone (1931), of which Jones was unaware at the time, adds another element to the rejection. Eventually, two more papers on the subject appeared from Thurstone and Jones: Thurstone and Jones (1957) and Jones (1959).

The more extensive discussion of Thurstone (1931) during the years following its publication was provided by Friedman and Wallis. Friedman started his academic career at Chicago under Schultz in the early 1930s, where he, with others, helped to establish Schultz's statistical laboratory from fall 1934 onward (Hands and Mirowski, 1998). Wallis also studied economics at Chicago in the 1930s and became close friends with Friedman and George Stigler (1911–1991). From 1942 to 1946, Wallis was director of the Statistical Research Group created by the U.S. Office of Scientific Research and Development at Columbia University. Together with Harold Hotelling (1895–1973), an economist from Columbia University and a collaborator of Schultz's in the 1930s, Wallis employed Friedman and other Chicagoans such as Stigler at the Statistical Research Group at Columbia University during the Second World War (Stigler, 1988, p. 61). In the late 1930s and early 1940s, Friedman became more critical of the statistical approach of Schultz and supported Burns and Mitchell's (1946) use of statistics and economic theory in the famous "measurement without theory" controversy of the late 1940s (Hands and Mirowski, 1998; Morgan, 1990).

Wallis and Friedman (1942) appeared in a volume composed in the memory of Schultz, who died in a car accident in 1938 and, like the other brief references by economists, was severely critical of Thurstone (1931). What is striking about Wallis and Friedman's criticism of Thurstone is, first, the repeated and explicit attempt by the two economists to distinguish between economics and psychology. Wallis and Friedman differentiated between the economic and the psychological significance of Thurstone's experiment and emphasized the economic use of the indifference curve as different from how it might be used in other disciplines. In other words, Wallis and Friedman saw psychology and economics as disciplines working from different premises and with different objectives. It seems that for Wallis and Friedman, in itself, this was almost enough reason to reject the psychological experiment of Thurstone.

Second, Wallis and Friedman wanted to convince the reader that their criticisms of Thurstone's work were fundamental and did not consist of minor issues that might perhaps be solved. When one does turn to Wallis and Friedman's objections, it is therefore surprising to see that the objectives were practical without exception. Wallis and Friedman did not object to the use of experiments in economics, to the nature of Thurstone's fundamental postulates, or to Thurstone's assumed link between observations and theory. Instead, they complained, for instance, that Thurstone's fundamental postulates were not so much "postulates" but rather "generalized observations." Subsequently, however, they agreed that Thurstone's generalized observations were valid generalized observations. In addition, Wallis and Friedman argued that one cannot assume that using hypothetical questions elicits the true preferences of the individual, that the individual's preferences may change during the experiment, and that the artificiality of the laboratory is not a good substitute for the economic situation supposedly studied. In short,

> The economic significance of Thurstone's experiments is vitiated by a number of serious limitations . . . its fundamental shortcomings probably cannot be overcome in any experiment involving economic stimuli and human beings. . . . The fundamental difficulty is that economic phenomena are so integral a part of life that effective experimentation would require control of virtually the entire existence of the subject. (Wallis and Friedman, 1942, pp. 179, 180)

It should be emphasized, however, that Wallis and Friedman not only criticized the possibility of inferring indifference curves through psychological experiments, but that they were also equally critical of doing so by means of statistical data of economic behavior. Also in the case of statistical inference, their criticism is best read as a practical, rather than as a theoretical or philosophical objection. Wallis and Friedman argued that one cannot suppose that the preferences of an individual are constant any longer than a relatively short period, that available income may affect preferences and is not constant over time, and that preferences are dissimilar across individuals, so adding individual preferences at one point in time also is not an option. For these reasons, they argued, indifference curves could not be constructed purely based on statistical data.

Instead of testing the indifference curve by means of laboratory experiments or statistics, Wallis and Friedman argued, "[t]he economist impounds in the indifference function all the psychological and sociological factors which determine consumer choice. The great merit of the indifference function is its ability to encompass these factors in their full generality and complexity and yet be free of irrelevant or erroneous assumptions about human psychology" (Wallis and Friedman, 1942, p. 176). This seems a puzzling statement. For if laboratory experiments and statistics are ruled out as sources of scientific input, where do the psychological and sociological factors come from? Moreover, how is it possible that the indifference function encompasses these psychological and sociological factors and yet be free of assumptions? The answer Wallis and Friedman gave was that "[t]he indifference function is *defined* for a single individual at a single time. Its purpose is to *abstract* from economics those psychological factors which, in conjunction with the cultural milieu, constitute the mechanism of choice" (Wallis and Friedman, 1942, p. 177, emphasis added). Thus, although partly grounded in observations of the economy, the indifference curve was also partly defined. In addition, the observations on which the indifference curve was partly based were not from the laboratory experiments and the statistics earlier criticized but were derived instead from clearly observable facts of economic life: "[t]he hypothesis that the indifference surfaces are negatively inclined rests on the fact that people generally prefer more of an economic good to less of it" (Wallis and Friedman, 1942, p. 176). At the same time, however, the indifference curve was also used to organize the facts of economic life. "A second use to which the indifference function might be put is the *organization* and analysis of empirical data on consumer expenditures. . . . giving quantitative *expression* to the indifference function" (Wallis and Friedman, 1942, p. 176, emphasis added). Other terms that Wallis and Friedman used were "to rationalize" and "to generalize" the facts of economic life.[4]

Wallis and Friedman used a twentieth-century language of facts, verification, and testing, but their rejection of experimental verification and purely statistical inference of indifference curves in favor of a method that "generalizes" or "rationalizes" observations that are readily available, in fact, is not unlike the method employed by Mill (1844). Wallis and Friedman implicitly argued that from reading the newspaper and other reports of the economy, and from buying groceries, insurance, houses, and vacations, the economist obtained a range of different "facts" of the economy. The economist then tried to structure these facts into one body of knowledge, using tools such as the indifference curve. For example, the indifference curve provided a rationalization for the "fact" that employees are only willing to work extra hours if their hourly wage increases for the extra hours worked. The indifference curve in this case rationalizes the available facts of employee behavior: it structures these facts. And to point immediately to a primary linguistic headache of twentieth-century economists, this rationalization of economic facts also rested on another economic tool: that of rational economic beings. We can only rationalize the extra wage demanded for the extra hours worked by using an indifference curve analysis of wages versus leisure, if we assume that individuals choose what they prefer, that is, that they choose rationally. In other words, to Wallis and Friedman, the

---

[4] A different question was whether indifference curves were proper economic tools *given* this epistemology. In that regard, Wallis and Friedman (1942) also had their doubts. See Lenfant (2012) for a careful exposition.

indifference curve was one example of a rationalization of the economic behavior of rational individuals.

It would be too easy to dismiss Wallis and Friedman's criticisms of Thurstone's experiment as an imperfect repudiation of something that did not sit well with existing economic theories. Similarly, it would be a mistake to understand the almost complete absence of discussions of Thurstone's experiment by economists in the 1930s through the 1970s as proof of economists' arrogance toward psychologists and their experimental method. Instead, the conclusion should be that Thurstone's experiment was simply not the way to do economics. To economists Wallis and Friedman, and the economic tradition they represented and developed, the indifference curve was not a theoretical proposition that could be tested; it was a tool with which one could rationalize readily available facts and observations of the economy.

4. Von Neumann and Morgenstern's Hilbertian Mathematics of Social Reality

The implicit Millian epistemology of Wallis and Friedman is very similar to the epistemology of von Neumann and Morgenstern's *Theory of Games and Economic Behavior* (2004 [1944]). In *Von Neumann, Morgenstern, and the Creation of Game Theory* (2010), Robert Leonard provides a detailed account of the background, construction, and subsequent influence of the *Theory of Games and Economic Behavior* (2004 [1944]). One of the many themes in Leonard's book is von Neumann's use of David Hilbert's (1862–1943) approach of founding the mathematical investigation of a scientific field on a set of independent and consistent axioms that produce the laws of the field. In the *Theory of Games and Economic Behavior*, von Neumann together with Morgenstern effectively created a "Hilbertian mathematics of social reality" (Leonard, 2010, p. 222).

Glossed over by many historians, philosophers, and other commentators, and even often only implicit in Leonard (2010), is the careful and subtle nature of the behavioral axioms by von Neumann and Morgenstern on which game theory was based. One reason arguably is the dominance of logical positivism, which left little room for other epistemologies even among historians and philosophers. A second reason for the neglect of the von Neumann-Morgenstern position, however, is that although some scientists clearly tried to adopt it, von Neumann's assistant Leonard "Jimmie" Savage (1917–1971) and Friedman among them, it quickly dissolved in the face of new interpretations and had largely disappeared by the mid-1950s. Yet to understand these reinterpretations of the nature of the behavioral axioms we first need to understand von Neumann and Morgenstern's approach.

Von Neumann and Morgenstern constructed game theory based on "a characterization of 'rational behavior' ... : a complete set of rules of behavior in all conceivable situations" (von Neumann and Morgenstern, 2004, p. 33). By "rational behavior" von Neumann and Morgenstern meant "the endeavor of the individual to obtain a maximum of utility, or, in the case of the entrepreneur, a maximum of profit" (von Neumann and Morgenstern, 2004, p. 1). Put differently, von Neumann and Morgenstern wished "to find the mathematically complete principles which define 'rational behavior' for the participants in a social economy, and to derive from them the general characteristics of that behavior" (von Neumann and Morgenstern, 2004, p. 31). Rational behavior was characterized by the following set of axioms.

We consider a system U of entities $u, v, w, \ldots$ In U a *relation* is given, $u > v$, and for any number α, $(0 < \alpha < 1)$, an *operation*

$$\alpha u + (1 - \alpha)v = w$$

These concepts satisfy the following axioms:
(A) $u > v$ *is a complete ordering of U.*
This means: Write $u < v$ when $v > u$. Then:

(A:a) For any two u, v one and only one of the three following relations holds:

$$u = v, u > v, u < v.$$

(A:b) $u > v, v > w$ imply $u > w$.

(B) *Ordering and combining.*
(B:a) $u < v$ implies that $u < \alpha u + (1 - \alpha)v$.
(B:b) $u > v$ implies that $u > \alpha u + (1 - \alpha)v$.
(B:c) $u < w < v$ implies the existence of an α with

$$\alpha u + (1 - \alpha)v < w.$$

(B:d) $u > w > v$ implies the existence of an α with

$$\alpha u + (1 - \alpha)v > w.$$

(C) *Algebra of combining.*
(C:a) $\alpha u + (1 - \alpha)v = (1 - \alpha)v + \alpha u.$
(C:b) $\alpha(\beta u + (1 - \beta)v) + (1 - \alpha)v = \gamma u + (1 - \gamma)v$
where $\gamma = \alpha\beta$.

(von Neumann and Morgenstern, 2004, p. 26, emphasis in the original)

Thus, rational behavior of individuals in the economy was characterized in three axioms, which each were decomposed into two or three parts.

Von Neumann and Morgenstern were only interested in characterizing rational behavior and tried to avoid taking any position in the discussion that always seemed to accompany rational behavior, that of measuring utility, without, however, denying the possibility that one day utility might be measured: "We wish to concentrate on one problem which is not that of the measurement of utilities and of preferences" (von Neumann and Morgenstern, 2004, p. 8). To von Neumann and Morgenstern, their book was not about measuring, verifying, and thus operationalizing the concepts of a specific theory, nor was it about the more philosophical question of whether and, if so, how and when individual utility can be measured. Instead, they argued, their book was about characterizing, or rationalizing, rational behavior. Yet, to determine the rational decision in each situation, von Neumann and Morgenstern nevertheless needed to compare and thus in a way measure the different options. They solved this matter by defining a numerical scale that allowed attaching numbers to the strength of the preference for each option of the individual, in much the same way as temperature defines numerically what we mean by heat (von Neumann and Morgenstern, 2004, p. 17). This definition is given by axiom C cited earlier.

However, in a move that would keep economists and others busy for years to come, von Neumann and Morgenstern labeled the numerically defined intensity of preference "utility" (e.g., Fishburn, 1989). Because of the eventually wide impact of the *Theory of Games and Economic Behavior*, this effectively constituted the second major redefinition of the concept of utility. As said, during the last quarter of the nineteenth century, utility changed from Bentham's measure of welfare of a society to a measurement of the mental state of a hedonistic economic subject (Maas, 2005; Hands, 2001). With von Neumann and Morgenstern, the meaning of utility changed again, from a psychophysical measure of the individual's preference for different goods to an axiomatically defined intensity of the individual's preferences.

The behavioral axioms, including numerically defined utility, derived from a specific view of the nature of science. As said, von Neumann and Morgenstern considered themselves to be building "a characterization of 'rational behavior'" (2004 [1944], p. 33). A key term here is *characterization*. Synonyms that were used were *exact description, rationalization,* and *generalization*. This method of "characterization" was distinguished from the descriptive method: "The aim of this book lies not in the direction of empirical research" (von Neumann and Morgenstern, 2004, p. 5). Instead, and not unlike Mill (1844) and Wallis and Friedman (1942), von Neumann and Morgenstern started from what they considered a few, well-known characteristics of rational behavior and tried to frame these characteristics into one consistent mathematical framework: "we wish to find the mathematically complete principles which define 'rational behavior' for the participants in a social economy, and to derive from them the general characteristics of that behavior" (2004 [1944], p. 31).

The axioms summarized rational behavior into a few characteristics that left out large amounts of empirical content, but not all: "We shall attempt to utilize only some commonplace experience concerning human behavior which lends itself to mathematical treatment and which is of economic importance" (von Neumann and Morgenstern, 2004, p. 5). In addition, it did not matter so much for the characterization of rational behavior whether individuals actually do behave rationally. What von Neumann and Morgenstern wanted to characterize was the "the *endeavor* of the individual" (2004 [1944], p. 1, emphasis added) to behave rationally, irrespective of whether the individual actually achieves this goal of rationality.

A further exposition of this scientific method can be found in von Neumann's "The Mathematician" (1988; see also Leonard, 2010).[5] In this account of the nature of mathematics, von Neumann started from the view that since Euclid, mathematicians had begun their mathematical analyses by formulating postulates. These postulates were subsequently combined and put to use in different contexts in what is best described as a creative and even an aesthetic process, von Neumann (1988) argued. The main question, however, was where these postulates originated. Up to the late nineteenth century, according to von Neumann, the idea had been that although these postulates may originally have derived from experience and empirical observation, their validity and justification could only come from mathematical reasoning. In other words, until the late nineteenth century, von Neumann said, the objective of mathematicians had been to de-empiricize the postulates on which the different branches of mathematics were founded. However, following Kurt Gödel's partial refutation of the Hilbertian program and the intuisionistic critique of Luitzen Brouwer and others in the first three decades of the twentieth century, it became clear that mathematics, one way or another, was always grounded in experience, intuition, or other expressions of empirical reality. Although von Neumann rejected the far-reaching consequences of Brouwer's intuitionist program, he also argued that this empirical basis of mathematics

---

[5] "The Mathematician" was first published in *Works of the Mind*, vol. 1 (University of Chicago Press, 1947), pp. 180–196. References here are to a 1988 reprint.

should be recognized more explicitly. Von Neumann argued, for instance, that where the fervent discussions around Euclid's fifth postulate of the infinite plane had been phrased as the question whether it could be derived from the previous four postulates throughout the nineteenth century, the real underlying discussion had always been whether the fifth postulate was grounded in experience and empirical observation: "The prime reason, why, of all Euclid's postulates, the fifth was questioned, was clearly the unempirical character of the concept of the entire infinite plane which intervenes there, and there only" (von Neumann, 1988, p. 2031).

At the same time, however, mathematics was more than the summing up of intuitions, experiences, and observations, von Neumann argued. Mathematics was the derivation of general rules (or principles, postulates, axioms, or whatever one wanted to call them) from these experiences, empirical observations, and intuitions. In other words, mathematics was a "science which interprets experiences on a higher than purely descriptive level" (von Neumann, 1988, p. 2029). Thus, von Neumann argued that "[t]here is a quite peculiar duplicity in the nature of mathematics" (von Neumann, 1988, p. 2030). Mathematics was always grounded in experience and empirical observation, but once the experiences and empirical observations had been summarized into a few postulates, mathematics set off on its own creative life of proof and derivation:

I think that it is a relatively good approximation to truth – which is much too complicated to allow anything but approximations – that mathematical ideas originate in empirics, although the genealogy is sometimes long and obscure. But, once they are so conceived, the subject begins to live a peculiar life of its own and is better compared to a creative one, governed by almost entirely aesthetical motivations, than to anything else and, in particular, to an empirical science. (von Neumann, 1988, p. 2038)

However, even this creative and aesthetic mathematical life of proof and derivation was not unrelated to empirical reality. Any derivation and proof always had to be related to the empirical world. The derivations did not have to be exact descriptions or predictions of the empirical world, but always had to be agreed on as useful summaries, characterizations, or rationalizations of the empirical world.

This, in other words, is what von Neumann meant when he sat down with Morgenstern to construct "a characterization of 'rational behavior'" (von Neumann and Morgenstern, 2004 [1944], p. 33). Von Neumann's understanding of the nature of mathematics recurred in a number of places

in the *Theory of Games and Economic Behavior*. Consider, for instance, the
following exposition of their choice of axioms:

A choice of axioms is not a purely objective task. It is usually expected to achieve
some definite aim – some specific theorem or theorems are to be derivable from
the axioms – and to this extent the problem is exact and objective. But beyond
this there are always other important desiderata of a less exact nature: The axioms
should not be too numerous, their system is to be as simple and transparent as
possible, and each axiom should have an immediate intuitive meaning by which
its appropriateness may be judged directly [fn]. In a situation like ours this last
requirement is particularly vital, in spite of its vagueness: we want to make an
intuitive concept amenable to mathematical treatment and to see as clearly as
possible what hypotheses this requires. (von Neumann and Morgenstern, 2004,
p. 25)

That is, the axioms were grounded in intuition *and* subject to "objective"
mathematical requirements. Intuition constituted the "the intuitive meaning – i.e. the justification – of each one of our axioms" (von Neumann and
Morgenstern, 2004 [1944], p. 27). Moreover, in the footnote (noted by [fn])
of the preceding quote, von Neumann and Morgenstern further explicated
that "[t]he first and the last principle may represent – at least to a certain
extent – opposite influences: If we reduce the number of axioms by merging
them as far as technically possible, we may lose the possibility of distinguishing the various intuitive background" (2004, p. 25). This is to say that
von Neumann and Morgenstern recognized that the two requirements of
intuition and mathematical usefulness were often at odds with one another,
in which case the scientist had to weigh the different arguments and decide
which of the two was the more important.

The "quite peculiar duplicity" of von Neumann and Morgenstern's mathematical approach also had another important implication. Because the
axioms were as much subject to the logic of mathematical reasoning as
they were grounded in empirical reality, when agreed on, they were also
rules for rational behavior. As much as von Neumann and Morgenstern
presented "a characterization of 'rational behavior,'" they wanted to provide "a complete set of rules of behavior in all conceivable situations" (von
Neumann and Morgenstern, 2004, p. 33). In fact, this was one of the main
objectives: "The immediate concept of a solution [in our approach] is plau-
sibly a set of rules for each participant which tell him how to behave in
every situation which may conceivably arise" (von Neumann and Morgenstern, 2004, p. 31). Thus, in the *Theory of Games and Economic Behavior*,
von Neumann and Morgenstern aimed to characterize rational decision

behavior while, at the same time, aiming to provide rules for how to make decisions rationally. In line with this epistemology, von Neumann rejected the idea that the game-theoretic solution could be tested experimentally (Leonard, 2010).

5. Conclusion

In the nineteenth century and the first half of the twentieth century, a number of authors not usually associated with one another understood the principles, premises, assumptions, or axioms upon which economics is based in quite similar ways. Relating Mill's (1844) interpretation of economic principles to Wallis and Friedman's (1942) rejection of Thurstone's indifference curve experiment clarifies the ways in which economists Wallis and Friedman clashed with psychologist Thurstone regarding the nature of economic reasoning. Similarly, Mill (1844) and Wallis and Friedman (1942) help to shed light on the subtle epistemology on which von Neumann and Morgenstern's *Theory of Games and Economic Behavior* (2004 [1944]) was based. According to these authors, the principles, premises, assumptions, or axioms on which economics is based should be understood as characterizations, or rationalizations, of economic behavior. Economic behavior itself was evident from observing the functioning of the economy in the grocery shop, from well-established facts of economic behavior, and from introspective knowledge of how economic agents operate.

Subsequently, however, this view of the nature of the principles on which economics is based disappeared. A general cause was the rise of logical positivism. According to the logical positivists, scientific statements were either definitions or empirical claims that by direct observation might be refuted or verified. In other words, characterizations or rationalizations of economic behavior did not qualify as scientific in the logical positivist framework and had to be discarded in favor of either definitions or empirical claims. In this story, Friedman is an important transitional figure for the economic discipline. On one hand, Friedman tried to maintain the nineteenth-century interpretation of the economic assumptions as characterizations while, on the other hand, trying to make this assumptions-as-characterizations view compatible to the new logical positivist framework of hypotheses, testing, assumptions, verification, refutation, and a general emphasis on the importance of empirical evidence.

The demise of the interpretation of economic principles as characterizations in favor of the logical positivist view sowed the seeds for the psychological criticism of economics in the 1970s and 1980s that gave rise to behavioral economics. The interpretation of the von Neumann and Morgenstern (2004 [1944]) axioms gradually evolved into a situation in which psychologists could understand economists' use of the axioms or assumptions as empirical claims to be verified or refuted. And refuting the axioms empirically is what the psychologists did.

But that story is told in Chapter 5. First, we turn to how economists and psychologists came to interpret the von Neumann and Morgenstern (2004) axioms along disciplinary lines between the mid-1940s and mid-1950s.

2

The Incorporation of von Neumann and Morgenstern's Behavioral Axioms in Economics and Psychology

1. Introduction

Von Neumann and Morgenstern's *Theory of Games and Economic Behavior* (2004 [1944]) and the subtle epistemology of the behavioral axioms on which it was based resulted in some ten years of intense discussion among psychologists and, in particular, economists on how to integrate the new theory and its axioms in existing theories and methodologies.[1] Initially, the discussions went in different directions, without any of the perspectives taking precedence over the others.

Leonard "Jimmie" Savage understood the axioms in the mathematical tradition of von Neumann as summarizing rational behavior on a higher than purely descriptive level. Milton Friedman understood the axioms in the Millian tradition as characterizations of economic behavior. Savage and Friedman briefly collaborated on a further application of the von Neumann-Morgenstern approach to economics. They could do so because the mathematical and economic interpretations were not unlike each other, as set out in Chapter 1. On the other hand, Paul Samuelson and, in particular, William Baumol took the von Neumann-Morgenstern axioms to be descriptive claims about the measurement of utility that might be refuted directly by empirical observations. Between 1950 and 1952, this led to a heated debate between Samuelson and Baumol on one side and Friedman and Savage on the other. Between 1952 and 1954, this discussion was repeated in less conciliatory tones by Savage and Maurice Allais, which, among others, produced the famous Allais paradox and the introduction of a distinction between a "normative" and an "empirical" domain of decision theory in

---

[1] In addition, the *Theory of Games and Economic Behavior* was picked up by mathematicians working for government-related agencies such as RAND (Leonard, 2010).

Savage's *The Foundations of Statistics* (1954). Others, including Kenneth Arrow and Jacob Marschak, tried to bridge the different views, with little success.

Around 1953 and 1954, the discussion settled into an interpretation along disciplinary lines. Generally, psychologists came to interpret the behavioral axioms in terms of a normative-descriptive distinction, in which the behavioral axioms functioned as stimuli defined by pure reason in the normative realm with which actual human decision behavior was compared under the rubric of the descriptive domain. Economists, on the other hand, came to understand the behavioral axioms in terms of Milton Friedman's (1953) positive-normative distinction. That is, choice or decision theory, as based on von Neumann and Morgenstern's axioms, was part of positive economics. It remained unclear how exactly the axioms should be understood – as generalized characterizations or as directly refutable descriptions – but their classification under positive economics was undisputed. Initially, Friedman's interpretation of the axioms as characterizations seemed to have the upper hand. However, from the 1950s through the 1970s this view was gradually replaced by the interpretation of the axioms as directly refutable descriptions.

The second section of this chapter introduces the incorporation of von Neumann and Morgenstern's (2004 [1944]) behavioral axioms in economics by Friedman and Savage (1948). Section 3 describes the discussion between, on one hand, Baumol and Samuelson and, on the other hand, Friedman, Savage, and Marschak regarding the nature of the behavioral axioms. The fourth section sets out the Savage-Allais debate, which led to the Allais paradox and to Savage's normative-empirical understanding of the axioms. Section 5 discusses the incorporation of the behavioral axioms in psychology in the mid-1950s, and Section 6, the understanding of the nature of the axioms in economics.

2. Friedman and Savage (1948)

While von Neumann was working with Morgenstern on the *Theory of Games and Economic Behavior* at Princeton in 1941, he hired a bright new research assistant from the University of Michigan, Jimmie Savage (1917–1971). At Michigan, Savage had written his PhD thesis in mathematical statistics, titled *The Application of Vectorial Methods to the Study of Distance Spaces*, under the supervision of Summer Myers (1910–1955). But he also credited the influence of Friedman and Wallis on his scientific education (e.g., Savage, 1954, p. xi). Wallis and Savage in particular would remain close friends for the rest of Savage's life, and it was Wallis who hired Savage for the Statistical Research Group, which resulted, among other things, in the collaboration between Friedman and Savage. However, the two years Savage spent as von Neumann's assistant at Princeton's Institute for Advanced Study from 1941 to 1943, and the discussions Savage had during these and following years with von Neumann on the *Theory of Games and Economic Behavior* arguably constituted the most important scientific influence on Savage. At the Institute of Advanced Study and later at Brown University (1943–1944), Columbia University (1944–1945), and New York University (1945–1946), Savage served the U.S. Army in different capacities as a mathematician and statistician. In June 1947, he joined the Department of Mathematics at the University of Chicago, where he would remain until 1964, when he took up a named professorship at Yale University.

Friedman and Savage felt that their respective approaches to the use of mathematics and statistics in economics (Friedman) and to the mathematical foundations of statistics (Savage) were compatible. Their "classic article" (Machina, 1982, p. 280), "The Utility Analysis of Choice Involving Risk" (1948), brought together the two lines set out by Wallis and Friedman (1942) and von Neumann and Morgenstern (2004 [1944]). Like von Neumann and Morgenstern (2004 [1944]), the purpose of Friedman and Savage's article was to "rationalize" a part of human behavior in the economy, namely individuals' responses toward risk. Thus, the very first sentence of the article stated that "[t]he purpose of this paper is to suggest that an important class of reactions of individuals to risk can be rationalized by a rather simple extension of orthodox utility analysis" (Friedman and Savage, 1948, p. 279). Specifically, they wanted to rationalize the observation that individuals in the economy both gamble and buy insurance, and hence seem both risk seeking and risk averse at the same time. To solve this apparent contradictory behavior, Friedman and Savage suggested a rationalization in the form of a "wiggly utility curve," depicted in Figure 2.1. Assuming that individuals on some parts of the wealth-utility curve are risk seeking and have a preference for gambling, while being risk averse and thus buy insurance on other parts of the curve, provided a rationalization of the contradictory behavior, they argued.

What is important here is not so much the exact rationalization Friedman and Savage constructed but the epistemological position they took. They emphasized that no new or separate empirical investigation was needed, as the behavior to be rationalized was clearly observable to everyone: "This choice among different degrees of risk so prominent in insurance and gambling, *is clearly present* and important in a much broader range of

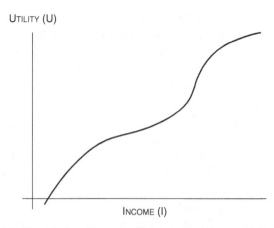

UTILITY (U)

INCOME (I)

Figure 2.1. The wiggly utility curve (Friedman and Savage, 1948, p. 297).

economic choices" (Friedman and Savage, 1948, p. 279, emphasis added), they argued, and "[t]his paper attempts to provide a crude empirical test by bringing together a few broad observations about the behavior of individuals in choosing among alternative risk... and investigating whether these observations are consistent with the hypothesis revived by von Neumann and Morgenstern" (Friedman and Savage, 1948, p. 282).[2] In addition, the second section of the article in which they described the simultaneous risk-seeking and risk-averse behavior was titled "Observable Behavior To Be Rationalized" (Friedman and Savage, 1948, p. 283).

Where for psychologists such as Thurstone or for the astronomer behind his or her telescope the most important question was whether the theory proposed was verified by the observations, and whether the observations were artifacts resulting from imperfect experiments or telescopes, to Friedman and Savage the key question was how to best rationalize a number of indisputable facts of human economic behavior. In this process, they

---

[2] Friedman and Savage (1948) did not base their analysis on the von Neumann and Morgenstern axioms directly, but instead argued to have made their own analysis "self-contained... by the paraphrasing of essential parts of [von Neumann and Morgenstern's] arguments" (p. 281). It is, hence, a matter of debate whether Friedman and Savage (1948) is indeed entirely in line with the axioms of von Neumann and Morgenstern (2004). For instance, von Neumann and Morgenstern (2004) suggested – but it was indeed only a suggestion – that "[i]t is not clear at all... what significance [marginal utility] has in determining the behavior of a participant in a social exchange economy" (p. 31), which seems at odds with Friedman and Savage's wiggly utility curve, reproduced in Figure 2. To Friedman and Savage (1948), however, their wiggly utility curve was in line with von Neumann and Morgenstern (2004) because its curve is constantly increasing.

rejected some well-known rationalizations of economic theory: "Diminishing marginal utility plus maximization of expected utility would ... imply that individuals would always have to be paid to induce them to bear risk. But this implication is clearly contradicted by actual behavior" (Friedman and Savage, 1948, p. 280). Using the ordinal-cardinal language introduced by English economists John Hicks and Roger Allen (1934a) in "A Reconsideration of the Theory of Value," Friedman and Savage argued that the indifference curve analysis of Francis Ysidro Edgeworth, Vilfredo Pareto, and Irving Fisher could be used to "rationalize riskless choices," whereas the new "numerical properties" of utility functions developed by von Neumann and Morgenstern (2004 [1944]) could be used to "rationalize choices involving risk" (Friedman and Savage, 1948, pp. 281–282).[3]

Thus, Friedman and Savage's (1948) method was in line with von Neumann's view of mathematics as expressed in von Neumann and Morgenstern (2004 [1944]) and von Neumann (1988), as well as with the methodology employed in Wallis and Friedman (1942) and by Mill (1844). Yet, like Wallis and Friedman (1942), Friedman and Savage did not operate in a historical vacuum, and had to justify their approach in the language and standards of their time. They repeatedly talked about verifying and testing their theory and labeled their theory a hypothesis that made predictions about actual behavior, in which the predictions constituted a test of the hypothesis. However, testing and verifying the theory simply meant investigating whether the proposed rationalization corresponded to observable behavior. Moreover, behavior observed in the lottery booth was as good a test as were more extensive empirical investigations. In other words, Friedman and Savage justified their approach using twentieth-century language that is perhaps best understood as loosely based on logical positivism and Karl Popper's falsificationism.[4] This justification also served to emphasize the distinction between economics and psychology, just as Wallis and Friedman (1942) had separated psychology from economics.

Whatever the psychological mechanism whereby individuals make choices, these choices appear to display some consistency, which can apparently be described by our utility hypothesis. This hypothesis enables predictions to be made about phenomena on which there is not yet reliable evidence. The hypothesis cannot be declared invalid for a particular class of behavior until a prediction about that class proves false. No other test of its validity is decisive. (Friedman and Savage, 1948, p. 298)

---

[3] No specific references were given.

[4] Friedman's crude Popperian methodology is better known in the context of Friedman (1953); see, for example, Blaug (1980) and Mäki (2009).

As stated in Chapter 1, synonyms for the "rationalization" of rational behavior that were used by Wallis and Friedman (1942) and von Neumann and Morgenstern (2004 [1944]) included "characterization," "exact description," and "generalization." Friedman and Savage (1948) offered a slight variation by suggesting a distinction between "generalization" and "rationalization," without, however, further explaining what exactly constituted this difference. More important, they added new synonyms. One new synonym was "in accordance with," in the sense that the individual behavior observed had to be "in accordance with" the axioms and wiggly utility curve proposed. But Friedman's well-known "as-if" language, which first appeared in Friedman and Savage (1948), should also be seen in this light. The as-if phrasing was an expression of the rationalization process and a part of the distinction drawn between economics and psychology. Thus, according to Friedman and Savage (1948), the psychological explanations for individual behavior were irrelevant: as long as the wiggly utility curve characterized individual behavior, as-if individuals made their decisions on the basis of that curve. The relevant test, again, was predicted (and observable) behavior. The point was not to reveal the underlying psychological mechanism of human behavior, but instead to construct a hypothesis that yielded correct predictions about individual behavior as if individuals behaved according to the hypothesis:

> The hypothesis asserts . . . that, in making a particular class of decisions, individuals behave *as if* they calculated and compared expected utility and *as if* they knew the odds. The validity of this assertion does not depend on whether individuals know the precise odds, much less on whether they say that they calculate and compare expected utilities or think that they do, or whether psychologists can uncover any evidence that they do, but solely on whether it yields sufficiently accurate predictions about the class of decision with which the hypothesis deals. (Friedman and Savage, 1948, p. 298, emphasis in the original)

Finally, two differences between Friedman and Savage (1948) and von Neumann and Morgenstern (2004 [1944]) that gave rise to many of the confusions and discussions in subsequent years need to be pointed out. First, whereas to von Neumann and Morgenstern rational behavior was something the individual "endeavored" to achieve, to Friedman and Savage (1948) the individual always behaved rationally. For if individuals did not always behave rationally, Friedman and Savage's theory could not be proven wrong by invalid predictions. To von Neumann and Morgenstern, the axioms of rational behavior were grounded in empirical reality, but an empirical test could never decisively verify or falsify the axioms as they had left open the possibility that although endeavoring to be rational, individuals might fail to be so. By emphasizing the theory's predictions as a decisive test of the theory, Friedman and Savage implicitly argued that individuals in the economy always behave rationally, because if they did not, the predictions could be wrong and the theory falsely rejected.

Second, Friedman and Savage intensified the confusion between numerically defined utility and money, as employed by von Neumann and Morgenstern. Strictly speaking, the two were not to be equated. Numerically defined utility was a rationalization, an axiomatic abbreviation of the relationship between individual choices and derived satisfaction. Numerically defined utility was not an ontological claim about the nature of that relationship, but rather an axiomatic characterization of how individuals decide. That is how it was intended by von Neumann and Morgenstern. But by stating that "[i]t simplifies matters, and involves no loss in generality, to regard the alternatives open to the consumer unit as capable of being expressed entirely in terms of money or money equivalents" (Friedman and Savage, 1948, p. 288), Friedman and Savage at least suggested that it was an ontological claim and that the utility the individual derives from different decisions can always be computed into money equivalents.

In addition to Friedman and Savage, other economists and mathematicians incorporated von Neumann and Morgenstern's new approach. Like his contemporaries, economist Jacob Marschak (1898–1977) struggled with the axiomatic method commenced by the *Theory of Games and Economic Behavior*, but in the end essentially followed it (e.g., Marschak, 1946, 1950).[5] Like von Neumann and Morgenstern, Marschak argued that "[t]he theory of rational behavior is a set of propositions that can be regarded either as idealized approximations to the actual behavior of men or as recommendations to be followed" (Marschak, 1950, p. 111). By implication, Marschak argued, the "use of setting" of these propositions was twofold: "to describe approximately the behavior of men who, it is believed, cannot be 'all fools all the time,' and to give advice on how to reach 'correct' conclusions. These two aspects of the rules of logic and arithmetic can be called, respectively, the descriptive and the recommendatory aspect" (Marschak, 1950, p. 112). Although Marschak considered the propositions to be idealized approximations, he also considered individuals to be "tolerably rational" (see also Marshak, 1946).

But because he regarded the propositions to be "idealized approximations," Marschak argued in contrast to Friedman and Savage (1948), and in line with von Neumann and Morgenstern (2004 [1944]), that the

---

[5] Marschak was director at the Cowles Commission for Research in Economics (1943–1948), then located at the University of Chicago.

propositions "cannot be tested by observation" (Marschak, 1950, p. 127). Like Friedman and Savage (1948), however, and in particular like Wallis and Friedman (1942), Marschak in addition argued that potential experiments in economics had so many practical difficulties that it was not possible to conduct experiments testing these "idealized approximations." There was no way to test whether individuals indeed are tolerably rational: "The difficulties [of testing whether someone is tolerably rational] are obvious and stem from the economist's inability to make experiments" (Marschak, 1950, p. 127). Like both von Neumann and Morgenstern (2004 [1944]) and Friedman and Savage (1948), Marschak argued that the behavioral postulates had to be based on intuition, or "immediate plausibility," and summarized observable behavior: "[We] desire to avoid behavior postulates which are neither immediately plausible nor show themselves as approximated by easily observable action" (Marschak, 1950, p. 134).

3. Economic Opposition to the von Neumann and Morgenstern and the Friedman and Savage Interpretation

A number of economists disagreed with the axiomatic approach to economic behavior offered by von Neumann and Morgenstern (2004) and Friedman and Savage (1948). Paul Samuelson (1915–2009) from the Massachusetts Institute of Technology, Princeton University economist William Baumol (b. 1922), and engineer-economist Maurice Allais (1911–2010) from the École Nationale Supérieure des Mines in Paris were particularly outspoken. This debate was understood by its participants, and by historians, to be about the measurability of utility, in which the Neumann-Morgenstern-Friedman-Savage-Marschak camp was accused of proposing a cardinal measure of utility that for different reasons was impossible to construct (Moscati, 2007b, 2010; Ingrao and Israel, 1990; Mandler, 1999; Mongin, 2009). But underneath, the question was what the behavioral axioms – and economic theory in general – aimed to provide: general characterizations or descriptions. Baumol, Allais, and Samuelson took the latter position, although by and large they did not seem to be aware of the fact that it was this different epistemological point of view that lay behind their disagreements with Friedman, Savage, and Marschak.[6]

---

[6] Paul Samuelson was an adversary of Friedman in other regards also, not in the least ideologically. Friedman, Allais, and, to a lesser extent, Savage and Wallis, were outspoken free-market advocates; Samuelson and Baumol were well-known Keynesians. An obvious question is thus whether opposite political ideologies played any role in the fervent debate on von Neumann and Morgenstern's behavioral axioms as discussed here. In the various publications and letters, there is not a single suggestion to that effect. Note also that whereas

As a result, the two sides failed to solve the dispute. Baumol gradually lost interest and switched to other topics. Samuelson nuanced his view and then left the matter. Allais was the last to arrive to the debate and was the most persistent in trying to convince Friedman and Savage that they were wrong. But Allais also did not seem to be able to refute conclusively the positions taken by Friedman and Savage. Around the mid-1950s, therefore, Friedman and Savage seemed to have won the argument. However, Chapter 5 shows that, for instance, Samuelson's influential undergraduate textbook *Economics* in its early editions of the 1940s and 1950s relied on the traditional, Millian interpretation of economic principles – somewhat contradictory given Samuelson's opposition to von Neumann and Morgenstern (2004 [1944]) – but came to explain the assumptions on which economic theory is based as positivist, descriptive claims in the 1970s and 1980s. By that time, Allais's counterexample to Savage's theory, which was little noticed in the early 1950s, had become the famous Allais paradox. These developments provide one explanation for why Baumol joined the advisory board of the newly created behavioral economics program at the Alfred P. Sloan Foundation in 1984, which sought to fund empirical research that further disproved the assumptions on which economic theory was based.

But that was all still decades away in the late 1940s and early 1950s. In late 1949, Baumol asked Samuelson if he intended to write something on the "Neumann-Morgenstern Measurability of Utility argument," urging that "What I am threatening to do in the event that you have no plans in that direction is to write it up in a note myself."[7] Samuelson replied that he did not have time or much interest in the matter and encouraged Baumol to put his ideas to paper. As Baumol initially considered there to be only a minor difference of opinion, he suggested to Marschak that together with Samuelson and Friedman they might issue a joint statement. Marschak and Friedman, however, were not interested.

Then, in a long letter dated May 5, 1950, Baumol wrote Samuelson that he took the von Neumann-Morgenstern utility index to be a description of the "introspective utility" individuals attach to different (bundles of) goods. In addition, he offered a few counterexamples he intended to use in a brief paper on the subject. Baumol's letter catalyzed Samuelson's interest in the matter. In his characteristically brash tone he replied to Baumol within days:

Friedman and Baumol remained on cordial speaking terms throughout the debate, Savage and Allais clashed irreparably.

[7] Baumol's letter to Smauelson, November 18, 1949, Box C1, William Baumol Papers, Economists' Papers Project, Duke University Rare Book, Manuscript, and Special Collections Library.

The N-M result is inadmissible and arbitrary: make no mistake about that. It *does* contradict the generally-admissible facts altho' Mosteller's truly-pathetic experiments are incapable of showing that [Mosteller and Nogee, 1951]. But to find where N and M introduced the arbitrary element is not easy. They truly don't know themselves. Axiom 3:C:b is not by itself objectionable: it is their treatment from the very beginning of the *utilities of a lottery-ticket or income-probability situation as their elements of their algebra* that introduces the hidden independence assumption.[8]

Fredrik Mosteller and Philip Nogee from Harvard University had attempted to measure the money-utility curve for some ten individuals, using a complicated, poker-like gambling experiment. The experimental results suggested individuals indeed maximize utility and derive marginally decreasing utility from increasing sums of monetary income. However, the results were far from conclusive and especially revealed the many practical difficulties associated with experiments in economics, which the authors extensively discussed.

Inspired by Baumol, Samuelson also sat down to put his arguments against the von Neumann-Morgenstern approach into a brief note. Samuelson's main objection was that the axioms were not a good description of human decision-making behavior. He bluntly stated: "I know of no empirical predictions that this theory has suggested which have turned out to be (1) valid and (2) novel or inexplicable without this special theory" (Samuelson, 1950, p. 168). More prosaically, Samuelson continued: "The most rational man I ever met, whom I shall call Ysidro [when] told that he did not satisfy all of the v. Neumann-Morgenstern axioms...replied that he thought it more rational to satisfy his preferences and let the axioms satisfy themselves" (Samuelson, 1950, p. 170).[9] This remark introduced the "Ysidro man" and "Ysidro functions" in the many letters between Samuelson, Baumol, Friedman, Savage, and Marschak that would follow over the next two years. In this correspondence, Samuelson also introduced his mother as an example of the archetypical noneconomist reasoning based on good sense. Samuelson's mother would, for instance, not compute introspective utilities of different lottery outcomes and would simply take $200 to be twice as valuable as $100. She was one counterexample to the

---

[8] Samuelson's letter to Baumol (emphasis in the original), May 9, 1950, Box C1, William Baumol Papers, Economists' Papers Project, Duke University Rare Book, Manuscript, and Special Collections Library.

[9] To economists at the time, "Ysidro" was an obvious reference to the already mentioned Francis Ysidro Edgeworth. Among others, Edgeworth further developed the mathematics of individual decision making and of utility theory and was the first to propose indifference curves as an illustration of economic theory. As such, Samuelson advanced Edgeworth as the first truly scientific, and hence truly rational, economist.

Neumann-Morgenstern-Friedman-Savage-Marschak approach, according to Samuelson and Baumol. Thus, for instance, Marschak would also discuss with Baumol how best to axiomatize the behavior of Samuelson's mother and why her behavior could or could not be considered rational. To drive home his objections, Samuelson argued: "If only the data knew what men know, planets might move in perfect circles" (Samuelson, 1950, p. 170).[10]

In a long letter to Samuelson, Savage argued in reference to Samuelson's article that the axioms were of course not intended as exact descriptions:

[Y]ou point out that the utility theory, as I shall for simplicity call it in this letter, is not consistent with every conceivable sort of behavior. This is, of course, true, and to the credit of the theory insofar as it shows that the theory is not simply tautological.... [Von Neumann's] interest, like Milton's and mine, is the theory stems from the belief that it is a skillfully chosen zero approximation to reality. As a matter of fact, if you and I have anything to argue about, it is the question of whether this particular approximation has been skillfully chosen.[11]

The "skillfully chosen zero approximation to reality" was a reflection of Savage's attempt to express and distinguish the epistemological position he had adopted from von Neumann. In addition, Savage argued that the behavioral axioms of von Neumann and Morgenstern were nothing more than a set of assumptions underpinning Daniel Bernoulli's (1954 [1738]) famous function of decreasing "moral value" with respect to monetary value.[12]

In 1738, Bernoulli had argued that individuals base their choice between two or more (uncertain) outcomes not on the monetary or objective value of the outcomes but on their individual, subjective valuation of these outcomes. Bernoulli labeled this individual valuation "moral value" and supposed its expansion decreases with increasing monetary outcome, as in the curve in the following figure.[13]

---

[10] A reference to the epi-cycle theory accounting for planets that deviated from the perfect circle orbit as predicted in the Ptolemaic system of astronomy, until Copernicus, Galileo, and Kepler put the sun instead of Earth at the center of the astronomical system. In other words, Samuelson accused von Neumann, Morgenstern, Friedman, Savage, and Marschak of building a Ptolemaic system that was incongruent with reality.

[11] Savage's letter to Samuelson, May 19, 1950, cc Friedman, Box C2, William Baumol Papers, Economists' Papers Project, Duke University Rare Book, Manuscript, and Special Collections Library.

[12] Letters not immediately copied to the others were often forwarded. The letter just cited, for instance, was forwarded by Samuelson to Baumol.

[13] For histories of Bernoulli's and others' solutions to the so-called St. Petersburg paradox, see Jorland (1987), Teira (2006), Jallais, Pardier, and Teira (2008), and Basset (1987).

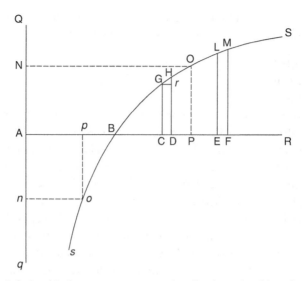

Figure 2.2. Relationship between monetary value (horizontal axis) and moral value (vertical axis; Bernoulli, 1954 [1738], p. 26).

In different words, Friedman argued as Savage did: "The significant problem is the construction of hypotheses about economic behavior that will enable predictions to be made about some part of behavior from the observation of other parts of behavior (i.e., that are not empty). These hypotheses will justify confidence only if there are many opportunities for contradiction, and the hypothesis repeatedly fails to be contradicted."[14] (Friedman's letter to Baumol, 3 June, 1950, cc Samuelson and Savage, Box C1). Thus, Friedman argued, to understand the von Neumann-Morgenstern axioms as a claim about the measurability of utility was a red herring. The axioms did not measure (that is describe) decisions one-to-one, but provided a characterization of the typical economic behavior by individuals.

Baumol quickly responded that "If utility measurement is a red herring, it was neither Paul Samuelson nor I who dragged it across the trail" and that

"even as a hypothesis about human psychology, the promise seems to me to be quite implausible and a fairly crude form of questioning of my friends serves to strengthen my doubts. . . . Perhaps some experiments designed explicitly to throw

---

[14] Friedman's letter to Baumol, June 3, 1950, cc Samuelson and Savage, Box C1. William Baumol Papers, Economists' Papers Project, Duke University Rare Book, Manuscript, and Special Collections Library.

light on this point are called for. Unfortunately the studies already undertaken by Mosteller and Nogi [*sic*] seem not to have been designed for this purpose."[15]

In a second letter to Savage, Baumol argued that "there are some people (Oskar Morgenstern among them) who feel that the correct measure of utility has been discovered"[16]

In the summer of 1950, Baumol submitted his comment on the von Neumann-Morgenstern-Friedman-Savage approach to the University of Chicago's *Journal of Political Economy*, where editor Earl Hamilton sent it to four reviewers. One of the reviewers was Milton Friedman – at the University of Chicago since the 1930s – who repeated his disagreement with Baumol but who also asked Hamilton, in view of the preceding discussions, to let Baumol know he was the reviewer. And despite his strong disagreement, Friedman did not object to the publication of Baumol's short article in the journal with which he identified intellectually and institutionally.[17] In his review of Baumol's article, Friedman again took the position that the "Bernoulli-Marshall-Neumann-Morgenstern-Friedman-Savage-Marschak hypothesis"[18] was an empirical claim of how economic behavior under uncertainty is best described. Hence, Friedman argued, if it is sometimes refuted, the first question should be if there is a hypothesis available that does better. In other words, Friedman understood the axioms as rationalizations of clearly observable behavior but framed this in a language of hypotheses, refutations, and description. As a result, it is clear how Baumol could understand Friedman as claiming that the axioms were empirical, refutable claims.

---

[15] Baumol's letter to Friedman, June 12, 1950, cc Samuelson and Savage, Box C1, William Baumol Papers, Economists' Papers Project, Duke University Rare Book, Manuscript, and Special Collections Library.

[16] Baumol's letter to Savage, July 27, 1950, cc Friedman and Samuelson, Box C1, William Baumol Papers, Economists' Papers Project, Duke University Rare Book, Manuscript, and Special Collections Library. Interestingly, neither Samuelson nor Baumol, Friedman, or Savage seemed interested in starting a correspondence with von Neumann or Morgenstern on the matter. With respect to von Neumann this is in all likelihood because it was common knowledge that von Neumann had moved on to other matters (Leonard, 2010). It is not clear why Morgenstern was not involved.

[17] Although not as close as with Samuelson, in general Baumol was always on good and cordial, if somewhat formal, terms with Friedman. Baumol and Friedman had been exchanging letters since the late 1940s on various economic issues, and continued to do so after the debate on the behavioral axioms. Baumol's revised version was accepted for publication September 29, 1950.

[18] Review Friedman of first submission Baumol, 1950, emphasis in the original, Box C1, William Baumol Papers, Economists' Papers Project, Duke University Rare Book, Manuscript, and Special Collections Library.

In his article, Baumol tried to disprove Friedman and Savage on their own terms – as he understood them – by showing the theory to be descriptively invalid. According to Baumol, it was "not at all difficult to construct examples in which the Neumann-Morgenstern [numerical utility] index leads to results conflicting with plausible preferences" (Baumol, 1951, p. 64). That is, Baumol claimed it was easy to construct examples that were at odds with the intuition of the axioms. Or, in Baumol's own words, these counterexamples had "introspective significance" and, hence, disproved the axioms. Baumol essentially produced the same kind of counterexamples that would later be made famous by Allais (1953a, 1979), Ellsberg (1961), Kahneman and Tversky (1979), and others. One counterexample ran as follows: call the numerical utility derived from choice options "utils," to avoid all unfortunate connotations and discussions related to equating numerical utility with money.[19] Now, which of the two options will you prefer?

a: a 5/6 chance of winning a 600 utils prize with a consolation prize of 60 if you lose

b: a 1/6 chance of winning the 600 utils prize with a consolation prize of 420

(Baumol, 1951, p. 64)

The von Neumann-Morgenstern and Friedman-Savage approach would argue for *a*, as the respective expected utilities (or perhaps one should say expected utils) of *a* and *b* are 510 and 450. However, Baumol argued, it was introspectively clear that many individuals would prefer *b* to *a* as a result of risk-aversion. Hence, the theory was flawed.

It was at this point, late in 1950, that Marschak became involved in the correspondence. As said, unlike Friedman and Savage but like von Neumann and Morgenstern, Marschak tried to distinguish between the axioms as characterizing rational behavior, the axioms as recommendations of how to behave rationally, and the possibility of actual behavior sometimes deviating from this rational standard. This introduced into the debate the question of what was meant by rationality. For instance, Baumol argued thus: "We are, I think, agreed that the empirical validity of the structure cannot be settled on a priori grounds, though I personally believe that it does not generally hold in practice.... [But t]here remains the largely semantic question whether it is "irrational" for a person to violate the hypothesis."[20] Subsequently,

---

[19] Note that a decreasing utility of money, or any other valuation of monetary income, is incorporated in the util. Thus, 100 utils by definition is twice as valuable to the individual as 50 utils.

[20] Baumol's letter to Marschak, January 9, 1951, cc Samuelson, Box C1, William Baumol Papers, Economists' Papers Project, Duke University Rare Book, Manuscript, and Special Collections Library.

Baumol and Marschak became entangled in an extensive correspondence in which Baumol challenged Marschak repeatedly on the descriptive validity of his and the von Neumann-Morgenstern axioms. Marschak responded by showing how Baumol's counterexamples actually did fit the axioms and by arguing that Baumol's counterexamples were self-contradictory. But Baumol quickly answered:

> I do not believe that people do in fact generally maximize their moral expectations. I do not maintain of course that no one ever does so or that it is irrational in any sense to maximize moral expectations. I believe merely that people often fail to behave so, and that it need not be more irrational in the standard sense of the term to fail to maximize moral expectations than to maximize them.[21]

Somewhat tired of failing to solve the dispute, Marschak replied that "[t]he existence of mathematics (and logic) is evidence of human limitations."[22] Thus, Marschak largely sided with the Friedman-Savage interpretation of the axioms and like the others initially assumed that the minor disagreements could be solved relatively easily. However, also Marschak and Baumol failed to bridge the different points of view because they failed to see that behind what appeared to be a dispute about the measurement of utility or the definition of rationality were in fact two different interpretations of the axioms on which decision theory was based.

Another attempt to strike a balance between the different voices and to bring the new decision theory in line with existing economic theories was undertaken by economist Kenneth Arrow (b. 1921) from Stanford University. Arrow (1951a) first of all sketched a broad overview of "the literature in economics, philosophy, mathematics, and statistics on the subject of choice among alternatives the consequences of which are not certain" (Arrow, 1951a, p. 404). Arrow then distinguished three categories: (1) "the axiomatic treatment of choice among probability distributions" stemming from von Neumann and Morgenstern and others; (2) "the modern theory of statistical inference," deriving from Neyman, Pearson, and Wald and understood as "a special form of the problem of (rational) behavior under uncertainty"; and (3) "Professor Shackle's new formulation of the whole problem of uncertain anticipations and actions based on them" (Arrow, 1951a, p. 405).[23]

---

[21] Baumol's letter to Marschak, March 5, 1951, Box C1, William Baumol Papers, Economists' Papers Project, Duke University Rare Book, Manuscript, and Special Collections Library.

[22] Marschak's letter to Baumol, 2 July, 1951, Box C1, William Baumol Papers, Economists' Papers Project, Duke University Rare Book, Manuscript, and Special Collections Library.

[23] In the 1950s, Geroge Shackle's (1903–1992) formalization of rational decision behavior was broadly considered an important alternative to the von Neumann-Morgenstern-Savage approach. However, after a period of canonization around von Neumann and Morgenstern

Subsequently, Arrow argued economists should not worry too much about questions of the empirical or normative status of these theories.

> Some of the theories discussed here purport to explain the actual behavior of individuals under conditions of uncertainty, some to give advice as to rational behavior, and some, by implication at least, to do both. . . . Almost all the theories discussed here seem to be rational in the first sense, but not in the second. In view of the general tradition of economics, which tends to regard rational behavior as a first approximation to actual, I feel justified in lumping the two classes of theory together. (Arrow, 1951a, p. 406)

In contrast to Baumol, Samuelson, Friedman, Savage, and Marschak, Arrow seemed to perceive the different ways in which one could understand the nature of the axioms, or principles on which the economic discipline was based as the crucial point of discussion. Subsequently, Arrow tried to incorporate the different new theories in economic theory and tried to brush over the apparently conflicting interpretations. As such, Arrow (1951a) may be understood as part of a broader development in post war economics to incorporate the new decision theory in its different varieties into economics by de-emphasizing the possible interpretations and the possible conflicts with existing economic theories (Amadae, 2003).

Just at the time when the unsolved dispute between Friedman-Savage-Marschak and Baumol-Samuelson subsided somewhat, French engineer-economist Maurice Allais (1911–2010) contacted Baumol. Baumol and Allais had been in irregular contact since the late 1940s, but never on this issue. The reason for Allais's contacting Baumol was the latter's *Journal of Political Economy* article: "I am pleased to send you a study on risk which, in view of your article in Journal of Political Economy, I think will interest you. Unfortunately, I have not taken account of your paper, my paper having been edited before receiving the corresponding Journal of Political Economy issue. I would of course be most delighted to receive your observations and suggestions."[24] Moreover, Allais referred to discussions he had been having

---

(2004 [1944]) and Savage (1954) in the 1950s, and after Shackle had turned more critical of the mainstream in Shackle (1961), his approach was put aside, including by Arrow (Zappia, 2008; Basili and Zappia, 2010).

[24] Allais's letter to Baumol, September 20, 1951, Box C1, William Baumol Papers, Economists' Papers Project, Duke University Rare Book, Manuscript, and Special Collections Library. The article to which Allais referred was "Fondements d'une Théorie Positive des Choix Comportant un Risque et Critique des Postulats et Axioms de L'Ecole Americaine" (1953a). Its English translation formed the basis of Allais and Hagen (1979). In their correspondence, Allais wrote in French and Baumol, Savage, and Friedman in English, a common

with Friedman regarding von Neumann and Morgenstern (2004 [1944]), Bernoulli (1954 [1738]), and Friedman and Savage (1948).[25] In a reply, Baumol dryly noted that "[i]t is interesting incidentally that while you were having this discussion with Friedman we were carrying on a similar debate by mail."[26] The two men quickly found each other in their disagreement with von Neumann and Morgenstern (2004) and Friedman and Savage (1948), but while to Allais this was only the beginning of a long and intense effort to refute von Neumann, Morgenstern, Friedman and Savage, Baumol had already begun to lose interest in the whole matter.[27]

Allais's attempts to prove wrong what he labeled the "American School" of utility theory famously erupted during the "Colloque International sur le Risque," held in Paris from May 12 through 17, 1952. For this symposium, Allais persuaded Samuelson to restate his views of the matter (Samuelson, 1952), a paper Baumol subsequently referred to as also describing his own position. Samuelson (1952) emphasized that he disagreed both on empirical, normative, and deductive grounds with what on this occasion he labeled the "Bernoulli utility theory." Samuelson saw only aesthetic or semantic value to the Bernoulli theory: "probably the largest part of human behavior is probably intrinsically and inescapably different from the utility hypothesis, precisely because the things it denies – pleasures of gambling or

---

practice between French- and English-speaking scientists at the time. Translations are the author's.

[25] Most likely, Allais and Friedman first met in person during the first meeting of the Mont Pelerin Society in Lausanne, Switzerland, in 1947. They started a correspondence early 1948 on various economic issues, including the question of whether the economic organization of France was such that France could attain the level of welfare of the United States, and regarding the price and revenue elasticities of various goods in the United States. The discussion on the measurement of utility to which Allais referred in his letter to Baumol consisted of Allais sending Friedman the same papers and questions as he was sending Savage. In contrast to Savage, Friedman never answered with more than one or two lines. The exception was the extensive questionnaire Allais also sent to Savage – to be discussed later – which Friedman patiently filled out while at the same time pointing to the many practical shortcomings that made the questionnaire in his view scientifically meaningless.

[26] Baumol's letter to Allais, October 18, 1951, Box C1, William Baumol Papers, Economists' Papers Project, Duke University Rare Book, Manuscript, and Special Collections Library.

[27] Next to Samuelson, Baumol and Allais there were others who disagreed with the von Neumann and Morgenstern approach. Robert Solow (b. 1924), from the Massachusetts Institute of Technology, suggested to Baumol that like Samuelson, he and many others were skeptical of the von Neumann-Morgenstern utility index: "Originally I was even more recalcitrant than Paul [Samuelson] in conceding special privilege to the linear index, if it exists. I would probably be more generous now, but in view of what we all seem to think about the whole circle of ideas, it hardly matters" (Solow's letter to Baumol, 14 May, 1952, Box C1).

of uncertainty, love of danger, taboos, etc. – are sociological and economically important for Homo sapiens" (Samuelson, 1952, p. 128).[28]

Friedman and Savage responded in print to Baumol (1951) in their own ingenious way, ignoring Samuelson's blunt axe. Friedman and Savage (1952) summarized Baumol's criticism in two points: (1) The axioms "are not introspectively obvious" (Baumol, 1951, p. 65), and (2) counterexamples can be constructed. Friedman and Savage defended themselves against the first point with the argument that the fact that the axioms are not introspectively obvious only speaks in favor of them. Friedman and Savage argued that science always advances by what initially seem rather implausible propositions. Hence, they argued, one could even say that the more implausible the hypothesis, the likelier it is to be true. Aside from philosophical or historical objections one could raise against this position, it clearly contradicted Friedman and Savage's (1948) epistemology of rationalizing and characterizing behavior that is plainly observable to all who are willing to spend a few minutes in the lottery booth or in a grocery shop.

Also Baumol's second objection was countered by means of a crude version of Popper's falsificationsim. Any theory or hypothesis, Friedman and Savage argued, has to be judged by how well it stands the scrutiny of attempted contradiction: "[i]f the statements about unobserved behavior are contradicted ('frequently' or more often and more flagrantly than statements suggested by an alternative hypothesis), then the hypothesis is wrong" (Friedman and Savage, 1952, p. 465). Therefore, the key question, according to Friedman and Savage (1952), was whether there exists an alternative theory or hypothesis that better predicts individual behavior involving risk than Friedman and Savage's (1948) and von Neumann and Morgenstern's (2004 [1944]) theory. The answer, said Friedman and Savage (1952), was that there was no such theory, and therefore their theory had the greatest "potential fruitfulness" and should not be discarded until a better theory showed up. They concluded that "[t]he important question for us is whether the postulates can be expected to correspond reasonably well with observable economic behavior," and that "[the postulates] and

---

[28] Around the same time, Samuelson gradually began to distinguish between, on one hand, Friedman and Savage's application of the von Neumann-Morgenstern axioms to economics and, on the other hand, Savage and de Finetti's work on Bayesian statistics. The latter was an important stepping-stone for Savage's (1954) *Foundations of Statistics*. Samuelson became increasingly impressed of Savage's Bayesian statistics over the course of 1952. In addition, around this time Samuelson's criticism of von Neumann and Morgenstern began to emphasize their use of separable probabilities in the individual's utility function as the key problem of the axioms. For further details, see Hands (2010).

closely related assumptions have been given much attention by economists. There is widespread agreement that they are introspectively very appealing and that their agreement with experience, though not perfect, is quite good enough to merit continued interest" (Friedman and Savage, 1952, p. 468). This position allowed Friedman and Savage (1952) to accept Baumol's counterexample while at the same time allowing them to maintain their original theory. Thus, Friedman and Savage (1952) neutralized Baumol's objections.[29]

To summarize, during the first ten years after the publication of the first edition of von Neumann and Morgenstern (2004 [1944]), a number of contrasting interpretations of the axiomatic method were discussed. Marshak (1946, 1950) closely tracked the von Neumann-Morgenstern interpretation of the behavioral axioms in their being general characterizations of rational behavior, recommendations of how to behave rationally, and predictions of some sort of actual behavior. Friedman and Savage (1948, 1952) ignored the recommendatory aspect but did see the axioms not as descriptions but as general characterizations of behavior. At the same time – and somewhat contradictory – they emphasized that the only valid test were predictions made by the axioms. As long as the axioms and the theories derived from them yielded more accurate predictions than did competing theories, their theory had to be maintained. By contrast, Samuelson (1950, 1952), and in particular Baumol (1951, 1958), took the von Neumann-Morgenstern axioms and their various derivatives as descriptive in the strict sense: any counterobservation or counterexample invalidated them.

When it became clear to the various participants in this debate that the dispute would not be resolved, they lost interest and moved to other issues. However, during the same years, Savage had also started a much bigger project than merely applying the behavioral axioms to gambling and

---

[29] Although Baumol shifted his research elsewhere from 1952 onward, he remained critical of the von Neumann-Morgenstern numerical utility index as a measurement of individual preferences. In Baumol (1958) he argued an important problem was that the von Neumann-Morgenstern theory suggests that the new numerical utility measurement index provides a measurement of "introspective pleasure intensity," "strength of feelings," or however one wants to call the utilitarian basis of individual behavior. That, Baumol strongly argued, is not true and is simply a confusion.

Apart from the different opinions on the usefulness of von Neumann and Morgenstern's behavioral axioms, there was a consensus that utility as the label for the numerical measurement index was rather unfortunate because of the link it suggested to utilitarianism and to earlier economic usage of the concept of utility. At the same time, no better label suggested itself (e.g., Savage, 1954; Baumol, 1951, 1958; Luce and Raiffa, 1957; Friedman and Savage, 1948, 1952; Fishburn, 1989).

insurance behavior. Fully aware of the fact that he was exploring new terri-
tory he sent parts of his book manuscript to different people. In late 1951, he
approached Allais. This brought the whole matter of how to understand the
assumptions or axioms on which the theory of individual decision making
was based back to fore.

4. The Savage-Allais Debate

After their two collaborative publications in 1948 and 1952, Friedman and
Savage went their separate ways. Friedman further developed the epistemological position taken in Wallis and Friedman (1942) and Friedman and
Savage (1948, 1952). This resulted among others in "The Methodology of
Positive Economics" (Friedman, 1953), heavily discussed by economists,
philosophers and historians during the rest of the twentieth century (Nagel,
1963; Archibald et al., 1963; Hausman, 1992; Mäki, 2009; Fourcade, 2009).
Savage, on the other hand, went back to his initial métier, the mathematical
foundations of statistics, and to the interpretation of the behavioral axioms
as envisaged by von Neumann.

In the late 1940s and early 1950s, Savage had been working on a book
that would combine the theory of von Neumann and Morgenstern and his
own work with Friedman, with recent developments in subjectivist probability theory and logical probability theory. It was eventually published in
1954 as *Foundations of Statistics*. Even before publication, however, Savage's
manuscript stirred a considerable amount of discussion. Allais in particular
strongly opposed Savage's approach as a theory of rational human decision
making. But despite Savage's Francophilia and a series of intense correspondence and face-to-face discussions that developed between the two,
Savage and Allais failed to agree and failed to acknowledge the other's different epistemological perspective. In many ways, the Savage-Allais debate
resembled the earlier Baumol/Samuelson–Friedman/Savage/Marschak discussion, of which Allais had only partial knowledge. But whereas Baumol, Friedman, Savage and Marschak, in particular, always strived to find
common ground despite their disagreements, Allais completely opposed
Savage and went to much greater length and detail to disprove Savage.
Savage refused to agree with Allais, but his discussions with Allais did led
Savage to adopt a new position regarding the nature of his and von Neumann
and Morgenstern's axioms, which in turn heavily influenced the interpretation of decision theory and its axioms by mathematical psychologists and
behavioral decision theorists. To see why and how Savage and Allais disagreed we need to look a bit further into the background of Savage's book

(in addition to the von Neumann-Morgenstern legacy), and in particular we need to appreciate Allais's position.

Between the 1920s and the 1950s, a number of ideas were introduced that thoroughly reshaped the way decision theorists thought about decision making under uncertainty.[30] Authors such as Bruno de Finetti (1906–1985; 1937, 1949, 1951) and Frank Ramsey (1903–1930; 1931) introduced the idea that probability theory could be applied not only to "objective" uncertainties out there in the world, such as the probability that a coin falls heads and the probability that the sun rises tomorrow, but also to "subjective" probabilities, that is, uncertainties inside the individual, for example, "How uncertain am I that it will rain tomorrow?" or "How certain am I that this secondhand car will last at least two years?" In a related development, authors such as John Maynard Keynes (1883–1946; 1921) and Rudolf Carnap (1891–1970; 1950) extended the theory of logic to include uncertain propositions, that is, propositions with a degree of probability less than 1.[31] In this logical probability approach, uncertainty stems from the subject's personal belief in the occurrence of an event. The difference between objective and subjective probability is that objective probability is a probability obtained based on the available information and mathematical theory, a probability that, by definition, is the same for all human beings. Subjective probability, on the other hand, is a number attached to the personal belief of an individual. Subjective probabilities of the same event may thus differ across individuals.

The distinction between the two has never been undisputed, for it is difficult to determine where to draw the line between them. Statistical data, the basis for objective probability, are information observed by human beings and can thus equally be considered input for subjective probability. Moreover, the calculations for objective probability are always conducted by human beings and can therefore also be considered as subjective probabilities instead of objective probabilities. Adherents of the so-called subjectivist or Bayesian school argued precisely this: that statistics is simply the extension of the process of human belief formation to a more formal domain

---

[30] This paragraph briefly indicates a few points in a large literature. For useful overviews, see Hájek (2012), von Plato (1994), and Eriksson and Hájek (2007). For the Ramsey-Keynes connection, see, for example, Skidelsky (2003).

[31] This research can be traced back to nineteenth-century authors such as George Boole and Augustus De Morgan (e.g., Maas, 2005b, pp. 111–122; MacHale, 1985). On the history of probability theory, decision theory, and statistics prior to the twentieth century see also Daston (1988), Hacking (1975), and Porter (1986). On Keynes's logical probability and its complicated relationship to the subjectivist school, see Skidelsky (2003).

(see also Giocoli, 2013). Ipso facto, this meant that the whole of statistics is a process of human decision making under uncertainty, albeit a process that is scrutinized more rigorously and recorded more formally.

In other words, the subjectivist probability theory commenced by de Finetti and Ramsey and the logical probability approach of Keynes, Carnap, and others made statistics a part of decision theory. Thus, Abraham Wald's (1902–1950) influential *Statistical Decision Functions* (1950) stated on the first page that "[a] statistical decision problem arises when we are faced with a set of alternative decisions, one of which must be made, and the degree of preference for the various possible decisions depends on the unknown distribution $F(x)$ of X" (p. 2; see also Fishburn, 1964).[32] Decision theory was no longer only about which decision we as human beings should make given our preferences and the objective probability of different states of the world; it was now also about which conclusion should be inferred by statisticians from statistical data. Decision theory had incorporated statistics and was now an all-encompassing theory of human decision making under uncertainty.

In his book, Savage combined the theory of decision making under risk with the theories of subjectivist probability theory and logical probability. More specifically, Savage's aim was to lay the groundwork from which each of these applications would derive. Building on the axiomatic approach of von Neumann and Morgenstern and his two papers with Friedman, Savage proposed to start from the following seven postulates:

Assuming a preference set F,

P1: A preference relation is a transitive and complete binary relation on F.

Binary means that either $f \leq g$ or $g \leq f$. Transitive means that if $f \leq g$ and $g \leq h$ then $f \leq h$.

P2: The preference relation is independent of other events or options. Also known as the Sure-Thing Principle.[33] More formally, for the possible outcomes f, g, and all the events B, either $f \leq g$ given B or $g \leq f$ given B.

P3: The preference between two outcomes is independent of the event that produces the outcomes.

P4: The preference relation does not depend on the probability of the occurrence of the outcomes. Thus, if $f \leq g$, then also $f_p \leq g_p$ for all $0 < p \leq 1$.

---

[32] Similarly, Savage argued that "[t]raditionally, the central problem of statistics is to draw statistical inferences, that is, to make reasonably secure statements on the basis of incomplete information" (Savage, 1951, p. 55).

[33] Or independence axiom.

P5: Preference relations in the set F exist.

P6: No outcome is infinitely worse or infinitely better than any other outcome.

P7: Monotinicity, i.e. people prefer more to less. Thus, if the individual prefers a portion of f to a full portion of g, she will also prefer any larger portion of f to g.

(Savage, 1954, pp. 1–104)

Late in 1951, Savage had his manuscript largely ready and sent a copy to Allais, asking him for suggestions.

Following the publication of the *Theory of Games and Economic Behavior*, Allais had also become interested in theories of rational behavior (see also Leonard, 2010). Although Allais liked to portray himself as the iconic founding father of a French school of rational choice theorists that opposed a corresponding U.S. school, Sophie Jallais and Pierre-Charles Pradier show Allais's research as having arisen from a broader development in French economic-engineering research (Jallais and Pradier, 2005). Two groups may be distinguished in France of the late 1940s and early 1950s, they argue, that extensively discussed expected utility theory. Based on research by Pierre Massé in the early 1940s, Allais and other engineer-economists attending Allais's seminar at the Ecole Nationale Supérieure des Mines de Paris – including Marcel Boiteux, Gerard Debreu, Edmond Malinvaud, and Jacques Lesourne – opposed using expected utility theory in any way and actively designed counterexamples and counter-theories to show it being invalid. By contrast, mathematicians from the Institut de Statistique de l'Université de Paris – including Georges Darmois, Geroges Guilbaud, Georges Morlat, Jean Ville, and Germain Kreweras – agreed on a prescriptive use of expected utility theory as providing decision rules for trained, rational decision makers (i.e., managers) in the public sector.

At the same time, no one went further and to greater detail in designing counterexamples and counter-theories than did Allais. More explicitly than von Neumann and Morgenstern (2004 [1944]) and Friedman and Savage (1948, 1952), Allais situated the *Theory of Games and Economic Behavior* in the mathematical probability tradition of the seventeenth century, the St. Petersburg paradox and its solution by Daniel Bernoulli of the eighteenth century, and the Weber-Fechner psychophysics of the late nineteenth century (Allais, 1953a, 1979).[34] Allais recalled how Daniel Bernoulli (1700–1782) had proposed to describe the human psychology of

---

[34] In addition to Allais (1953a, 1979), the next few paragraphs draw on Allais' position as set out in his letters to Savage, to be found in Savage's archives at Yale University. Allais (1979) is the English translation of Allias (1953b).

choosing between outcomes of different probability not in terms of expected monetary value but in terms of expected moral value. He argued that this expected moral value was a form of "cardinal" utility in the sense that it suggested that subjective valuation of (monetary) outcomes could be measured numerically.[35] Allais subsequently equated this Bernoullian cardinal utility with the Weber-Fechner equation of psychophysics, thus linking it to psychology.

In experimental psychology and psychophysics as they arose in late-nineteenth-century Germany, the Weber-Fechner equation referred to the experimentally observed decreasing sensation with which individuals perceive an increasing value of a stimulus, thus producing a curve similar to the Bernoulli curve depicted earlier. Linking the two, the lower sensation of, say, adding one kilogram on top of twenty-five kilograms one is already carrying compared to adding it to five kilograms one is already carrying is psychologically the same situation as the lower sensation/utility resulting from adding an extra euro to twenty-five euro as opposed to adding it to five euro. As said, psychophysics played a major role in the early years of English neoclassical theory, when, for instance, Stanley Jevons and Edgeworth employed psychophysics to base economics on individual perception, valuation and hence demand of goods, rather than on the supply of goods (Maas, 2005). Also to Allais, the Bernoulli money-moral value curve was one example within the broader Weber-Fechner theory of the relationship between objective stimulus and subjective perception. Moreover, Allais understood Bernoulli-Weber-Fechner explicitly as a descriptive claim or hypothesis about the functioning of the human mind.

However, Allais argued that the Bernoulli-Weber-Fechner hypothesis of "psychological value" did not go far enough and offered his own extension of the theory by introducing the idea that the individual values a stimulus (including monetary gains) with respect to his or her own "psychological mean." In other words, Allais argued that the Bernoulli-Weber-Fechner hypothesis was correct but that it had to be defined not with respect to the mathematically or economically determined origin, but with respect to the individual's own psychological origin, or mean. This psychological mean, then, varied among individuals. For instance, in the choice between a certain gain of five euro and a four in ten chance at ten euro, the (implicit) mathematical or economic origin is zero euro. The psychological mean, by contrast, asks how these two outcomes relate to the psychological situation

---

[35] Allais did not refer to Hicks and Allen (1934a,b) and considered ordinal versus cardinal utility to be an established distinction.

the individual is currently in regarding the monetary stimuli. That psychological situation is different for a billionaire and a waitress, possibly leading the two to make a different choice.[36]

In addition, Allais understood the discussions of rational behavior in terms of a distinction between reason-based philosophy on the one hand, and empirically-grounded science on the other. He thus took a position that differed both from von Neumann and Morgenstern (2004 [1944]) and Friedman and Savage (1948, 1952), but that was similar to Baumol (1951, 1958) and Samuelson (1950, 1952; see also Fishburn, 1989). Allais distinguished clearly and rigorously, but largely implicitly, between reason as a basis of knowledge in the domain of philosophy, and systematic and controlled observation as the basis for knowledge in the domain of empirical science. This made the scientific investigation of the Bernoulli-Weber-Fechner hypothesis a difficult enterprise. As "psychological value" referred to the value attached to an outcome inside the individual human mind, the only way to reach it was through introspection by the individual.

In the most general case, the link between psychological and monetary values and the influence of the shape of the distribution of psychological values are *inextricably interwoven, and no experiment concerning choice among uncertain prospects can be relied on to determine psychological value (cardinal utility)* . . .

In the most general case, the psychological value (cardinal utility) can be determined *only* by introspective observation of either psychologically equivalent increments or minimum perceptible thresholds. (Allais, 1979, p. 35, emphasis in the original)

Based on this distinction between reason and experimental observation, Allais understood there to be two ways of defining rational behavior. The first one was that of rational behavior as the abstract criterion of consistency, noncontradiction, and the other components of philosophical reason. Although Allais did not say so explicitly, it is safe to suppose that such a definition of rational behavior could also only be refuted through reasoning/introspection. To emphasize Allais's position, remember that von Neumann, Morgenstern, and Savage would have disagreed with this interpretation, and would have argued that even these abstract criteria had to derive somehow from experience and observation. Allais, however, argued that the only way a rational definition could be changed was when one individual convinced another individual that his or her reason-derived definition was flawed.

---

[36] Allais's theory of the "psychological mean" is thus essentially the same as the reference dependence later introduced by Kahneman and Tversky.

The second definition of rational behavior, Allais argued, was "experimentally, by observing the conduct of persons who, one has reason in other respects to believe, act rationally" (Allais, 1979, p. 24). This, in other words, was the experimental psychology route as taken by Thurstone (1931). The empirical definition depended crucially on the assumption that the individual used in the experiment indeed acted rationally. For if the individual did not behave rationally, it would obviously be impossible to infer descriptions and theories of rational behavior from observing the individual.[37] Also this empirical definition of rationality conflicted with von Neumann and Morgenstern (2004 [1944]) and with what would become Savage's (1954) manuscript. To von Neumann and Morgenstern (2004 [1944]) and Savage (1954), it was perfectly fine if the individual behavior deviated from the rational norm, as long as the individual intended to behave rationally. Under Allais's second definition of rationality, however, the individual used in the experiment had to be assumed to behave rationally. And, importantly, Allais believed that also von Neumann and Morgenstern (2004 [1944]), Friedman and Savage (1948, 1952), and Savage (1954), in his manuscript, held this view, and, hence, believed that evidence that showed individuals to not behave rationally would refute their "American school" of rational decision theory.[38]

Late in 1951, Allais and Savage started a correspondence on decision theory in which Allais continuously challenged Savage on his approach and in which Savage reluctantly but seriously and sometimes extensively took account of Allais's arguments, although in the end, he only adjusted

---

[37] This use of the experiment seems somehow at odds with the declared impossibility of conducting experiments on the psychology of monetary values in the longer quote above. Implicitly, Allais seems to have made a distinction between two types of experiments, broadly in line with the historical development of the experiments in experimental psychology (e.g., Danziger, 1990, 1997). Historically, the first use of the experimental method in psychology is to ask individuals in a controlled environment to report on their internal, introspective sensation of an external stimulus – which originally did not, but very well could, include valuations of choice options or assessments of what is the rational course of action. The second use of experiments tries to track the natural sciences more closely by looking only at measurable output and by thus ignoring introspective reports of the experimental subject. Allais forcefully argued in favour of a strict distinction between reason and empirics, in which the experiment was a method solely of the latter. His rational choice experiments, however, employed the older type of psychological experiments in which philosophical, or rational introspection was a crucial part of the experimental practice.

[38] Allais was always self-conscious about his own work. In opposition to the "American School of utility, founded by von Neumann-Morgenstern," he recognized "the French School of utility represented by its founder Allais" (Allais and Hagen, 1979, p. vii).

his theory in a minor way.[39] From the first letter onward, Allais explicitly understood Savage's manuscript as an investigation of the object of "psychological attitude" or of "psychological value" of the individual toward different choice options and considered Savage's axioms to be an empirical description of this human psychology. At the same time, Savage's position, as expressed in his letters, seemed somehow different, which quickly frustrated Allais[40]:

I admit not to understand your position all that well . . . Naturally, we may define rational man as a man who obeys your postulates, but this definition of rationality appears to me considerably cut off from the concept of rationality as it is obtained by scientific logic. . . . It is necessary to acknowledge the observations I sent you in my last two letters.[41]

During the already mentioned 1952 symposium in Paris organized by Allais, the famous (what would later be called) Allais paradox arose.[42] The Allais

---

[39] Savage's archive at Yale University contains eight letters from Allais to Savage (Box 1, Folder 11). The first is dated March 21, 1952; the last, December 30, 1952. One of Allais's letters, however, refers back to a letter from Savage to Allais, dated December 20, 1951, the same letter to which Allais referred in his correspondence with Baumol. As said, that letter seems to have been the first between Savage and Allais and the letter in which Savage asked Allais to comment on his manuscript. In addition, the Savage archive contains a lengthy letter from Savage to Allais dated March 10, 1953 (Box 1, Folder 11), which more or less concluded the discussion. Yale University and Savage's family have put considerable effort in making the archive as inclusive as possible, so that one must conclude that other correspondence has been lost. As said, translations are the author's.

[40] Savage was generally interested in German and French and spent a few months in Paris on a Guggenheim Fellowship in 1952, during which he among others closely befriended Maurice Fréchet (1878–1973). As a result, Savage's reading of French in particular seems to have been fluent. In the mix between the serious and the tongue-in-cheek way of writing that was his trademark, Savage stated under "Foreign languages" on the Guggenheim application form: "Read mathematical German fluently, other German fairly well. Can understand lectures in German and increasing due to current study and practice of spoken French. Expect to be able to lecture in French, and can already converse reasonably well, especially about mathematical subjects" (Savage's Guggenheim application, late 1950, Box 2, Folder 11).

[41] Allais's letter to Savage, April 2, 1952, Box 1, Folder 11, Jimmie Savage's papers, Yale University, New Haven, Connecticut.

[42] Other participants besides Allais, Samuelson and Savage who attended the symposium included Kenneth Arrow, Bruno de Finetti, Milton Friedman, Ragnar Frisch, William Jaffé, Jacob Marschak, Jimmie Savage, George Shackle, and, of course, Allais himself. It is not exactly clear why Baumol did not attend the symposium. Given Allais's remarks in his letters to Baumol, it seems unlikely that Allais would have invited Samuelson, Friedman, and Marschak, but not Baumol. In view of the fact that in 1954 Baumol had to decline an invitation by Allais to attend a conference on dynamic models in Paris because Princeton would not fund such a visit, a possible explanation is that Baumol did not have the means to attend the symposium in 1952. Alternatively, it may be that Baumol was simply

paradox is among the best known in modern decision theory, and its peculiar history has been well documented by Jallais and Pradier (2005). During the symposium, Allais presented Savage with a decision problem over lunch that was set up with the same purpose as Baumol's (1951) counterexample: to show that the von Neumann-Morgenstern-Savage theory was descriptively invalid. The problem ran as follows:

1. Which of the following two gambles do you prefer?
   a) A 100% chance at 100 million francs
   b) A 89% chance at 100 million francs
      A 1% chance at nothing
      A 10% chance at 500 million francs
2. Which of the following two gambles do you prefer?
   c) A 89% chance at nothing.
      A 11% chance at 100 million francs
   d) A 90% chance at nothing
      A 10% chance at 500 million francs[43]

(Allais, 1953b, p. 527; translation by author)

Savage, like many human beings, chose option a) in the first question. This does not maximize the monetary outcome but could be explained by risk aversion and/or a decreasing utility of wealth such as suggested by Bernoulli (1954). In the second question, however, Savage chose (d), thus maximizing the monetary gain. Because one cannot prefer maximizing and non-maximizing at the same time, this contradicted the axioms as laid out by Savage in his forthcoming book. Thus, Savage had to choose between two unappealing options. Either he had to admit that his seven postulates were invalid, or he had to decide that he, Savage, the mathematician and *the* expert on his own theory and its postulates, had behaved irrationally.

The important detail in the Allais-Savage history is that Savage gave this outcome some thought (Jallais and Pradier, 2005). Had he, like Allais, taken the position that the empirical evidence directly and necessarily verified or refuted the theory, he could have decided immediately that the theory was false. But Savage, like his mentor von Neumann, believed that although individuals intend to behave rationally as defined by his postulates, they

overwhelmed by the different obligations he had at the time and did not have the time and energy a trip to Europe required (William Baumol, e-mail to author, October 18, 2011).

[43] Savage took the exchange rate at the time to be 350 francs to the dollar, which makes the 100 million francs equal roughly 285,000 1952 dollars. Similarly, 500 million francs equals about 1,400,000 1952 dollars.

may fail to do so. However, violating the axioms could also mean that the axioms were invalid characterizations of rational behavior. Thus, Savage needed some time to reflect on whether Allais's set of questions and his own answers to them had convinced him that his postulates were not a good characterization of rational behavior or that he had behaved irrationally. When Savage came back to Allais, he declared to believe he had been irrational and that he considered the seven postulates to still be good characterizations of rational behavior.

Allais, on the other hand, interpreted his lunch questionnaire discussion with Savage as the first observation in an empirical investigation into the validity of the von Neumann-Morgenstern-Savage theory as a description of the psychological valuation of monetary outcomes. According to Allais, Savage's responses showed that a linear, monotonic description of individual valuation of expected monetary outcomes as postulated in Savage (1954) and in von Neumann and Morgenstern (2004 [1994]) was invalid. Allais clearly saw Savage's answers as a first wedge in the postulates. To capitalize on this result, Allais wrote Savage (who was still in Paris) a letter two days after the symposium in which he further developed his attempts to disprove Savage by offering a question to which, he argued, Savage could not answer in a fashion that was in accordance with his own theory or with Bernoulli's theory of decreasing marginal utility. Allais came straight to the point. It is worthwhile to quote Allais at length here.

I suppose a lottery consisting of 1000 tickets and one unique price of 200 million francs.

In a first situation, individual X possesses 999 tickets and agrees to buy the 1000th ticket for price S_0

...

In the second situation, he possesses only 998 tickets and he is proposed only to buy one ticket, the last ticket out of his reach in any situation.

Let S_1 be the sum he is willing to pay for the 999th ticket in the second situation.

...

A number of people whom I have posed this question, and who are commonly regarded as rational, have given me without exception a value of S_0 that is superior to that of S_1.

Do you consider such a situation irrational?

...

I intend to conduct a questionnaire regarding this question on two groups of people: To students from the Ecole des Mines in Paris who, on average, may probably be considered to be rational; and to members of a seminar series ["groupe de conférence"] which I am chairing and who might equally be considered rational.

In any case, before organizing this questionnaire, I would like to have your opinion through *a reply to this letter* if possible, on these different questions, in such a way that I can take them into account.[44]

Within a day, Savage responded that he saw no reason why a rational but prudent person could not be risk averse and thus value increasing amounts of expected monetary outcomes with decreasing margin. A week later, however, Allais replied that he was "not convinced by [Savage's] answers."[45] The reason, Allais argued, was that the same result would obtain if the exercise were done with 50, 200, 300, 400, or 1,000 francs instead of 200 million. This implied that at each possible interval, one would have to draw a curve of marginally decreasing utility of expected monetary outcome while the curve as a whole would have to be increasing up to 200 million francs. Thus, Allais implied, the Bernoulli and von Neumann-Morgenstern-Savage idea of a constantly increasing valuation of expected monetary outcomes was invalidated. Clearly, Allais felt he had cornered Savage into a paradox of his and of von Neumann and Morgenstern's axioms.

Subsequently, Allais sent Savage as promised a "Sondage sur le risque."[46] This questionnaire – published in French as "Questionnaire destiné a tester la validité de la formulation de l'école Américaine pour les hommes rationnels" (Questionnaire intended to test the validity of the definition of rational men by the American School) – consisted of ten sets of questions regarding the risk attitude of the respondent (Allais, 1953c). The third set, for instance, posed the two questions which would later become the famous Allais paradox and eight other but similar questions. Set 4 presented four questions along the lines of the question Allais posed to Savage in his letter of May 19, 1952, just quoted. Along more or less similar designs in the other sets, the tenth set asked twenty-one questions such as "Do you play poker, and if so, which fraction of your monthly income do you spend on poker?" "Do you practice sports of high, or very high risk?" and "When you lose at a game of chance, up to which fraction p of your monthly income are you indifferent regarding your total loss during the game?" In addition, Allais asked Savage "to send me an indication of which are your different values for possible gains of 100 to 1 billion francs."[47]

---

[44] Allais's letter to Savage, May 19, 1952, Box 1, Folder 11, emphasis in original, Jimmie Savage's papers, Yale University, New Haven, Connecticut.

[45] Allais's letter to Savage, May 28, 1952, Box 1, Folder 11, Jimmie Savage's papers, Yale University, New Haven, Connecticut.

[46] Ibid.

[47] Allais's letter to Savage, June 18, 1952, Box 1, Folder 11, Jimmie Savage's papers, Yale University, New Haven, Connecticut.

Savage, meanwhile, was busy and apparently not very eager to comply with the extensive request by Allais, which is not surprising after what Savage must also have realized was a paradoxical outcome of his postulates. Over the course of June-November 1952, however, Allais continued to insist in a number of letters, indicating among others that he intended to use Savage's response in "a general study on Risk and in two articles for Econometrica."[48] In addition, in his letters, Allais copied a few times his earlier questionnaire and accompanying valuation question, should Savage have lost the earlier copy.

In March 1953, Savage finally responded, and quite extensively. In his answer to the list of questions of Allais and in the separate request to sketch his own utility curve, Savage proceeded by first assuming zero income or wealth to have zero utility, and one million dollars to have one unit of utility. Subsequently, he estimated, "by self interrogation,"[49] how much money he would want to receive to forego a gamble between an even chance of obtaining a certain income or nothing at all for a few different incomes between zero and 1 million dollars. He then estimated his utility curve[50] in the area of zero to 1 million dollars to be

$$U(x) = 0.035578(1 - e^{-0.001x})$$

Having established an estimation of his own income-utility curve, Savage then "gave [Allais's] questionnaire to a computer with instructions to answer those questions on it, the answers of which are implicit ... in the exponential formula." The reason for letting the computer determine the answers was that "my long experiences with the questionnaire is such that I can't fill it out spontaneously any more."[51] But of course, letting a computer provide the answers based on a pre-determined equation also ensured that no irrational answers would come out. After the computer had done its work, Savage examined the answers given by the computer "to see whether any of the mechanically-given answers seemed hopelessly inappropriate to my own tastes."[52] Savage was pleased to report that "I believe I can honestly say, for

[48] Allais's letter to Savage, May 28, 1952, Box 1, Folder 11, Jimmie Savage's papers, Yale University, New Haven, Connecticut.

[49] Graph, Savage, December 23, 1952, see appendix, Box 1, Folder 11, Jimmie Savage's papers, Yale University, New Haven, Connecticut.

[50] Graph, Savage, December 23, 1952, Box 1, Folder 11, Jimmie Savage's papers, Yale University, New Haven, Connecticut. Attached at the end of this chapter are Savage's initial sketches of his own utility curve, as well as the final version that was sent to Allais.

[51] Savage's letter to Allais, March 10, 1953, Box 1, Folder 11, Jimmie Savage's papers, Yale University, New Haven, Connecticut.

[52] Ibid.

what little it may be worth, that while my spontaneous answers to many of the questions would have been different I am not grossly dissatisfied with the answers chosen for me by the curve, especially after reflection, though the curve does make me out to be somewhat bolder than I really am."[53]

Savage's extensive response was completely in line with the von Neumann-Morgenstern-Savage theory, or, for that matter, with the Bernoulli curve on which Allais liked to elaborate. And although Savage ignored to mention it, his response to Allais flatly denied Allais's suggested invalidation of the well-formed income-utility curve. Thus, it is no surprise that Savage's letter was the last in the correspondence between Allais and Savage. In late 1953, Savage was asked by the editor of *Mathematical Reviews*, John Weyhausen, to review Allais's 1953 *Econometrica* article. Clearly not very inspired, Savage noted that the utility theory adhered to by "what the author calls the American School... is in fact shared by many others and is not confined to America."[54] Subsequently, Savage summarized Allais's position and concluded that he knew of no one who agreed with Allais. After this episode, Allais, not unlike Baumol two years earlier, shifted his attention to other issues, and his arguments against expected utility theory were largely forgotten, to be revived only in the 1970s, as a result of the publication of Allais and Hagen (1979), among others (Jallias and Pradier, 2005).[55]

However, Savage did incorporate Allais's critique by introducing in his nearly completed manuscript a distinction between a normative and an empirical "interpretation" of the theory (Savage, 1954, pp. 19–20). The normative interpretation comprised the von Neumann-Morgenstern-Savage approach of characterizing rational behavior irrespective of whether individuals actually do behave rationally all the time and derived from this characterization rules for behaving rationally. The empirical interpretation, on the other hand, investigated under which circumstances individuals behave rationally and under which circumstances they do not. This new normative-empirical distinction of Savage's *The Foundations of Statistics*

---

[53] Ibid.

[54] Draft, Box 11, Folder 251, Jimmie Savage's papers, Yale University, New Haven, Connecticut.

[55] In 1988, Allais won the Nobel memorial Prize in economics. Officially, Allais received the prize for "for his pioneering contributions to the theory of markets and efficient utilization of resources" and not for the paradox that bore his name ("The Sveriges Riksbank Prize in Economic Sciences in Memory of Alfred Nobel 1988," *Nobelprize.org*, accessed June 9, 2012, http://www.nobelprize.org/nobel_prizes/economic-sciences/laureates/1988/). That said, to the French engineer-economists expected utility theory and its counterexamples had always been part of an engineering approach towards the economy.

did not basically change the von Neumann-Morgenstern-Savage approach, but recognized that scientists, and in particular psychologists, should also empirically investigate how individuals actually do behave. Moreover, it took Savage away from the position taken in Friedman and Savage (1948, 1952), and back more closely to von Neumann and Morgenstern's *Theory of Games.*

More explicitly and forcefully than Baumol (1951, 1958), Samuelson (1950, 1952) and Arrow (1951), Allais understood the von Neumann-Morgenstern-Savage axioms to be descriptive claims of human behavior. Apart from the interpretation of the axioms, one cannot but agree that Allais had indeed pointed to a weak point in the von Neumann-Morgenstern-Savage theory and that Savage simply refused to acknowledge this. Savage's distinction between a normative and an empirical interpretation of the axioms is hence best read as an attempt to save the axioms while at the same time accommodating the questionnaire results by relegating them to a different, empirical, domain. Indeed, one equally has to appreciate this clever move by Savage. It silenced Allais and contributed to the impact of Savage's book. In addition, however, Savage's normative-empirical distinction unintentionally produced a whole new development in the communities of mathematical psychology and behavioral decision research.

5. Mathematical Psychology and Behavioral Decision Research

Two months after the Paris symposium, in the summer of 1952, mathematical psychologist Clyde Coombs (1912–1988) and mathematician Robert Thrall (1914–2009), both from the University of Michigan, organized an eight-week seminar on "The Design of Experiments in Decision Processes" at the RAND Corporation in Santa Monica, California. The seminar had evolved from Coombs's Mathematical Psychology seminar, which he had initiated at the University of Michigan in 1950 (see Chapter 3 for further details). The Santa Monica Seminar was supported either directly or indirectly by the Ford Foundation, the RAND Corporation, the Office of Naval Research, and the Cowles Commission and has been described as both an important catalyst for the development of game theory by historians of economics (Leonard, 2010; Weintraub, 1992; Dimand, 2005; Mirowski, 2002; Lee, 2004) and as a catalyst for the development of mathematical psychology by mathematical psychologists and their historians (Tversky, 1991; Frederiksen and Gulliksen, 1964; Laming, 1973; Luce et al., 1963a). The seminar resulted among others in an experimental test of non-cooperative game theory by Kalish, Milnor, Nash and Nering (1954), "Some Experimental n-Person Games," which appeared to show that people do not behave competitively and purely self-interested. Others who attended and presented at the seminar included psychologists Leon Fetsinger (1919–1989), William Estes (1919–2011) and Coombs; mathematicians Merill Flood (1908–1991) and Thrall; and economists Marschak, Howard Raiffa (b. 1924), and Gerard Debreu (1921–2004). The only scientist who attended both the Allais symposium in Paris and the Santa Monica seminar was Marschak.

The starting point of the seminar was the observation that "what we may call the modern look in decision theory is somewhat less than ten years old" (Davis, 1954, p. 2). In other words, the seminar's organizers and participants understood von Neumann and Morgenstern (2004 [1944]) to have started a new branch of social science, which was yet to be fully explored. At the same time, "decision theory" was defined a little broader than the cooperative game theory of von Neumann and Morgenstern (2004 [1944]). It also included rational decision making under given uncertainty (as opposed to the strategic uncertainty of game theory), noncooperative game theory as commenced by John F. Nash, and decision making under certainty started by economists such as Pareto, Edgeworth, and Samuelson.[56] In the introduction to the collection of papers that emerged in 1954, Coombs, Thrall, and Davis tried to side themselves with the epistemological position of von Neumann-Morgenstern-Savage, and thus against the position taken by Allais, but at the same time, they introduced a new interpretation in the form of a normative versus descriptive realm:

There is a ... distinction which, as often as it is recognized and properly described, nevertheless keeps obscuring communication and understanding between various scientists. That is the distinction between the theory which is in some sense principally descriptive or predictive and that which is solely normative....

The words "normative" and "rational man" seem unfortunate. It may be that the first economists to think in these terms actually intended to set forth what a man *should* do if he were rational; the intention of modern formulators of normative theory is usually more modest. Each constructs an abstract system about which he says in effect: "if a person's behavior is such that under the proper interpretation it can be said to satisfy the requirements of this system, then his behavior is what is called 'rational' in my theory." (Davis, 1954, p. 4, emphasis in the original)[57]

---

[56] The introduction did not provide specific references to articles or books of these authors.

[57] The conference organizers Thrall and Coombs "delegated to [Robert L. Davis] the task of writing a chapter designed to serve as introduction.... While he is responsible ... many of the ideas ... are outgrowth of numerous editorial conferences.... the word 'we' ... refers to all three editors" (Davis, 1954, p. 1).

Note first of all that the authors presumed the equation of rationality with normativity to stem from economics. Second, the last two sentences of this quote illustrate how Coombs, Thrall, and Davis considered themselves to be acknowledging the von Neumann-Morgenstern-Savage position while at the same time emphasizing the scientist's knowledge of what constitutes rational behavior at the expense of the individual subjects. In other words, they slightly reinterpreted the von Neumann-Morgenstern-Savage position. In addition, they emphasized the difference between the recommendatory and the descriptive elements of the von Neumann-Morgenstern-Savage position: "Game theory illustrates another source of confusion in interdisciplinary discussions. For von Neumann and Morgenstern evidently intended not only a normative interpretation for their theory, but also that it provide foundations for a new analysis of the empirical processes of economic exchange" (Davis, 1954, p. 5).

This normative-descriptive interpretation of the von Neumann-Morgenstern-Savage theory was taken over and reinforced by behavioral psychologists such as Ward Edwards (1927–2005; see also Chapter 3). Like Coombs, Thrall, and Davis, Edwards understood Savage's distinction between a normative and an empirical interpretation to be the same as experimental psychology's distinction between a normative and descriptive domain of scientific investigation (Edwards, 1954, 1961). Decision theory was understood by Edwards as providing a theoretical framework for the objective stimuli that the subject is presented with in the case of decision making under uncertainty. The self-assigned task of behavioral decision researchers was to measure experimentally which decision subjects make with respect to this objective stimulus. In the traditional framework, experimental psychology investigated individuals' subjective perception of objective values, such as weight or brightness differences (Danizger, 1990, 1997). In behavioral decision research the weights and lightbulbs were replaced with the probabilities and monetary values (or equivalents thereof) of decision theory. Given the objective values of the monetary outcomes and probabilities, decision theory determined the objective, that is, the normative decision. Behavioral decision research then measured experimentally which decision the subject actually made.

The distinction between the normative and the descriptive was often and clearly made by behavioral decision researchers (see also Amadae, 2003). Here is an example:

Decision theory is the study of how decisions are or ought to be made. Thus it has two faces: descriptive and normative. Descriptive decision theory attempts to describe and explain how actual choices are made. It is concerned with the study of variables that determine choice behavior in various contexts. As such, it is a proper branch of psychology. Normative decision theory is concerned with optimal rather than actual choices. Its main function is to prescribe which decision should be made, given the goals of the decision maker and the information available to him. Its results have a prescriptive nature. They assert that if an individual wishes to maximize his expected gain, for example, then he should follow a specified course of action. As such normative decision theory is a purely deductive discipline. (Coombs et al., 1970, p. 114)

Thus, in contrast to von Neumann and Morgenstern (2004 [1944]), von Neumann (1988), and Savage (1954) and to Edwards and other behavioral decision researchers (as well as to mathematical psychologists such as Coombs), there was no longer a "peculiar duplicity" in the normative part of decision theory. There was no longer an intricate relationship between experience, observation, and the derived axiomatic characterizations of decision theory. Instead, the normative realm had a purely deductive meaning that it derived from pure reason only. The only reference to observed behavior was in the descriptive realm, in which observed behavior was compared to the normative benchmark of pure reason.

It was in this regard that Edwards was interested in economics, as exemplified by his extensive and knowledgeable discussion of economics in Edwards (1954).[58] Edwards understood economics as a normative, deductive theory of human decision making, and he discussed it on an equal footing with statistics, mathematics and philosophy. Thus, Edwards noted that economics is an "armchair" science (Edwards, 1954, p. 14), not because he denounced economics but because he understood economics to be an armchair science just as mathematics, statistics, and philosophy. Edwards's discussion of "economic man" should also be read in this light. Economic man for Edwards and for the majority of psychologists was someone who makes his choices according to the normative theory, making it therefore a normative concept. If you asked what economic man would do in a certain decision problem, you asked what the normative solution is. At the same time, economic man as the embodiment of the normative theory formed a hypothesis about actual decision making that can be tested: "if economic man is a model for real men, then real men should always exhibit transitivity

---

[58] In January 1954, Edwards approached Savage with an early draft of his paper to check two references to papers of Savage. At the time, Savage and Edwards did not know each other personally, and it seems that prior to Edwards's letter, Savage was unaware of Edwards's work. Yet, Savage responded with an eleven-page letter, carefully discussing a total of fifty-two comments. Savage's letter started a correspondence that lasted a few years and formed the basis for Edwards's eventually successful attempt to lure Savage back to Michigan where he remained from 1960 to 1964 (Phillips and von Winterfeldt, 2006).

of real choices. Transitivity is an assumption, but it is directly testable. So are the other properties of economic man as a model for real men" (Edwards, 1954, p. 16). This experimental psychological interpretation of economics was thus not unlike what Thurstone had in mind during his conversations with Schultz.

It was as a result of expositions such Davis (1954), Edwards (1954, 1961), Coombs et al. (1970), and others that the terms *normative* and *descriptive* became the concepts in which decision theory was discussed in psychology and mathematics. This categorization into a normative and descriptive realm implied a different understanding than the von Neumann-Morgenstern-Savage position of the axioms as simultaneously generalized characterizations and rules for rational decision making. To the mathematical psychologists, and to the behavioral decision researchers, the norms of the normative realm were given by reason and hence were not subject to empirical investigation. The descriptive claims about actual decision making of human beings, by contrast, were directly amenable to experimental validation and falsification. In addition, the normative-descriptive distinction of the psychologists differed markedly from how economists would come to interpret decision theory and its axioms.

6. Friedman and the Methodology of Positive Economics

As stated earlier, Friedman's view of the proper epistemology of economics first explored in Wallis and Friedman (1942) and Friedman and Savage (1948, 1952) was further developed in "The Methodology of Positive Economics" (Friedman, 1953). Friedman's (1953) exposition is indicative of economists' view of the nature of their discipline in the postwar period and as such is indicative for economists' understanding of decision theory and its behavioral axioms. In "The Methodology of Positive Economics," Friedman firmly reinstated a conception of positive and normative science among economists that went back to John Stuart Mill and John Neville Keynes, which sharply contrasted with both Savage's normative-empirical interpretation and with Coombs, Edwards, and the other psychologists' normative-descriptive understanding of decision theory. To Friedman, "normative" meant ethical and thus nonscientific, and "positive" meant nonethical, not normative, and, hence, scientific (Hands, 2001). Such a very different interpretation of the word normative might seem odd, but note that Friedman (1953) was published one year before the first introduction of the mathematical-psychological meaning of "normative" in Savage (1954).

Moreover, by that time, Friedman and Savage had moved in different directions, and there was no pressing reason to resolve the fact that each used "normative" in such a different way.

What used to be called "rationalizations," "generalizations," "characterizations," or "exact descriptions" of rational behavior in Wallis and Friedman (1942), von Neumann and Morgenstern (2004), and Friedman and Savage (1948, 1952) were relabeled "assumptions" in Friedman (1953). Thus, in the language of Friedman (1953), economists made certain "assumptions" about individual behavior in the economy, and thus did not need psychology. Second, economists, according to Freidman (1953), derived specific predictions about not yet observed behavior from these assumptions. When the predictions were right, the proper assumptions had been made. And, in what would become one of the biggest controversies surrounding Friedman (1953), the realism (i.e., descriptive accuracy – recall his discussions with Baumol and Samuelson) of these assumptions was largely irrelevant. In fact, Friedman (1953), like Friedman and Savage (1952), suggested that because there is a strong rationale for scientific theories to be as simple and as general as possible, by definition they should leave out as much empirical content as possible. Thus, in a way, one could say that the more unrealistic the assumptions the better. The law of gravity is also best formulated without disturbing factors such as air resistance or the boy holding a ball. However, leaving this empirical content out makes the theory of gravity and its assumptions – no air, no boys holding balls – more unrealistic.

Friedman (1953) clearly struggled to find the right terms and always put quotation marks around "assumptions." In addition, Friedman (1953) slipped back a few times into his older language of "generalizations" and other terms:

Positive economics is in principle independent of any particular ethical position or normative judgments. As [Neville] Keynes says, it deals with "what is," not with "what ought to be." Its task is to provide a system of generalizations that can be used to make correct predictions about consequences of any change in circumstances. Its performance is to be judged by the precision, scope, and conformity with experience of the predictions it yields. In short, positive economics is, or can be, an "objective" science, in precisely the same sense as any of the physical sciences. (Friedman, 1953, p. 4)

Thus, to Friedman (1953), the positive realm was free of any ethical values; normative economics, on the other hand, was reasoning based on what is good, just, or ethical in any other sense. As such, Friedman placed himself in the tradition of Nassua Senior, John Stuart Mill, John Neville Keynes, and

Lionel Robbins (Hands, 2001). Although Friedman argued that normative economics could never be independent of positive economics, as one needed an understanding of the economic world to achieve the ethical goals one had set, positive economics could and should be as free from ethical values as possible. This remained the most prominent and, perhaps, the only understanding of positive and normative among economists until the rise of behavioral economics in the 1980s and 1990s (e.g., Hands, 2001).

One important difference between the normative-descriptive position of Coombs, Edwards, and others, and the positive-normative position of Friedman (1953) was their perceived relation to science. To the psychologists, the normative and the descriptive were both in the realm of science. Under the rubric of normativity, scientists determined the rules for rational behavior; in the descriptive realm, actual decision behavior of individuals was investigated. To Friedman (1953), however, normative first of all defined what scientific economics is *not* and what it should not be. Scientific economics to Friedman was first of all not being normative as a scientist (see also Stapleford, 2011). Following Friedman (1953), normative became a stigma to be avoided by economists; it became a label of non-scientificity. Thus, in addition to simply being about two different things – rationality or ethics – the two ways of using "normative" obtained very different roles in their respective communities. To mathematical psychologists, behavioral decision researchers, and other decision theorists, normative became the standard of behavior as determined by scientists to be followed by all and the benchmark by which to compare all behavior. To the majority of economists in the postwar decades, normative was everything scientific economists should not do.[59]

---

[59] Both the normative-descriptive distinction of the psychologists and the positive-normative distinction of the economists neglected the subtleties of the initial von Neumann and Morgenstern position, which explains why, towards the end of his life, Morgenstern felt compelled to reinstate their position. Morgenstern (1972) noted with some condescension that von Neumann and Morgenstern (2004 [1944]) had simply done what any good science had done since David Hilbert: use the axiomatic method. Axioms, Morgenstern asserted, are a description of the world, but not just any, they are its "highest degree of description" (Morgenstern, 1972, p. 700). This form of description, Morgenstern argued, is completely separate from the normative in the ethical sense as set out for instance by Friedman (1953). However, Morgenstern reasoned, there is a second meaning of normative, which applies to the situation in which the individual expresses the desire to base his or her behavior on an axiomatic system. For instance, when the individual expresses the wish to build a rocket to go to the moon, the individual may ask the axioms of physics what to do. In this sense, the axioms are normative. Similarly, when the individual desires to behave rational in a specific situation the von Neumann-Morgenstern axioms may be used to determine

7. Conclusion

Von Neumann and Morgenstern's *Theory of Games and Economic Behavior* (2004 [1944]) and the subtle epistemology of the behavioral axioms on which it was based led to intense discussion among psychologists and economists on how to integrate the new theory and its axioms in existing theories and methodologies. Around 1953 and 1954, however, the discussion settled into an interpretation along disciplinary lines. Generally speaking, psychologists came to interpret the behavioral axioms in terms of a normative-descriptive distinction, in which the behavioral axioms functioned as stimuli defined by pure reason in the normative realm with which actual human decision behavior was compared under the rubric of the descriptive domain. Economists came to understand the behavioral axioms in terms of Friedman's (1953) positive-normative distinction. That is, choice or decision theory, as based on von Neumann and Morgenstern's axioms, was nonethical, scientific, and, hence, part of positive economics. It remained somewhat unclear exactly how the axioms should be understood – as characterizations or as directly refutable descriptions – but its classification under positive economics was undisputed.

The different interpretations of the von Neumann-Morgenstern behavioral axioms by psychologists and economists was not an accidental diversion, but reflected different ways of talking about individual behavior present well before the publication of the *Theory of Games and Economic Behavior*. Thurstone's experimental investigation of economists' indifference curve following the conversations with his friend and economist Schultz and its subsequent rebuttal by Wallis and Friedman (1942) – as discussed in Chapter 1 – illustrates this point. But to understand which different interpretations psychologists and economists developed with

what to do. A year later, Morgenstern again neatly summarized this position: "There is no a priori notion of 'rationality' in the theory; rather, that is a concept to be derived and given meaning to from the theory. The theory is 'absolutely convincing' in the sense that if behavior deviates from that predicted by the theory, after explanation of the theory, behavior would be adjusted. The von Neumann-Morgenstern 'expected utility theory' was the first approximation to an undoubtedly much richer and far more complicated reality. In that sense, the attacks on the theory are misplaced. It is common knowledge throughout scientific circles that axiomatic systems are often modified as axioms are more precisely specified, qualified, or, at times, replaced, as our understanding of physical laws is expanded. Not unexpectedly, the evolution of the von Neumann-Morgenstern 'expected utility theory' over the past thirty years is in complete concordance with scientific progress" (Morgenstern, 1973, p. 175).

respect to the axiomatic method as introduced by von Neumann and Morgenstern, one equally needs to appreciate the epistemological position developed by von Neumann and Morgenstern with respect to their behavioral axioms. The point is perhaps not so much the subtlety of the von Neumann-Morgenstern position itself, but the room it left for diverging interpretations. Had von Neumann and Morgenstern sided with either position from the start, it would have been much more difficult for the other discipline to incorporate the behavioral axioms in the tradition of its own discipline.

At the same time, in 1944 it was by no means obvious whether economists and behavioral psychologists would adopt the new method and theory of von Neumann and Morgenstern, let alone how they would interpret it epistemologically. The mid-1940s to mid-1950s saw a number of heated discussions surrounding the behavioral axioms that evolved around the question how to interpret the von Neumann-Morgenstern and later the Savage axioms. The normative-descriptive distinction of the psychologists and the positive-normative distinction of the economists in which these discussions eventually resulted, determined the terms in which subsequent discussions between psychologists and economists in the 1960s and 1970s would be put.

Appendix 1

Savage sketching his own utility curve for $0 to $1,000,0000, through "self interrogation on 23 dec[ember] 1952" in response to Allais's questionnaire on risk. Dollars ("$") are on the horizontal axis, "utiles" on the vertical axis. The estimated utility function on the graph-sketch is $U(x) = 0.11754(1 - e^{-0.0025x})$, which is different from the utility function eventually mentioned in Savage's letter to Allais: $U(x) = 0.035578(1 - e^{-0.001x})$.[60]

---

[60] Box 1, Folder 11, Jimmie Savage's papers, Yale University, New Haven, Connecticut.

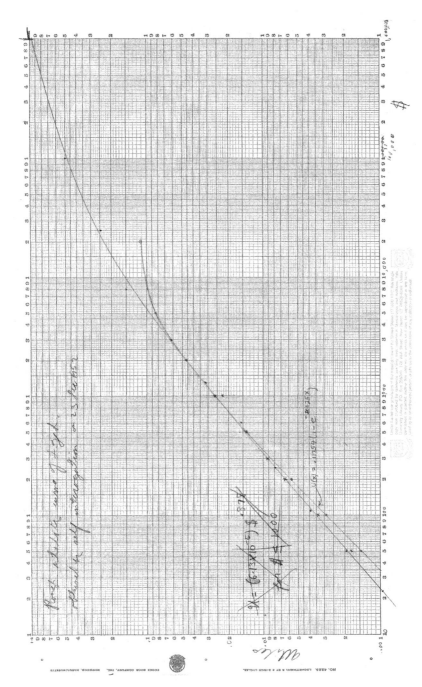

Savage sketching his own utility curve.

Savage sketching his own utility curve.

3

"Measurement Theory in Psychology Is Behavior Theory"

1. Introduction

The previous chapter's discussion about how a few psychologists in the 1950s adopted Savage's postulates and adapted his normative-empirical dichotomy into a normative-descriptive distinction is one element within a broader history of American psychologists' new emphasis on human engineering. In this process, psychologists understood themselves explicitly to draw on the work of economists. Both economists and psychologists incorporated von Neumann and Morgenstern's *Theory of Games and Economic Behavior* (2004 [1944]) and Savage's *The Foundations of Statistics* (1954). Moreover, also economists increasingly perceived themselves as social engineers (e.g., Mirowski, 2002). It is therefore tempting to view these developments as part of one broader story. Yet, this chapter argues, it cannot be emphasized enough how different the psychological program was from the economic approach.

The normative and the descriptive have always been closely related in psychology. In Freudian psychoanalysis as well as in military recruits' IQ testing during World War I, the object was as much to describe and classify human behavior as it was to steer it in more desirable directions. In the words of James McKeen Cattel (1860–1944), the first professor of psychology in the United States at the University of Pennsylvania, the aim of psychology was "to describe, to understand, and to control human conduct" (Cattel, 1930, p. 31). A field such as experimental psychology might emphasize the descriptive element, whereas applied psychologists focused more on improving actual human behavior in society; all of them were members of the American Psychological Association (APA), the principal authority of the field in the United States (Capshew, 1999). In fact, the APA's authority increasingly reached beyond the United States as the psychological profession became progressively dominated by U.S.-based psychologists. At the time of the Ninth International Congress of Psychology in September 1929, held for the first time in the United States, the *Psychological Register* already counted 678 U.S. psychologists compared to a total of 551 elsewhere (Murchison, 1929; Caphsew, 1999, p. 16). However, although the descriptive and the normative were closely linked, and although both the university-based and the applied psychologists were represented by the APA, experimental psychologists such as Edwin Boring (1886–1968) drew a clear line between the two and looked down on applied psychology as not very scientific.

Social engineering, the desire to subject the cause of societal improvement to the laws and machines of rational science, is an U.S. phenomenon that dates to the early twentieth century (Jordan, 1994; Mills, 1998; Lemov, 2005). The newly created philanthropic foundations played a major role in this development (Dowie, 2001). For instance, in 1929 the Rockefeller Foundation pledged nearly $10 million to establish the Institute of Human Relations at Yale University in an attempt to forge an interdisciplinary and cooperative scientific attack on the roots of social and individual problems. At Yale, it hoped to create a science that would present the basis for a rational management of human affairs, that is, of social and mental engineering (Capshew, 1999; Lemov, 2005; Morawski, 1986; Samuelson, 1985). The Second World War provided a strong catalyst to this engineering aspect of U.S. society, with science and engineering stepping forth as primary components in winning the war and in organizing society. These developments also drew in psychology, boosting the discipline with a wealth of new funds, career opportunities, and areas of psychological research and application, while drawing the different branches of psychology together in one discipline of human engineering (Capshew, 1999; Cordeschi, 2002; Mindell, 2002).

One consequence of the increasingly complex machines and organizations on which modern U.S. society and warfare had come to rely was that the functioning of the human being became crucial. Human beings had to operate the machines, fight the wars, and man the institutions. This is where psychologists saw a chance to contribute to the war and a chance to obtain a part of the funds made available through the war effort. Walter Hunter put it thus:

Wars are not fought by machines nor by men alone, but by man-machine units. The machine must be designed for the man, and the man must be selected and trained for the machine. . . . Efficient human performance depends on a multitude of capacities and abilities which must be analyzed and correlated with the demands of the total job if an efficient man-machine unit is to result. (Hunter, 1946, p. 479)

The war "brought together psychologists, physiologists, physicists, design engineers, and motion-and-time engineers to solve some of these problems" (Chapanis et al., 1949, p. v). In psychology, a new impetus was given to what had been called, during the First World War, "mental engineering" but had been relabeled "human engineering" in the Second World War following the rise of behaviorism (Dodge, 1919; Capshew, 1999).

Particularly explicit was Robert Yerkes (1876–1956), who stepped into the limelight during World War II as the initiator and organizer of the Intersociety Constitutional Convention, which sought to reorganize the psychology profession on behalf of the APA and a few other major associations. A gap existed, Yerkes argued, "between the human needs which are partially met by the physician and those which the clergyman or priest is expected to satisfy" (Yerkes, 1941, p. 535). Psychology, as the science concerned with the needs and requirements of the normal individual (as compared to the abnormal or severely maladjusted individual who required therapy or medial attention), "must stand as a basic science for such universally desirable expert services as the guidance and safeguarding of an individual's growth and development, education and occupational choice, social adjustments, achievement and maintenance of balance, poise, and effectiveness, contentment, happiness, and usefulness" (Yerkes, 1941, p. 536). The Convention reconfirmed the APA as the profession's primary authority and declared that "[t]he object of this society [the APA] shall be to advance psychology as a science, as a profession, and as a means of promoting human welfare" (Intersociety Constitutional Convention, quoted in Capshew, 1999, p. 67).

The new emphasis on engineering in addition stressed the importance of rationality. On one hand, engineering psychology was defined as dealing with normal, healthy – that is, rational – individuals. On the other hand, engineering psychologists sought to understand and enhance this rationality of normal, healthy individuals. In turn, the focus on rationality added a new component to established experimental psychological topics such as investigating human perception, decision making, and a new component to the understanding of the human being as the ultimate measurement instrument (Heidelberger, 2004; Michell, 1999). Measurement was a perception by a human being, be it a scientist or anyone else. It was the human being who perceived, say, weight A to be heavier than weight B and thus measured A as heavier than B. The new element was that this measurement/perception needed to be performed by an individual who was recognized as capable of correctly perceiving and reporting the difference between the two stimuli. That is, the measurement needed to be conducted by a rational individual, or, put differently, a proper scientific perception/measurement came to be understood as a rational decision between different stimuli.

The different branches within psychology incorporated the new focus on human engineering in different ways. Under the leadership of Boring, experimental psychologists argued that their knowledge of the skills, abilities, and limits of performance of the human being was crucial for the design and operation of military machines (Capshew, 1999, p. 145). An example of this new experimental psychological focus on human engineering was Boring and Van de Water's *Psychology for the Fighting Man: Prepared for the Fighting Man Himself* (1943), a handbook for every officer and soldier capable of reading the newspaper to improve their fighting skills that eventually sold 400,000 copies (National Research Council, 1943; Capshew, 1999).

When the psychologists returned to their academic departments after the war, some experimental psychologists and psychometricians returned to their more fundamental research. Others, however, continued to work in what was now the well-established field of human engineering. There was no need to worry that psychology's newly found status would abate or that research funds would dwindle. As a result of the G.I. Bill, the number of psychology students, among others, increased dramatically and funds continued to flow to psychological research in large amounts. Not only traditional major psychology departments such as Yale and Harvard profited, also departments at other universities gained from the postwar boom and established flourishing psychology departments. One psychology department that stood out as capitalizing extremely well on the new developments and that consequently propelled itself to a place among the nation's top two or three programs was the psychology department at the University of Michigan.

2. Psychology at Michigan

In 1942, Walter Pillsbury (1872–1960) retired as the head of the psychology department at the University of Michigan after a service of forty-five years (Raphelson, 1980). The new head of the department was Donald Marquis (1908–1973), a rising star in postwar psychology, a former researcher at Yale's Institute of Human Relations, and, until 1942, the head of the psychology department at Yale (Pooley and Solovey, 2010). Marquis rapidly built the Department of Psychology at the University of Michigan into one of the foremost in the United States (Capshew, 1999; Sears, 1973; Duderstadt, 1994; Peckham, 2005, pp. 245–266; Frantilla, 1998). The number of psychology PhDs rose from 16 between 1935 and 1939 to 133 between 1950 and 1954 and to 147 between 1960 and 1964.[1] The department's faculty grew from 8 to 40 members between 1945 and 1950 and then to some 220 faculty members in the second half of the 1960s, making up about sixty full-time equivalents.[2] In 1956, University of Michigan dean Hayward Keniston asked the chairmen of the twenty largest U.S. psychology departments to list the top ten departments in order of merit. The survey placed Harvard, Michigan, and Yale as the numbers one, two, and three, respectively.[3] Among others, Marquis was a master in expanding the psychology department through joint appointments between the psychology department and other university units.[4]

Related to, but organizationally distinguished from the Department of Psychology, were the centers organized under the heading of the Institute for Social Research. The Survey Research Center was established by psychologist George Katona (1901–1981) in 1946, who pioneered a social survey research on consumer sentiment (House et al., 2004; Bulmer, 2001; Hyman, 1991; Hollinger, 1989). To finance the war, the U.S. government had issued a large number of war bonds, and with the end of the war in sight, it wanted to know how likely it was that U.S. consumers would maintain or liquidate these bonds. Because Katona felt that he could not immediately ask people what they would do with their money, he proposed starting with some general questions that would comfort the respondents and would get them to start thinking about their own budgets and future prospects. In these consumer confidence surveys, Katona employed the term *behavioral economics* as early as 1947 (Juster, 2004, p. 120). Two years later, in 1948, following the death of its founder Kurt Lewin (1890–1947), the Research Center for Group Dynamics relocated from the Massachusetts Institute of Technology (MIT) to the University of Michigan. The two groups remained separate but were brought together under the newly created Institute for Social Research 1949.[5] In order to protect its general university funds, in 1946, Marquis

---

[1] Composed from various documents in the Department of Psychology archives at the Bentley Historical Archives, University of Michigan, Ann Arbor.

[2] Capshew (1999); David Krantz, interview with the author, Columbia University, New York, June 20, 2008; and Robert Pachella, interview with the author, University of Michigan, Ann Arbor, April 8, 2009.

[3] Letter from Head of Department of Psychology to Dean and Executive Committee of Literature, Science, and the Arts, November 8, 1961, Clyde Coombs papers, Bentley Historical Archives, University of Michigan, Ann Arbor.

[4] Capshew (1999); Krantz, interview, 2008; and Pachella, interview, 2009.

[5] Since 1949, the Institute for Social Research has been joined by other centers, and new centers have been created within the body of the Institute for Social Research, such as the Center for Political Studies and the Population Studies Center. In the 1960s, the Institute

insisted on creating the Survey Research Center and that it be funded entirely through grants and contracts, a policy that was also applied to the Institute of Social Research when it was created in 1949. As a result, the Institute of Social Research could not offer tenure to those it employed. There were always certain researchers who were the last to leave whenever funds ran out, but even these senior researchers and directors could never obtain tenure at the Institute for Social Research.[6]

In 1955, another component was added to the Michigan empire in the form of the Mental Health Research Institute. It was founded by Anatol Rapoport (1911–2007) and others and was subsequently headed by James Grier Miller (1916–2002), a University of Chicago psychologist working on behavioral science theory and related research (Capshew, 1999; Pooley and Solovay, 2010).[7] Other, smaller groups of researchers included the Michigan Mathematical Psychology Group, created by Clyde Coombs (1912–1988) after he came to Michigan in 1949, and the Engineering Psychology Laboratory, set up by Ward Edwards (1927–2005) under the auspices of the then recently created Human Performance Center when he arrived at Michigan in 1958.[8]

As result of a general availability of research funds in the postwar years, but not in the least because of the organizational and funding skills of Marquis as well, there was enough money for nearly everyone to pursue his or her ideas and interests in a general atmosphere of "live and let live."[9] (Krantz, interview, 2008; Dawes, interview, 2008). Moreover, although Marquis undoubtedly to some extent constrained the research, it was generally not a strong constraint. Robyn Dawes (b. 1936), for instance, was employed

for Social Research for a while contained the Center for Research and the Utilization of Scientific Knowledge, which later dissolved and disappeared. The scientists staffing the different centers of the Institute for Social Research were social scientists and a few statisticians. Many were sociologists or political scientists, but the majority in the 1940s through the 1970s were the psychologists (Krantz, interview, 2008).

[6] Krantz, interview, 2008; Juster (2004); and Hollinger (1989). Leon Festinger (1919–1989), elected on the advisory board of the Alfred P. Sloan behavioral economics program in 1984 (see Chapter 5), was employed by Lewin's Research Center for Group Dynamics and by Katona's Survey Research Center after the former had moved to the University of Michigan.

[7] Rapoport was a Russian-born mathematician employed, among others, as professor of Mathematical Biology at the Department of Mathematics of the University of Michigan from 1955 to 1970. He is best known for his application of game theory to the psychology and politics of conflict resolution (e.g., Rapoport, 1989).

[8] Pachella, interview, 2009; Phillips and von Winterfledt (2006); and Fryback (2005).

[9] Krantz, interview, 2008; and Robyn Dawes, interview with author, Carnegie Mellon University, Pittsburgh, June 23, 2008.

for a year by the Institute of Social Research and had an office in their building but conducted very little work for them and continued working with Coombs and the mathematical psychologists.[10] By consequence, scientists could pursue their own research without regard to other research programs, even if they seemed closely related. Thus, although it would seem that Rapoport and Miller's Mental Health Research Institute, Katona's Survey Research Center, Edwards's Engineering Psychology Laboratory, and Coombs's Michigan Mathematical Program would naturally seek cooperation, in practice, they largely went their own ways. It is in this light that the relationship between Coombs and Edwards should be seen. Both were strong but had very contrasting personalities, and each had his own research program. The large number of people around and the general availability of funds ensured that they could conduct their own research programs without ever really having to confront one another. Something similar held for the relation between Coombs's Michigan Mathematical Program and the Institute of Social Research. Coombs and the other mathematical psychologists were aware that their work concerning the axioms of measurement should in one way or another be related to the measurement methods used at the Institute of Social Research, and, in turn, the researchers at the Institute of Social Research were equally aware of the work of Coombs and others.[11] But in day-to-day practice, both groups simply pursued their own research agendas.

Because of the rapid growth, in 1959 the Department of Psychology was divided into ten fields of specialization[12]: experimental, mathematical, physiological, developmental, personality, social, community, industrial organization, and, the two largest, clinical and counseling psychology. Later, physiological psychology was relabeled biological psychology, and mathematical psychology became part of experimental psychology, illustrating the close connection between the two. However, this classification was relatively loose and more a matter of cataloguing what people were doing rather than assigning them what to do. Coombs was only associated with mathematical psychology, but Edwards's Engineering Psychology Laboratory was associated with both mathematical and experimental psychology. Amos Tversky (1937–1996) was also associated with both specializations. David Krantz (b. 1938) was related to experimental, mathematical, and physiological psychology, and Dawes, to mathematical and clinical psychology. Thus, the

---

[10] Dawes, interview, 2008.
[11] Krantz, interview, 2008.
[12] Pachella, interview, 2009.

Department of Psychology had an organization both in terms of where the money came from and in terms of fields of specialization.[13] But, because of the large number of faculty members and the availability of funds, from 1940s through the 1960s, the organization was not tightly knit, so everyone could more or less do what he or she wanted.[14]

3. Mathematical Psychology and Behavioral Decision Research

In the 1930s, Clyde Coombs had been a student of Chicago psychometrician Thurstone, whose work has been introduced in Chapter 1. After his service in the U.S. Army during World War II, Coombs went to the University of Michigan in 1949, where he remained until his retirement in 1982. Coombs made his researchers work long hours, but largely without his imposing constraints or specific research subjects and in an atmosphere of celebrating the good life in general, and academia in particular.[15] Edwards, on the other hand, was a Harvard man, and very much aware of it. Edwards always pushed his own program but at the same time was supportive of his brightest students, which certainly included people such as Tversky.[16]

The mathematical psychology program that Coombs initiated at the University of Michigan has a clear background. The use of mathematics in the study of psychological phenomena goes back to Gustav Fechner (1860) and is closely related to experimental psychology (Heidelberger, 1993, 2004; Daston and Galison, 2007; Michell, 1999, 2007). In 1935, Thurstone cofounded the Psychometric Society and the journal *Psychometrika* during the annual APA conference at the University of Michigan and gave a new boost to theoretical reflection of measurement in psychology and to psychologists' use of mathematics, as briefly mentioned in Chapter 1 (see also Gigerenzer, 1987a,

---

[13] Krantz, interview, 2008.

[14] Krantz, interview, 2008; and Dawes, interview, 2008.

[15] Tversky (1991); Krantz, interview, 2008; Pachella, interview, 2009; and Dawes, interview, 2008.

[16] Krantz, interview, 2008; Pachella, interview, 2009; Dawes, interview, 2008; and Phillips and von Winterfeldt (2006). In a letter to James March, Dean at the University of California, Coombs wrote, "I have no concern for [Edwards's] integrity but probably some remarks should be made about his personality. He has very firm opinions and is not reticent in bringing them out in open discussion. There is no question but what he has annoyed some people. I think he perhaps presents a different personality to those he perceives as above him than to those he perceives as below him. He is tough and demanding with students but on the other hand he gives of himself fully and so long as the student is as totally committed and hard working as Ward he has no problem" (Coombs's letter to March, February 2, 1966, Box 1, Folder Correspondence 1966, Clyde Coombs Papers, Bentley Historical Library, University of Michigan, Ann Arbor).

1987b; Dunlap, 1942). Thurstone's measurement program was soon joined by another measurement program. In the 1940s and 1950s, the so-called representational theory of measurement rose to prominence, with Stanley S. Stevens (1906–1973) as its most important contributor (Boumans, 2007; Michell, 1999). The main question Coombs was interested in was whether it was possible, and, if so, how, to combine Thurstone's measurement approach with the representational measurement tradition.

The term *mathematical psychology* was coined by Thurstone in the 1930s but acquired common usage in the early 1950s following the creation of Coombs's Michigan Mathematical Psychology Program in 1949. The key importance of Thurstone is always mentioned when the origins of mathematical psychology are set out (e.g., Frederiksen & Gulliksen, 1964; Laming, 1973; Luce et al., 1963a; Tversky, 1991; Stevens, 1951a), but the driving force behind mathematical psychology as a separate field in psychology was Coombs. A first important catalyst was what was officially called the Seminar on the Mathematical Aspects of the Social Sciences, but which was commonly referred to as the Mathematical Psychology Seminar.[17] Organized by Coombs, the Mathematical Psychology Seminar met once or twice monthly from fall 1950 onward and included speakers from various disciplines working on the application of mathematics to social and behavioral phenomena, including Edwards, Kenneth Arrow, and Kenneth Boulding. A second important catalyst, and an extrapolation of the Mathematical Psychology Seminar to the summer months, was the already mentioned two-month summer institute in Santa Monica in 1952, organized by Coombs and University of Michigan mathematician Robert Thrall (Davis, 1954). The Santa Monica conference brought together a range of psychologists, economists, and other scientists working on the mathematical and experimental investigation of decision making and facilitated the start and progress of much prominent research in mathematical psychology. Leading mathematical psychologists from the late 1950s onward include, besides Clyde Coombs, David Krantz, Amos Tversky, R. Duncan Luce (1925–2011), Patrick Suppes (b. 1922), and William Estes (1919–2011).

The contributions made to the field increased so much that in 1964 the *Journal for Mathematical Psychology* was founded.[18] This gave self-proclaimed mathematical psychologists a more solid basis. However, it had

---

[17] Krantz, interview, 2008.
[18] The founding committee consisted of Richard C. Atkinson, Robert R. Bush, William Estes, R. Duncan Luce, and Patrick Suppes. This paragraph draws on letters and minutes from Luce's archive at Harvard University.

not yet become a society. Only in 1975 did the board of editors of the *Journal for Mathematical Psychology* discuss the possibility of a merger with the Psychometric Society and its journal, *Psychometrika*. This effort was due to the financial mismanagement of *Psychometrika* and the general desire of both groups to secure their financial future by combining conferences, journal administration, and so forth. In addition, subscribers and the board of editors of both the *Journal for Mathematical Psychology* and *Psychometrika* argued that the merger might also be beneficial from the standpoint of content. In the end, two proposals were put forward to the two groups to vote on – one in which the two would be completely merged into one society with two journals and one in which two divisions would exist, each having its own journal under the umbrella of one overarching society. Although Coombs, Krantz, and Tversky had all indicated to Luce (one of the editors of the *Journal for Mathematical Psychology*) that they would vote in favor of a merger, both proposals were rejected. In response, the editors of the *Journal for Mathematical Psychology* proposed in 1976 to create the Society for Mathematical Psychology.[19] This proposal was accepted, and the society was officially founded in 1977.

Mathematical psychologists defined their field not based on a particular understanding of psychological phenomena, but instead based on a method of investigation of psychological phenomena. The field was characterized as "the attempt to use mathematical methods to investigate psychological problems," and it was thus "not defined in terms of content but rather in terms of an approach" (Coombs et al., 1970, p. 1). It signified "not the study of a particular type of behaviour or the delineation of some new class of psychological phenomena but, rather, the application of new techniques to traditional psychological problems" (Laming, 1973, p. 1). In other words, mathematical psychology was defined rather broadly as an attempt to use theories and techniques from the field of mathematics to represent and investigate psychological phenomena. All research that applied mathematics to what could be considered psychological phenomena in principle fell under the heading of mathematical psychology. This is illustrated by the three-volume *Handbook of Mathematical Psychology* (1963–1965), which started its exposition of what mathematical psychology is with a list of thirty-nine "Basic References in Mathematical Psychology."[20] Mathematical

---

[19] The journal editors were Wlliam Batchelder, William Estes, B. F. Green, and R. Duncan Luce.

[20] These basic references include among others Arrow's *Social Choice and Individual Values* (1951b), N. R. Campbell's *Foundations of Science* (1957), Chomsky's *Syntactic*

psychology aimed to synthesize all mathematical approaches to individual human behavior.

The scope of this list of basic references turned out to be more wishful thinking than an actual reflection of research conducted by mathematical psychologists. The inclusion of economist Arrow and political scientist Simon suggested a synthesis that did not exist. Mathematical psychology was supposed to include all mathematical reasoning related to human behavior, but in day-to-day practice, it was almost exclusively focused on psychophysics, measurement theory, and decision theory (Gigerenzer and Murray, 1987; Coombs et al., 1970). Mathematical psychology of the 1950s, 1960s, and 1970s was about the mathematics of measurement theory and about the mathematics of decision theory.

The experimental counterpart to mathematical psychology's theoretical research was Ward Edwards's behavioral decision research. In 1958, Edwards joined the University of Michigan, where he began to apply mathematical psychology's work on measurement to his empirical investigation of Savage's decision theory, as developed in the latter's *The Foundations of Statistics* (1954). Edwards was strongly influenced by von Neumann and Morgenstern's and by Stevens's work on measurement, and was one of the first promoters of Savage's normative-empirical decision-making program. Edwards admired Savage as one admires a genius, something Edwards shared with others who had read *The Foundations of Statistics*, such as Luce, Tversky, and Krantz.[21] Edwards's 1954 article on the historical background of decision-making research, "The Theory of Decision Making," and its 1961 follow-up, "Behavioral Decision Theory," created the field of behavioral decision research.[22] Behavioral decision research was dominated by Edwards until the early 1970s. From that point on, a number of his students started to develop their own interpretations. The most successful were

---

Structures (1957), Guilford's *Psychometric Methods* (1954), Luce and Raiffa's *Games and Decisions* (1957), Simon's *Models of Man* (1957), Stevens's *Handbook of Experimental Psychology* (1951b), and Thurstone's *Multiple Factor Analysis* (1947) and *The Measurement of Values* (1959).

[21] Krantz, interview, 2008.

[22] Different names exist for Edwards's program and its offspring. Behavioral decision research, behavioral decision theory, and behavioral decision making are all used to refer to the same psychological program. It is not clear exactly when and how these terms originated, although behavioral decision theory has been around at least since Edwards published his second overview article in 1961. Behavioral decision research, the most commonly used label, seems to have originated in the 1970s, but has been applied in retrospect to the research of the 1960s and late 1950s also. To avoid confusion, I use the term *behavioral decision research*.

Paul Slovic and Sarah Lichtenstein, who developed a constructed preferences approach that drew connections with Simon (e.g., Slovic and Lichtenstein, 1971, 1973, 1983), and Daniel Kahneman and Amos Tversky (e.g., Tversky and Kahneman, 1974; Kahneman and Tversky, 1979).

4. Decision Making and Measurement

Despite the loose organization at the University of Michigan and the opposing characters of Coombs and Edwards, mathematical psychologists and behavioral decision researchers developed closely related research agendas evolving around the themes of measurement, decision theory, and the empirical measurement of actual decision making by human beings.

The theory of measurement developed by the mathematical psychologists was, as described, inspired by both Thurstone's and Stevens's theories on measurement. Moreover, the effort to set up a mathematical psychology program by Coombs was principally influenced by Thurstone. Yet, after a while, the work on measurement of the mathematical psychologists drifted away from Thurstone and toward Stevens. The self-perceived task of the mathematical psychologists became to develop further the mathematical structure of Stevens's view of measurement. Indeed, the three volumes of *Foundations of Measurement* (1971, 1989, 1990), a coproduction of Krantz, Luce, Suppes, and Tversky, is best seen as a thorough set-theoretical reformulation of Stevens's representational theory of measurement (Michell, 2007). *Foundations of Measurement* became the standard work on the representational theory of measurement in psychology and one of mathematical psychology's lasting influences on the psychological discipline. Stevens's program was strongly inspired by Bridgman's operationalism (Bridgman, 1927), and defined measurement as the operation of assigning numerals according to a rule (Boumans, 2007; Michell, 1999, 2007). The theoretical background and the new perspective of *Foundations of Measurement* have been extensively treated by Michell (1999, 2007). Here, I concentrate on its organizational and contextual history.

In the summer of 1965, at the end of a three-week measurement workshop held at the University of Michigan, the already established scholars and longtime friends Luce and Suppes invited the "then two brightest young people working in the area"[23] to write a book on measurement that would summarize and synthesize all the recent work done on measurement in

---

[23] Luce's letter to Hamada, June 23, 1986, R. Duncan Luce Papers, Unprocessed Archive Harvard University Archives, Cambridge, MA.

mathematical psychology. Despite the gap between the publication of the first volume and the second and third volumes, most of the three volumes of *Foundations of Measurement* was written in the late 1960s.[24]

The main author of the first volume was Krantz, who consequently was also made its first author. The editor and first author of the second volume was Suppes, whereas the third volume was edited by Luce. The main initiator and contact person throughout the whole project was Luce. Luce and Tukey (1964), the very first article published in the *Journal for Mathematical Psychology*, formed the basis for much of the measurement work in mathematical psychology and hence formed an important basis for *Foundations of Measurement*. Interestingly, the authors discovered along the way that much of what they were doing had been done before by mathematician and economist Gérard Debreu (e.g., Debreu, 1954, 1958, 1959a, 1959b, 1960). But Debreu had taken a topological approach that was difficult for economists and psychologists to understand.[25] The reference to Debreu is intriguing because it again illustrates that economists and psychologists could be working on the same phenomenon but understand it differently. For mathematical economist Debreu, his work was on utility theory; for the mathematical psychologists, it was about measurement.[26]

In the first two sentences of the first chapter of the first volume of *Foundations of Measurement*, the authors stated their belief in the representational theory of measurement and the object of their book explicitly: "When measuring some attribute of a class of objects or events," they argued, "we associate numbers (or other familiar mathematical entities, such as vectors) with the objects in such a way that the properties of the attributes are faithfully represented as numerical properties. In this book we investigate various systems of formal properties of attributes that lead to measurement in this sense" (Krantz et al., 1971, p. 1). *Foundations of Measurement* thus referred to the mathematical properties used in the numerical structure in the representational theory of measurement. The first chapter put forth what was called the three basic procedures of measurement: (1) ordinal measurement, (2) counting of units, and (3) solving inequalities. It differs

---

[24] This and the following paragraph draw on the interview with Krantz and on letters from Luce's archive at Harvard University.

[25] Krantz, interview, 2008.

[26] Also historians of economics have focused only on the economic interpretation of Debreu's work. For instance, Weintraub and Mirowski (1994) note that "Debreu is best read as providing a handbook for the working economic theorist of the neoclassical components of economic theory. In retrospect, it is hard to read *Theory of Value* (1959b) as anything else" (p. 266).

from the approach set out by Stevens (1939, 1951a) only in that it was mathematically more refined and sophisticated. The remainder of the book was based on these three procedures. This view of measurement not only served as an important component in decision theory and behavioral decision research, as set out in the following, but it also illustrates which approach mathematical psychologists took toward the world they investigated.[27]

The point of departure in the representational theory of measurement is that if the scientist wants to measure, the appropriate mathematical system needs to be used. Thus, it assumed that the phenomena to be measured are clearly defined. If the scientist wants to measure length, temperature, wealth, or utility, what he or she needs to do is specify mathematically all the characteristics used in the measurement procedure *and* in the empirical system to be measured and then apply this system of representation to the observations. For instance, when the scientist starts from the observation or assumption that the natural phenomenon of temperature has transitive properties, the measurement system used must likewise have transitive properties. This is equally true for situations in which the human being is used as a measurement instrument. If the psychologist wants to measure the human perception of utilities through human beings, using a measurement framework that employs transitivity, he or she needs to assume that human perception of utilities has transitive properties. Ideally, one would have first discussed whether transitivity made sense in the case of temperature, religious attitudes, or utility, but if this stage was forgotten, the mathematical framework used simply determined that these phenomena were understood as being subject to transitivity.

The mathematical psychologists brought their measurement theory in line with recent developments in theories of human behavior. The new theory they were particularly keen to incorporate were von Neumann and Morgenstern (2004) and Savage's (1954) decision theory. According to the authors, the two-sided theory of measurement and decision making was described as follows at the beginning of chapter 9, *Foundations of Measurement*, volume 1:

Unlike most theories of measurement, which may have both physical and behavioral interpretations, the theory of expected utility is devoted explicitly to the problem

---

[27] For a methodological discussion of measurement in general and the representational theory of measurement in particular, see Boumans (2005, 2007) and Michell (2007). For a thorough exposition of the history of measurement theory in nineteenth-century experimental psychology and of the link of this psychological literature to interwar logical positivism, see Heidelberger (1993, 2004). For a discussion of postwar measurement theory of the *Foundations of Measurement* and its link to logical positivism/empiricism and Stevens, see Michel (1999).

of making decisions when their consequences are uncertain. It is probably the most familiar example of a theory of measurement in the social sciences. (Krantz et al., 1971, p. 369)

No economist, perhaps with the exception of Edgeworth, would have understood utility theory as a theory of measurement. But for the mathematical psychologists the representational theory of measurement and the theory of expected utility theory, or decision theory, were two sides of the same psychological coin.

In addition, behavioral psychologists such as Edwards, Krantz and Tversky understood the *Theory of Games and Economic Behavior*'s (2004) behavioral axioms to have introduced the concept of stochastic preference, which can be found either in a weak or in a strong form (see Tversky, 1969, for the distinction between the two). Stochastic preference embodies the idea that an individual who has only a very small preference for A as opposed to B may not always correctly perceive this small difference and may mistakenly choose B. The difference is so small that the individual cannot consciously perceive it and considers itself to be indifferent toward A and B. However, if the choice is repeated a large number of times, the individual will nevertheless choose A more often than B. Therefore, this individual is said to stochastically prefer A to B. Stochastic preference, as the behavioral psychologists understood it, eliminated the concept of indifference.[28] Even if the individual has an infinitely small preference for A as opposed to B, this preference would show up if the choice was repeated often enough. The individual was unaware of its preference for A as opposed to B and considered itself to be indifferent, but the individual was not, and the mathematics therefore needed to be modeled as such.

In turn, that drew attention to the question how exactly the relation between the normative rules of rational behavior and actual, empirically observed behavior by rational individuals should be understood. Savage's theory, as understood by Savage and by the behavioral psychologists, investigated what a rational person does in the face of uncertainty. Rationality to Savage was a theory of reasoning, either formalized or not. For certain propositions, Savage argued, it is generally accepted that this theory is logic. That is, the axioms of logic are widely accepted as characterizing and as providing rules for reasoning about certain propositions. As set out in Chapter 2, for the extension of logic to uncertainty Savage presented in the book, this was less clear, as the theory still had to be developed. That is, Savage contended that it was as yet unclear whether the axioms he presented were

---

[28] No direct link to economics or to Thurstone (1931) was established in this context.

indeed the best description, and provided the best rules, for reasoning under uncertainty. The reader thus must subsequently verify for him- or herself the axioms Savage presented. "I am about to build up a highly idealized theory of the behavior of a 'rational' person with respect to decisions," he wrote. But "[i]n doing so I will, of course, have to ask you to agree with me that such and such maxims of behavior are 'rational.' . . . So, when certain [i.e., some] maxims are presented for your consideration, you must ask yourself whether you try to behave in accordance with them, or, to put it differently, how you would react if you noticed yourself violating them" (Savage, 1954, p. 7).[29]

But what conclusion needed to be drawn when a subject in an experimental setting was observed to make a decision that violated the rules governing the theory of reasoning, without showing that the rules themselves were invalid? First, the theory could only be applied experimentally to subjects that can reason. Roughly, this included all normal and healthy adults. As for the engineering psychologists in general, children, the mentally disabled, and animals were therefore excluded from experimental investigation. But when subjects capable of reasoning were observed making decisions that violated the axioms and did not present a convincing argument of how the axioms should be changed, such decisions were deemed irrational decisions or simply errors. To Savage, these errors were the result of failed or too little reasoning. The individual had made a mistake in his or her reasoning or had not given it enough thought. When the subject would think further or when its error would be explained, the subject would recognize his or her mistake and correct his or her behavior. Savage noted that

[t]here is, of course, an important sense in which preferences, being entirely subjective, cannot be in error; but in a different, more subtle sense they can be . . . A man buying a car for $2,134.50 is tempted to order it with a radio installed, which will bring the total price to $2,228.41, feeling that the difference is trifling. But, when he reflects that, if he already had the car, he certainly would not spend $93.85 for a radio for it, he realizes that he has made an error. (Savage, 1954, p. 103)

---

[29] It is no accident that Savage put quotation marks around "rational." As in Friedman and Savage (1948, 1952), he continued struggling to find the right words. In a lecture titled "Some Remarks on the Relations Between Decision Theory and the Social Sciences," delivered in Coombs' Mathematical Psychology Seminar on May 10, 1956, Savage alternated between describing decision theory as theorizing about "*wise* decisions in the face of uncertainty," describing homo economicus as "an idealized rational man," and decision theory as describing "homo economicus *as though* there were probability measures on states of nature, as though he sought to maximize expected income on this basis" (Savage, 1956, Savage's archives, Yale University Library, New Haven, Connecticut, emphasis in the original).

When Edwards and his fellow behavioral psychologists subsequently incorporated Savage's theory into their experimental psychological methodology, the way in which individuals could deviate from the rational norm was rendered more precise. First of all, individual subjects could have their own, subjective, perception of the values of the probabilities and the outcomes. In that case, the individual might make a different decision than the rational scientist while still being rational. For this reason, Edwards and his associates emphasized that in experiments the outcomes and probabilities of the different options should be defined as unambiguously as possible, for instance, by letting the individual throw the dice him- or herself and by putting the money to be gained on the table. Also stochastic preferences and errors made by the individual, such as in the case of accidently buying the car with the radio installed or, more generally, errors resulting from stress, too little time, and other external constraints, were understood to fall in this category.

The second way in which an individual could deviate from the rational decision was by making irrational decisions systematically, as a result of insufficient capacity to reason rationally. The largely implicit distinction between these two types of deviations is important. Edwards investigated under which circumstances individuals deviated in the first sense and believed, like Savage that by and large individuals would not systematically commit deviations of the second type. The core objective of the research of Kahneman and Tversky in the 1970s was to show that the individual actually does systematically commit deviations of the second type.

The value of the different options was to be measured in utilities. On the interpretation of the theory of utility, Savage (1954), like Friedman and Savage (1948, 1952), sided with von Neumann and Morgenstern (2004). Savage suggested that economists and others had been somewhat led astray in constructing complicated theories of utility. "[E]conomists were for a time enthusiastic about the principle of diminishing marginal utility, and they saw what they believed to be reflections of it in many aspects of everyday life" (Savage, 1954, p. 95). However, thanks to von Neumann and Morgenstern, we were now back on the right track of understanding utility as nothing more than a convenient measurement scale of preferences:

A function U that ... arithmetizes the relation of preferences among acts will be called utility ... I have chosen to use the name "utility" in preference to any other, in spite of some unfortunate connotations this name has in connection with economic theory, because it was adopted by von Neumann and Morgenstern when they revived the concept to which it refers, in a most stimulating way. (Savage, 1954, p. 95)[30]

---

[30] Savage's main source regarding economic utility theory was, of course, Friedman.

Following Savage, Edwards and his behavioral decision researchers evaluated decisions in terms of utility and, like Savage, understood themselves to draw on economists and their use of the concept of utility. Nevertheless, Edwards and his behavioral decision researchers did not understand utility in the same way as economists. For behavioral decision researchers, utility was merely a new concept for an already existing idea in experimental psychology, that of valence. "The notion of utility is very similar to the Lewinian notion of valence. Lewin conceives of valence as the attractiveness of an object or activity to a person. Thus, psychologists might consider the experimental study of utilities to be the experimental study of valence, and therefore an attempt at quantifying parts of the Lewinian theoretical schema" (Edwards, 1954, p. 25; see also Frijda, 1986). Valence measures the intrinsic attractiveness or averseness of an individual to a certain event, object, or situation. Thus, if an individual is more attracted to Islam than to Christianity, Islam has a higher valence. In addition, emotions can be classified in terms of valence. Anger and fear are emotions with a negative valence; joy has a positive valence. By equating utility with valence, Edwards and behavioral decision research understood utility to be a general measurement of an individual's attitude toward events, objects, and situations. As a result, an individual preferring ten to eight dollars was psychologically in the same situation as an individual preferring Allah over Yahweh.

An illustrative example is Edwards's exposition "Experiments on Economic Decision Making in Gambling Situations," delivered on November 20, 1952, at Coombs's Mathematical Psychology Seminar. During the talk, Edwards used *value* to refer to the actual monetary outcome of a gamble, and *expected value* to denote the expected monetary outcome. Similarly, *utility* referred to the subjective perception of the monetary outcome, and *expected utility* to the subjective perception of the expected monetary outcome. In the same way, *objective probability* referred to probability as defined by the scientist, whereas *subjective probability* denoted the perceived probability of the individual subject in the experiment. However, in an illustrative twist that makes the behavioral psychological literature of this period sometimes seem sloppy, a synonym for *utility* that Edwards used was *subjective value*, as opposed to the *objective value* of the actual monetary outcome. Another synonym was *subjective utility*, again as contrasted with *objective value* (*objective utility*, by contrast, seems never to have been used). To complicate matters further, in the context of the problem of measuring utilities, Edwards also discussed how best to construct a "scale of values" for utility. Finally, in Edwards's approach individuals could have a "probability preference" for a specific probability (say 0.5 or 0.8) in addition to their subjective perception of the objective probability.[31]

Savage and other decision theorists investigated the normative decision theories. It was the task of psychologists, according to Edwards, to investigate the descriptive part and in turn to see how well human beings in their actual everyday decision making behave according to the normative principles set out by decision theory. What was at least as important for Edwards, however, was the question how human decision making could be improved. The research conducted and favored by Edwards was explicitly called "engineering psychology."[32] For Edwards, the starting point was that the human being is highly capable of making complicated decisions in situations based on uncertain information. It is just that there is only so much a single human being can do. For that reason, human beings may sometimes deviate from what is normatively the right decision, and it may be useful to think about how to help human beings decide when, for whatever reason, the decision-making process is especially difficult or especially important. As such, Edwards's behavioral decision research was closely related to operations research as frequently discussed in the context of the history of economics (Klein, forthcoming; Mirowski, 2002). As behavioral decision research, operations research aimed to gather all information available relating to a particular problem and then use decision theory to calculate the optimal decision: "Operations research makes the claim that, by pitting the forces of research against large-scale problems, the decision maker (manager, president, general, etc.) will be freed to devote his time to other tasks" (Fishburn, 1964, p. 4).

The self-assigned task of behavioral decision researchers was to measure experimentally which decision subjects make with respect to this objective stimulus. As a basis for their measurements in the laboratory, the behavioral decision researchers used the measurement theory of the mathematical psychologists. Measurement theory could be used to measure rational decision making: the human being was expected only occasionally and only randomly to deviate from the rational decision and, hence, was also expected

---

[31] Another example is Coombs and Komorita (1958), which measured experimentally "social utilities," seeing it as an empirical contribution to Arrow's *Social Choice and Individual Values* (1951b).

[32] In a letter from the Head of the Psychology Department to the Dean and Executive Committee of the College of Literature, Science, and the Arts (8 November, 1961, Clyde Coombs Papers, Bentley Historical Archives, University of Michigan, Ann Arbor), Edwards's Engineering Psychology Laboratory was described as providing "unique opportunity to make advances in the areas of research where psychology and engineering intersect."

to fail only occasionally and randomly as a measurement instrument. Thus, Savage's normative decision theory and measurement theory became two sides of the same coin. The behavioral decision researchers simultaneously used measurement theory to measure actual decision behavior and used their experiments to empirically test measurement theory.

More specifically, in behavioral decision research and mathematical psychology, the human being was considered a measurement instrument that reasons logically and applies Bayesian statistics. In other words, the individual was considered a logician and a Bayesian statistician of some sort. The purpose of behavioral decision research, then, was to figure out whether this human being is a good logician and Bayesian statistician. This particular type of understanding human behavior was neatly summarized in a paper by Rapoport and Tversky: "[The behavioral decision research] approach to the study of choice behavior," they argued, "is based on the comparison between the normative solution of a decision problem and the observed solution employed by subjects." As a consequence, "man is viewed as an intuitive statistician who acts in order to maximize some specified criteria while operating on the basis of probabilistic information" (Rapoport & Tversky, 1970, p. 118).[33]

Edwards and the developing behavioral decision research approach compared actual human decision making with respect to this "normative solution," measured the decisions made in terms of "utility," and looked for ways to improve, that is, engineer human decision making toward better outcomes. But behavioral decision researchers sometimes also recognized that matters were a little more complicated than they usually portrayed them. In their introduction to *Decision Making* (1967), for instance, Edwards and Tversky noted that "the distinction between what an organism should do and what it does do is slippery" (1967, p. 8). The problematic distinction between the normative and the descriptive was a recurring theme, although it was far outnumbered by the instances in which the distinction was regularly used. The underlying problem was that in Savage's decision theory the normative and the empirical were closely related. The normative rules were rules that every healthy adult should agree with when thinking them through carefully. Savage's normative decision theory was as much a

---

[33] Under the broad definition of mathematical psychology as incorporating all mathematical treatments of human behavior, Rapoport may be classified as a mathematical psychologist. At the same time, it seems he was only loosely affiliated with Coombs's Mathematical Psychology Group – whose members were not working on game theory directly.

prescription for optimal behavior because it was a characterization of the behavior of an adult who had carefully thought through which decision to make. In experimental psychology, however, the distinction had become much stronger. In experimental psychology, the subjective perception of the stimulus, the sensation, was supposed to deviate from the objective norm. Thus, when decision theory was integrated into the experimental framework, the normative-descriptive distinction of decision theory risked becoming a much stronger and much more absolute distinction than it was meant to be by Savage (1954). This was unproblematic as long as the experiments showed that most of the time, subjects did indeed make their decisions according to the norms of decision theory, and it was what Edwards expected to find and actually did find. However, when the experiments indicated that there might be systematic differences between the norms of decision theory and actually observed behavior, an idea that gradually developed during the 1960s, it did become problematic.

5. Measurement and Decision Making in Psychology

To sum up, in the 1950s and 1960s mathematical psychology and behavioral decision research considered themselves to be directly related to economics and drew on substantial amounts of economic literature. Edwards's extensive knowledge of economics in particular tempts the reader to conclude that here we have a case in which psychology and economics were truly integrated into one research project (e.g., Edwards, 1954, 1961). But the way in which Edwards, Tversky, Krantz, and others talked about economics does not resonate with the way in which economists spoke about economics. Such different prominent economists as, say, Lionel Robbins, Paul Samuelson, and Milton Friedman would not have agreed to be engaged in constructing a normative theory of decision making or with equating utility with Lewinian valence.

Mathematical psychologists sought to develop the application of mathematics in psychology, and as behavioral decision research used a great deal of mathematics, a natural and direct link existed between the two. How to formulate mathematically how people should behave and how people actually do behave in situations under uncertainty were research questions that belonged to mathematical psychology as well as to behavioral decision research. Hence, the same scientist could naturally be perceived as being a contributor to these different fields at the same time. Tversky, Luce, and Suppes serve as examples.

But the link between mathematical psychology and behavioral decision research went further than the mere use of mathematics. Mathematical psychology's representational theory of measurement and behavioral decision research's experimental investigation of human decision making started from different perspectives, but were partly about the same subject: normative decision behavior. Mathematical psychology's representational theory of measurement used the human body as a measurement device. In the case of values and probabilities, for instance, the human being was used to measure human perception of these values and probabilities. But in order to make this a valid procedure, it had to be assumed that the human being as a measurement device functions consistently. Indeed, the validity of the measurement instrument was a major concern in the psychological experimental methodology of the time (Heukelom, 2011). The representational theory of measurement's definition of consistency was: according to the normative rules of decision theory. The assumption needed to be made was that the human measurement instrument behaved according to the normative decision theory.

Behavioral decision research, on the other hand, compared behavior of individuals in its experiments to the norms of decision theory, for which it used the representational theory of measurement. The two fit neatly together. Assuming that subjects behave according to the normative rules, the mathematical psychologists set up measurement frameworks that measured the perception of utilities, risk averseness, and so on. Assuming that, in general, subjects behave according to the normative rules, behavioral decision researchers investigated under which circumstances subjects made mistakes. Mathematical psychologists provided behavioral decision research with a solid theory of measurement, and behavioral decision research informed mathematical psychologists under which circumstances its human measurement instrument was less accurate.

To illustrate why for mathematical psychologists "measurement theory in psychology is behavior theory," (Coombs, 1983, p. 36), it is useful to ask how experimental psychologists measured the phenomena they were interested in. How did they measure the attitude of religious people who go to church twice a day? How did they measure the perception of "rape" in terms of good versus bad? How did they measure the perception of a probability of 0.01 percent? How did they measure the relative utility of receiving a certain ten dollars as opposed to a 0.8 chance of receiving fifteen dollars? The answer is that they measured all these psychological phenomena through the human being. "In psychological measurement, the individual is the measuring device; he plays the role of the pan balance, the meter stick, or the thermometer" (Coombs, 1983, p. 36). The psychologist used individuals to measure the value of psychological phenomena of *the* individual. This could be the human being in general, it could be the representative or average member of a culture, and it could even be the individual itself. For instance, one could use individuals as a measurement instrument to measure that same individual's risk averseness. "Psychological measurement theory is concerned with the empirical regularities in [the individual's] behavior that justify numerical assignments to the stimuli he is responding to and/or justify numerical assignments to him" (Coombs, 1983, p. 36).

However, to "justify numerical assignments" to stimuli and to "justify numerical assignments" to the individual based on "empirical regularities in this behavior," the psychologists needed to understand that behavior. In other words, they needed a theory describing human behavior. The psychologists needed to understand how humans function to be able to use them as measurement instruments, just as the physicist needs to understand how the thermometer works in order to use it as an instrument. But in the case of the human being as a measurement instrument, this could not be just any understanding; it needed to be an understanding in terms of rationality.

Mathematical psychology and behavioral decision research showed that in order for the human being to function as a measurement instrument, the human being needed to be understood as behaving rationally. For that reason, the scientist needed to have a behavioral explanation of the individual's response toward different stimuli in terms of *rationality*. In the case of decision making based on utilities and probabilities, that behavioral theory of rationality was decision theory. Decision theory explained how an individual would rationally respond to different stimuli and thus informed the psychologist which numeral to assign to the different stimuli. To make the link between measurement theory and decision theory, one had to assume that the individual that is used as the measurement instrument by and large behaves rationally.

Finally, what happens if we find out that the individual's behavior does systematically deviate from the rational norm? That question did not come up seriously until the late 1960s. However, from the preceding, we can see what happens. If individuals are found to behave irrationally, this is problematic for decision theory because it means that decision theory does not provide a good characterization of human behavior. As long as the deviations from decision theory are random, this is not too problematic. It would be the same problem as knowing that some or even all thermometers do not measure exactly right but that they measure correctly on average. However, when individuals are found to deviate systematically from the norms of decision theory, it becomes a serious problem. It not only means that decision theory is not a good description of actual human behavior; it also implies that measurement theory is based on flawed assumptions. In other words, it implies that the individual is not a valid measurement instrument. For instance, if the psychologist wants to measure what the relative value of two uncertain outcomes is and assumes that people have decided rationally, he or she may simply ask a few people which of the two they prefer and thus measure which of the two has the highest expected value. But if it now turns out that human beings systematically deviate from rational behavior, the psychologist cannot infer from their choices (i.e., from the measurement) which of the two options has the higher expected value.

6. Conclusion

In the 1950s and 1960s, both psychologists and economists elaborated on von Neumann and Morgenstern (2004) and Savage (1954), in which psychologists understood themselves explicitly to draw on the work of economists. Moreover, the concept of rational behavior played a key role in the psychological and economic research that drew on these authoritative sources. Nevertheless, it is difficult to overemphasize how distinct the two approaches were. The substantial difference between the normative-descriptive interpretation of the von Neumann and Morgenstern axioms in psychology and their interpretation in terms of the positive-normative distinction in economics is one expression of this disparity.

In postwar psychology, the normative and descriptive realms were closely related in a program of human engineering. In this program, measurement and rational decision making were two sides of the same coin, in which the rational individual served as a measurement instrument for its own subjective perception of the values and probabilities of the different decision options. Heidelberger (1993, 2004) and others (Michell, 1999, 2007; Boumans, 2007; Daston and Galison, 2007) have shown how the German experimental psychological tradition both laid the basis for the experimental investigation of human perception and, in a direct extension, argued that the human being is the ultimate measurement instrument in all science. The mathematical psychologists and behavioral decision researchers extended perception to decision making and added the requirement of rationality to the process of human decision making/measurement. The central question was no longer how the human being perceives, but rather how the human being infers a decision based on his or her perceptions and whether this is the correct (that is, the rational) decision. Thus, the theory of rational decision making fundamentally altered the experimental investigation and theoretical perspective of measurement and perception in experimental psychology. Rationality arose as a key concern both in the experimental investigation of human perception/decision making and in the understanding of the human being as the ultimate measurement instrument. Moreover, the reformulation in terms of decision making and rationality connected experimental psychology to statistics, thus adding a new chapter to the well-documented history of statistics (Daston, 1988; Porter, 1986; Krüger, Daston, et al., 1987; Krüger, Gigerenzer, et al., 1987).

The University of Michigan's preeminence in psychology lasted until the 1970s. One reason for the relative decline was the departure of prominent scientists such as Coombs, who retired in 1982, and Edwards, who relocated to the Highway Safety Research Institute in 1971 and then to the University of Southern California in 1973. Michigan's standing was also influenced by a general decline in the visibility of mathematical psychology and behavioral decision research, although both continue to be active research programs to this day.[34] More importantly, students of Edwards such as Slovic, Lichtenstein, and Tversky took behavioral decision research in directions that contradicted the assumption that human beings generally make their decisions rationally. Together with Daniel Kahneman, Tversky, in particular, came to strongly oppose the fundamental assumption of Savage and Edwards that, by and large, human beings make their decisions in accordance with the normative rules of decision theory. During the 1970s, Kahneman and Tversky's heuristics and biases, and later their prospect theory, arose as a new and appealing theory of decision making in behavioral psychology.

---

[34] Krantz, interview, 2008; and Pachella, interview, 2009.

Kahneman and Tversky

Heuristics, Biases, and Prospects for Psychology and Economics

1. Introduction

The human engineering project, which had received such a strong boost from the Second World War and early Cold War years, underwent a significant change in the 1960s and 1970s. In retrospect, the mid-1940s to the mid-1950s are best characterized as a period of generally undirected discussions of how best to formalize human decision making and of how such formalizations related to experimental evidence and to the concept of rationality. A few important elements of this discussion have been set out in Chapter 2. The mid-1950s to the late 1960s, then, are best understood as a period of canonization based on the *Theory of Games and Economic Behavior* (2004) and *Foundations of Statistics* (1954) (Zappia, 2008; Basili and Zappia, 2010). These books by von Neumann and Morgenstern and by Savage became the canonical standards for reasoning about individual rational behavior. The psychologists did so in the normative-descriptive framework of experimental psychology, whereas the economists employed a postivie-normative framework reinforced by Friedman (1953).[1]

That does not mean that criticism was absent, far from it. George Shackle (1903–1992) continued to develop his alternative theory of decision making (Shackle, 1949, 1961). Daniel Ellsberg (b. 1931) published his well-known criticism of Savage's Sure-Thing Principle (or independence axiom) in "Ambiguity, and the Savage Axioms" (Ellsberg, 1961). Herbert Simon (1916–2001) began to develop his staunch critique of the neoclassical economic and Savagian conception of rational human behavior and bit by bit developed his own alternative theory of bounded rationality (Simon, 1955,

---

[1] The interest in game theory waned among economists during the 1950s, only to return in the 1980s (Weintraub, 1992).

1959, 1986; Sent, 2001, 2005; Crowther-Heyck, 2005; Augier and March, 2004). However, the mainstream advanced based on the axiomatic approach as set out by von Neumann and Morgenstern (2004) and Savage (1954). Mathematicians proceeded to further develop the theory mathematically (e.g., Fishburn, 1964, 1981), behavioral and mathematical psychologists investigated its empirical application (Edwards and Tversky, 1967; Goldstein and Hogarth, 1997; Diamond and Rothschild, 1978), and mainstream, neo-classical economists integrated the axiomatic approach of rational behavior in the older economic theory of demand (Amadae, 2003; Mirowski and Hands, 1998).

This changed in the early 1970s. A number of newly recruited behavioral psychologists, among others, started to look for ways to maintain the behav-ioral axioms, its related models, and the associated normative-descriptive distinction, while at the same time taking account of the intuitive and empir-ical evidence against the axioms. Prominent examples include Paul Slovic (b. 1938) and Sarah Lichtenstein's (b. 1933) research of preference reversals (e.g. Slovic and Lichtenstein, 1971, 1973; Lichtenstein and Slovic, 2006) and Daniel Kahneman (b. 1934) and Amos Tversky's (1937–1996) program of heuristics and biases and, later, their prospect theory (e.g., Tversky and Kahneman, 1974; Kahneman and Tversky, 1979).[2]

These new developments in behavioral psychology occurred within the broader context of the rise of cognitive science. Cognitive science did not evolve around one center or confined group of scientists, and its objec-tives were hence manifold and not clearly circumscribed. As a consequence, also historical and philosophical discussions of cognitive science tend to emphasize different authors, time periods, and theoretical characteristics (e.g., Mirowski, 2002; Mindell, 2002; Cordeschi, 2002; Dupuy, 2009). But that said, cognitive science was (and is) first of all defined by the aim to open the mind's black box and to investigate how its different constituents such as memory, cognition, and perception interact to produce behav-ior. As such, it was directed explicitly against the behaviorism of Watson and Skinner, although it was in line with the behavioralist or engineer-ing approach of twentieth-century U.S. psychology (Mills, 1998; Capshew, 1999). A second aim of cognitive scientists was to bring together scien-tists from all disciplines and backgrounds who in one way or another were

---

[2] For detailed overviews of these and the many other behavioral programs of the 1960s and beyond, see, for example, Gigerenzer and Murray (1987), Goldstein and Hogarth (1997), Hogarth and Reder (1987), Guala (2000), Fishburn (1981), and Diamond and Rothschild (1978).

investigating human behavior and to thus construct one broad research program of the mind and of behavior (Cohen-Cole, 2007). Given its broad and only vaguely defined scope, Simon's program of bounded rationality, Slovic and Lichtenstein's research of preference reversals, and Kahneman and Tversky's alternative behavioral theories could be regarded as falling under the heading of cognitive science, next to, say, Noam Chomsky's (b. 1928) new approach to linguistics and Jerry Fodor's (b. 1935) new philosophy of mind.

Of the postwar research on decision making, Kahneman and Tversky's collaboration stands out as among the most influential in psychology and economics, as exemplified by Kahneman's 2002 Nobel Memorial Prize in Economics, the number of times their work has been cited (Laibson and Zeckhauser, 1998) and the rapid ascent of Kahneman and Tversky–inspired behavioral economics in the 1980s through the 2000s (Sent, 2004; Camerer and Loewenstein, 2004; Angner and Loewenstein, 2012). Their research introduced the idea that although rational individuals should adhere to the normative theories of logic, Bayesian updating, and expected utility calculation in their decision making, individuals in fact systematically and predictably deviate from these norms. To understand Kahneman and Tversky's collaborative research, it is crucial to understand their individual scientific backgrounds. These are discussed in Sections 2 and 3. The fourth section discusses their heuristics and biases program and prospect theory of the 1970s, and the fifth section seeks to offer three reasons for Kahneman and Tversky's influence among psychologists and economists.

2. Tversky Caught between A Priori Axioms and Behavioral Deviations

Tversky received a BA in the human sciences from Hebrew University in Jerusalem, Israel, in 1961. His teacher at Hebrew University, Israel Gutman (b. 1923), recommended him to mathematical psychologist Clyde Coombs (1912–1988), after which Tversky entered graduate school at the University of Michigan. In 1965, Tversky obtained his PhD from the University of Michigan under the supervision of Edwards and Coombs, combining Coombs's mathematical psychology with Edwards's behavioral decision research. Tversky's stay in the United States was never meant to be permanent, if only because he was from time to time required to serve in the Israeli army. But more in general Tversky was deeply involved with Israeli society and politics (his mother Genia was a member of the Knesset from 1948 until her death in 1964). However, as his wife, fellow cognitive psychologist

Barbara Tversky, whom he had met in Michigan, still had to complete her PhD, Amos Tversky spent the next four years as a postdoc and assistant professor at Michigan and Harvard. In 1969, the couple went back to Hebrew University where Tversky's collaboration with Kahneman started.

In his work on decision theory in the 1960s, Tversky adhered to the model and approach set out by Savage: "Utility theory, or the subjective expected utility (SEU) model, is a theory about decision making under risk. It is based on a set of seemingly reasonable axioms (Savage, 1954) which imply that an individual's choices between risky alternatives can be described as the maximization of his subjective expected utility" (Tversky, 1967c, p. 27). Tversky also accepted Edwards's interpretation and application of Savage's decision theory in terms of psychologists' normative-descriptive distinction. Thus, we read that utility theory "has been widely applied as a normative principle in economics and operations research, it underlies game theory and detection theory, and it has stimulated extensive experimental investigation" (Tversky, 1967c, p. 27). Tversky's experiments, then, compared the actual decision making of individuals in experiments with the normative rules for rational decision making as taken from Savage (1954).

Like the other mathematical psychologists introduced in Chapter 3, Tversky equated measurement theory with decision theory. To Tversky, the individual in psychological experiments served as the measurement instrument, just like the thermometer or pan balance in the experiments of the physicist and the chemist. As a consequence, the axioms of the representational theory of measurement that described the working of the measurement instrument were exactly the same as the axioms that described rational, normative behavior in decision theory. The direct link between measurement and decision making is a crucial part of Tversky's approach to individual decision making and clearly set out in *Foundations of Measurement I*:

Unlike most theories of measurement, which may have both physical and behavioral interpretations, the theory of expected utility is devoted explicitly to the problem of making decisions when their consequences are uncertain. It is probably the most familiar example of a theory of measurement in the social sciences. (Krantz et al., 1971, p. 369)

Thus, to Tversky, the axioms of normative decision theory were at the same time axioms that described the functioning of the psychologist's measurement instrument and axioms that described optimal decision behavior. Conceptually, this is only possible when one assumes that actual human decision behavior deviates very little from the norms of decision behavior.

The axiom assumes that if actual decision behavior deviates from the norm, it is somehow distributed evenly around the norm and does not deviate from the norm systematically. It also assumes that if human beings are found to deviate from the norms in certain situations, their mistakes can be relatively easily explained to them after which individuals will correct their behavior.

Tversky's work on the representational theory of measurement and on decision theory came together in his experimental work on behavioral decision research. The measurement models were applied in experimental testing and actual decision behavior was tested against normative decision theory. It is important to emphasize that in this early experimental work of Tversky, the question was *not* whether, let alone how, human beings deviate from the norms of decision theory. Tversky's basic research question in the 1960s, just as that posed by Edwards, was how to apply the normative model to human decision-making behavior. The axioms of decision theory indicated how individuals should, and usually do make decisions given the objective utilities and probabilities implied by the different options. But what the axioms neglected to specify was how a human being perceives utilities and probabilities. In Savage's subjective expected utility (SEU) model, for instance, it was assumed that subjects have a subjective perception of both objective values and probabilities and that subjects base their decisions on these subjective probabilities and subjective values (i.e., utilites). In a closely related descriptive model, the subjective expected value (SEV) model, it was assumed that subjects have only a subjective perception of the probabilities but perceive the values as what they objectively are. Tversky's experiments were first and foremost an investigation of how to employ the axioms of measurement theory and decision theory in the descriptive context of the experiment.

At the same time, Tversky used his experiments to test whether the human instrument indeed functioned properly. Tversky's experiments were set up to measure the utility curve of, for instance, candy and cigarettes, but the experiments at the same time checked whether the subjects behaved according to the axioms of decision theory and measurement theory. For instance, because the axiom of transitivity was the "cornerstone of normative and descriptive theories" and underlay "measurement models of sensation and value" (Tversky, 1969, p. 31), the experiments were used as an opportunity to also test the axiom of transitivity in actual human decision behavior. Thus, in one and the same experiment, Tversky would apply the representational theory of measurement, checked whether its human measurement instrument functioned properly, measured subjective perception of probabilities and values, and monitored whether human beings indeed behave according to the axioms of decision theory.

Let me give two examples. Tversky (1967a) tested the additivity and the independence axiom, two key axioms of normative decision theory and measurement theory, in a gambling experiment with eleven male inmates at the State Prison of Southern Michigan.[3] The subjects had to gamble for, and were paid in, candy and cigarettes. Six normative decision models were compared for both the set of candy gambles and the set of cigarettes gambles. In both cases, it turned out, Savage's SEU model provided the best description of the behavior displayed by the subjects. Given the SEU model, both additivity and the independence of subjective probability and utility were confirmed. That is, assuming that people make their decisions according to the normative theory, the SEU model provided the best description. Nevertheless, Tversky was cautious and concluded that "[a]fter more than 15 years of experimental investigation of decisions under risk, the evidence on the descriptive validity of the SEU model is still inconclusive" (Tversky, 1967a, p. 199).

In a related paper, Tversky (1967b) set out a measurement model that tested the descriptive validity of different normative models of decision making, among them Savage's SEU model, the power utility theory, and the strict additive model. To do so, the eleven inmates from the State Prison of Southern Michigan had to choose between different gambles but did not know the relevant probabilities beforehand. Savage's SEU model provided the best description, but failed in the sense that the subjects consistently overestimated low and underestimated high probabilities. The model was therefore extended with a power utility function that allowed utility to be a non-monotonic function of money (vs. monotonic in the standard case), and to vary across individuals. Tversky stressed the proven

---

[3] As mentioned earlier, engineering psychologists considered themselves to fill the gap between the priest, the teacher and the psychiatrist. As also mentioned earlier, Tversky collaborated on a few papers with Anatol Rapoport, who, among others, was associated with the Mental Health Research Institute at the University of Michigan. In addition, Tversky shared Rapoport's social/liberal political orientation (Erickson, 2010). It seems therefore relevant and quite intriguing that for the experiments mentioned here, Tversky relied on inmates. However, the reason for Tversky's using inmates simply seems to have been that candy, cigarettes, and (small amounts of) money were relatively scarce among the prison population, which enabled Tversky to conduct experiments with comparatively high stakes for the subjects, thus ensuring they would do their best. Tversky selected the inmates explicitly based on normal, mentally healthy individuals, and thus as being as similar to the population of normal, healthy individuals outside the prison walls.

independence of subjective probability and utility in the experiment and concluded that the best descriptive model (SEU plus power utility) was incompatible with decision theory as axiomatized by Savage (1954). To maintain the idea that individuals make decisions rationally, it had to be concluded that Savagian decision theory was a systematically incorrect description of actual/empirical behavior by individuals. Thus, Tversky went a step further than Edwards did in testing the axioms of measurement theory and decision theory. Tversky gradually allowed the possibility that sometimes the axioms were systematically violated by the experimental subjects.

In 1969, Tversky published a paper titled "Intransitivity of Preferences," in which experiments were described and discussed that had the sole purpose of testing the axiom of transitivity. Transitivity, Tversky stated, "is of central importance to both psychology and economics. It is the cornerstone of normative and descriptive decision theories." Furthermore, it was the essential assumption in measurement theories because "it is a necessary condition for the existence of an ordinal (utility) scale" (Tversky, 1969, p. 31). The article described a number of experiments that falsify weak stochastic transitivity (WST).[4] Tversky's experiments showed that WST does not hold descriptively. That is to say that the subjects' actual decisions were not in the least stochastically transitive.

Yet, Tversky was reluctant to give up on this foundation of both measurement theory and decision theory, as transitivity was "one of the basic and the most compelling principles of rational behavior" (Tversky, 1969, p. 45). Tversky suggested that normative decision theory could be maintained because apparent intransitivities could always be attributed to an unobserved change of preference that takes place between the decisions made. He concluded somewhat paradoxically that "[t]he main interest in the present results lies not so much in the fact that transitivity can be violated but rather in what these violations reveal about the choice mechanism and the approximation method that govern preference between multidimensional alternatives" (Tversky, 1969, p. 46). If Tversky had accepted that the axioms were wrong, the representational theory of measurement and normative decision theory as description of human behavior would be falsified. Another reason why Tversky was reluctant to give up the axioms was that the experimental results did not always indicate falsification.

---

[4] In WST, transitivity of preferences is defined in terms of probabilities, hence, x is weakly preferred over y if and only if $P(x,y) \geq 1/2$, meaning that the probability of choosing x over y is larger than or equal to a half.

For instance, in the previously mentioned experiments conducted in the State Prison of Southern Michigan, the decision behavior of the subjects largely corresponded to the norm.

The methodological tension Tversky was struggling with involved the question how a theory that is considered introspectively, or intuitively, true can be combined with experimental results that point in many directions, but only occasionally in the direction of the intuitive theory. Tversky could not proceed as an experimentalist who seeks to test whether a theory is right or wrong. As the axioms were understood as introspective or intuitive truths, they could ultimately only be proved wrong based on introspective or intuitive reasoning. Measurement theory and normative decision theory were simply not understood and employed as theories that could be falsified experimentally. At the same time, Tversky wanted to do justice to the experimental results he had obtained. Sticking to the axioms of measurement theory and decision theory would have implied that whenever a systematic behavioral deviation was observed in the experiments, there was something wrong with the experiment. This would mean that the majority of Tversky's experiments were invalid. Thus, Tversky was effectively caught between the intuitive truth of the axioms of measurement theory and decision theory and the behavioral deviations that surfaced in his experiments. He had to decide between taking his experiments seriously, or accepting the axioms of measurement theory and decision theory.

In the end, Tversky chose the former and endeavored to develop a new normative measurement and decision theory. "Elimination by Aspects: A Theory of Choice" appeared as a monograph in 1971 and as an article in *Psychological Review* in 1972.[5] "Elimination by Aspects: A Theory of Choice" began by introducing decision theory's twofold problem with the independence axiom. The independence axiom was first of all problematic on empirical grounds because it was "incompatible with some observed patterns of preferences which exhibit systematic dependencies among alternatives" (Tversky, 1972, p. 281). Even though he had observed this problem before, Tversky now concluded that this behavioral deviation could not be solved within existing decision theory:

data show that the principle of independence from irrelevant alternatives is violated in a manner that cannot be readily accounted for by grouping choice alternatives. More specifically, it appears that the addition of an alternative to an offered set

---

[5] Another illuminating example of Tversky's struggle with Savage's normative decision theory and its experimental falsifications is Slovic and Tversky's "Who Accepts Savage's Axiom?" (1974).

"hurts" alternatives that are similar to the added alternatives more than those that are dissimilar to it. (Tversky, 1972, p. 283)

Because of the impossibility of solving the behavioral deviations within the existing theory, decision theorists and behavioral decision researchers required "a more drastic revision of the principles underlying [the] models of choice" (Tversky, 1972, p. 283).

Tversky accepted the intuitive or introspective status of the independence and other axioms, but moved on to show that based on intuitive thinking doubts could also be raised. "Suppose," Tversky argued, "you are offered a choice among the following three records: a suite by Debussy, denoted D, and two different recordings of the same Beethoven symphony, denoted B_1 and B_2." Assume furthermore "that the two Beethoven recordings are of equal quality, and that you are undecided between adding a Debussy or a Beethoven to your collection. Hence, $P(B_1;B_2) = P(D;B_1) = P(D;B_2) = 1/2$." That is, being undecided between two options to Tversky implied a probability of choosing one or the other equaling one-half. It then "follows readily that $P(D;B_1;B_2) = 1/3$." However, this conclusion "is unacceptable on *intuitive grounds* because the basic conflict between Debussy and Beethoven is not likely to be affected by the addition of another Beethoven recording" (Tversky, 1972, p. 283, emphasis added). The empirical evidence had made the normative theory less useful for practical purposes, but it was this last introspective argument that dealt the final blow.

Thus, a new normative decision theory was required, Tversky argued, and this should preferably be a theory that could serve both the normative and the descriptive domain. Elimination-by-aspects was as simple and elegant as it was convincing. Rational human decision making, Tversky argued, occurs not through a process of expected utility maximization, logic, or Bayesian updating, but through a sequential process of eliminating the alternative with the lowest expected value. Here I quote Tversky at length.

The present development describes choice as a covert sequential elimination process. Suppose that each alternative consists of a set of aspects of characteristics, and that at every stage of the process, an aspect is selected (from those included in the available alternatives) with probability that is proportional to its weight. The selection of an aspect eliminates all the alternatives that do not include the selected aspects, and the process continues until a single alternative remains. If a selected aspect is included in all the available alternatives, no alternative is eliminated and a new aspect is selected. Consequently, aspects that are common to all the alternatives under consideration do not affect choice probabilities. Since the present theory describes choice as an elimination process governed by successive selection of aspects, it is called the elimination-by-aspects (EBA) model. (Tversky, 1972, p. 285)

Tversky's elimination-by-aspects accepted his experimental results as valid and constructed a whole new basis for measurement theory and decision theory. It did so by disproving Savage's decision theory on intuitive grounds, that is, by accepting that ultimately only an introspective "test" of the axioms could prove them wrong. But elimination-by-aspects turned out to be a road not taken. In the late 1960s and early 1970s, Kahneman offered Tversky a solution that accepted the experimental behavioral deviations as valid while at the same time leaving intact the fundamentals of measurement theory and decision theory.

3. Kahneman's Cognitive Mistakes

To understand how Kahneman solved Tversky's problem, we need to examine the research Kahneman conducted before his collaboration with Tversky. Kahneman obtained a BA from Hebrew University in 1956 while working as a psychologist in the Israeli army. In 1958, he moved to San Francisco and obtained a PhD from the University of California at Berkeley in 1961 under the supervision of Susan Ervin (b. 1927). After completing his PhD, Kahneman returned to the psychology department at Hebrew University where he would remain until 1978. In the meantime, however, he was a visiting scholar at the University of Michigan in 1965–1966, a visiting scientist and lecturer in psychology at Harvard University in 1966–1967, a visiting scientist during the summer terms of 1968 and 1969 at the Applied Psychology Research Unit of Cambridge, the United Kingdom, and a lecturer in the graduate program of the University of Michigan in 1968–1969. While teaching at Michigan, Kahneman invited his younger colleague Tversky to lecture a class on recent developments in judgment and decision making (Kahneman, 2002). In the 1960s, Kahneman's research was about semantic differentials, optometry, vision research, and related themes. Kahneman's research during this period was unrelated to mathematical psychology, unrelated to decision theory, unrelated to behavioral decision research, and despite some retrospective hints of Kahneman to the contrary, entirely unrelated to economics.

Based on Kahneman's recollections in his autobiography and the one publication that emerged from it, his early work for the Israeli army in the early 1950s and at the Hebrew University is best characterized as correlational psychology (Kahneman and Ghiselli, 1962; Kahneman, 2002; Danziger, 1990, 1997; Gigerenzer, 1987a, 1987b). Correlational psychology builds theories based on correlations in statistical data, for example, between IQ and the degree of education. Using methods developed by the British army in World War II, the aim of Kahneman's early research was to develop reliable predictions about the future performance of people based on character traits, be it in the army or in different kinds of jobs. For instance, to find out at an early stage which new recruits in the army would eventually be successful leaders on the future battlefield, tests were designed to evaluate the differences between recruits with respect to a few behavioral and personal characteristics that were thought to relate to leadership capacities.

It is not difficult to see that in this kind of research the ability of the researcher to predict the future performance of the subjects investigated is an important, and perhaps the only way to measure success. A classification of new recruits in the army along different dimensions might be an interesting exercise, but if it does not predict better than chance, then it is of no use. In his autobiography (Kahneman, 2002), Kahneman recalls how frustrating it was when time and again he was confronted with the fact that his predictions were anything but reliable. Extensive questionnaires and tests were set up, but in the end, it turned out that the intuitive guesses of the staff members who conducted the tests and collected the questionnaires proved better than the scientific predictions.

Dissatisfied with the results of this research and eager to develop his research skills, Kahneman switched to the experimental psychology of vision, resulting in some twenty-five articles over a period of ten years, including two publications in *Science* and a whole range more in prominent experimental psychology journals such as the *Journal of Experimental Psychology*. There is not one particular theme or article that stands out during the decade from 1961 to 1971. Kahneman's overarching view of the human mind emerges when the different themes and articles are considered next to each other.

Kahneman's career continued with the models used in experimental studies of semantic differentials. Semantic Differential (SD) research investigates people's attitude toward words (Heise, 1970, p. 235) or, put differently, measures the meaning of abstract objects to the individual (Kiddler, 1981). A distinction is made between the denotative and the connotative meaning of a word, or a concept, or an object. Thus, it is assumed that apart from the dictionary, or the denotative meaning, words are also assigned connotative meanings by the individual. The words *massacre* and *rape*, for instance, are attributed different connotations than are *flower* and *sunny day* in terms of good versus bad. SDs are measured on a bipolar scale, for which in principle all opposites can be used, such as good-bad, soft-hard, fast-slow, clean-dirty, valuable-worthless, and so forth.

Articles on SD make up a small, but important part of the publications of Kahneman's early work. Apart from his dissertation, it was the subject of one published article. It also provides a good illustration of Kahneman's take on experimental psychology.[6] Within the field of SD research, Kahneman's focus was on the theory behind the models that are used to infer conclusions about the connotative meanings. In Kahneman (1963), he showed that models that are used to measure SDs are mathematically not sufficiently sophisticated and may give rise to wrong interpretations of what is observed. Kahneman considered the following model for the rating s_{ijk} of the concept j by individual i on scale k:

$$s_{ijk} = T_{jk} + C_{ik} + d_{ijk}, \qquad (4.1)$$

in which T_{jk} is the "true score" of concept j on scale k, computed as the average score of a number of judges. C_{ik} is the "constant deviation" of subject i on scale k, computed as the average deviation of subject i from the true score over a large number of concepts. d_{ijk} is the "specific deviation" (or "error of judgment") on a particular rating. Put differently, like the mathematical psychologists and behavioral decision researchers of Chapters 2 and 3, Kahneman used the individual to measure the individual's own rating and deviations from the average. C_{ik}, then, is the accuracy, or the validity of the individual-as-measurement-instrument, d_{ijk} is the precision or reliability (see also Heukelom, 2011).

Kahneman argued that the practice of contemporary SD research wrongly assumed that the specific deviations of ratings were uncorrelated. For example, deviating from the true score could very well be correlated during the course of one experiment. Improvement should be sought in the direction of more "precise algebraic" models. Kahneman's research focused not so much on the theory of SDs as such, but on the improvement of the analysis of variance in the statistical models it employed. Specifically, he focused on the notion of the "error of judgment" in SD research. The object of investigation was to understand how people deviate from what is true or correct. In effect, that meant that the analysis of the actual process of how people make judgments was black boxed.

In 1962 and 1963, Kahneman set up a vision lab at the Department of Psychology of Hebrew University (Kahneman, 2002, p. 6). Many of the articles he published in the following years were derived from the experimental results of this lab. In this research, Kahneman investigated the relationship

---

[6] Daniel Kahneman, interview with author, Princeton University, Princeton, New Jersey, April 16, 2009.

between the "energy" of different stimuli and visual perception capacities. "Energy" was employed as a general concept to define the strength of a stimulus; the brighter, the more illuminated, the more contrasted, the longer, and so forth the stimulus was, the more energy it had. Visual perception was measured in terms of the reaction times of the subjects. In the typical experiment, the subject had to decide as quickly as possible whether the opening of a so-called Landolt C was directed up-, down-, left-, or rightward.[7] The conditions in terms of brightness, contrast, and so on in this setting could be varied in numerous ways. The visual task could also be combined with other cognitive tasks. Kahneman's textbook on the psychology of vision and attention, *Attention and Effort* (1973), was still used in the early twenty-first century as standard reference on the subject.[8]

Examples of this research include Kahneman's (1965a) "Control of Spurious Association and the Reliability of the Controlled Variable" and Kahneman's (1966b) "Time-Intensity Reciprocity in Acuity as a Function of Luminance and Figure-Ground Contrast."[9] In Kahneman and Norman (1964), the relation between the minimal amount of time subjects need to identify a visual stimulus (labeled the "critical duration" t_c) and the energy in terms of brightness and duration of the stimulus was investigated. It was shown that stimuli of equal energy do not necessarily produce the same critical duration and that a given visual stimulus does not trigger one but multiple sensory processes. The second conclusion particularly opposed the general view held in the psychophysical community that one stimulus triggers only one sensory process.

In the psychophysical paradigm Kahneman was working in, visual perception was seen as one of many cognitive tasks. Other cognitive tasks included conversation, or more generally, speech, learning, and calculation. How different cognitive tasks influence one another was investigated in Kahneman and Beatty (1966, 1967), Kahneman et al. (1967, 1968), and Kahneman and Peavler (1969). The explicit emphasis in these articles was on how the combination of different cognitive tasks could lead to "errors of judgment." In Kahneman et al. (1967), for instance, it was shown that the capacity to visually perceive substantially decreases when subjects were

---

[7] The Landolt C is one of the standard symbols used in psychophysics of vision and optometry. It consists of a C in which the opening can be varied and is either surrounded by bars the width of which equals the C's opening or not surrounded.

[8] Robyn Dawes, interview with author, Carnegie Mellon University, Pittsburgh, June 23, 2008.

[9] Other examples include Flom et al. (1963), Kahneman (1964, 1965b, 1966a, 1967), Kahneman and Norman (1964), and Kahneman et al. (1967).

engaged in other mental tasks such as speech or calculation. The "error of judgment" in these cases is very real, because it explains, for instance, why car drivers may miss a stop sign when engaged in conversation. It again illustrates Kahneman's focus on the psychology of mistakes.

Thus, in Kahneman's vision research, an emphasis was placed on the question under which circumstances the human mind makes cognitive errors. Kahneman showed that there is a trade-off between different cognitive tasks in perception capacities, and that as a result people may sometimes "fail" to perceive the stimulus and make an error in judgment. Furthermore, the research conducted by Kahneman in the period between 1961 and 1971 was in line with the behaviorist drive to eliminate all introspection from psychology started in the interwar period (Danziger, 1997). In Kahneman's experiments, self-reports were not necessary to establish how the cognitive system operates. The behavior of the cognitive system could be inferred from observed behavior and physical responses that cannot be controlled, such as pupil dilation and restriction. The human mind was considered to not permit introspective access, whereas its functioning could be inferred from the uncontrollable and unconscious responses made by the individual subjects.

Both elements are important in gaining an understanding of Kahneman's psychology and his subsequent influence on Tversky. The recurring theme of the cognitive errors shows that in Kahneman's view psychology was about discovering how people deviate from a norm behavior. This aspect of experimental psychology dates back to the beginning of experimental psychology in nineteenth century Germany. But in nineteenth-century German and interwar U.S. experimental psychology, this framework was adopted for the purpose of discovering what the *true* value was. The experimental psychologists wanted to know the true value of, for instance, the smallest amount of difference in weight people could perceive, and for this purpose devised a framework, which in spite of all the individual errors, could establish the true value (Fechner, 1860; Heidelberger, 2004; Boring, 1929). Thurstone, for instance, wanted to measure *the* attitude toward religion of a group of people, and for this purpose, he constructed a method that would elicit the attitude from a series of observations in which each individually deviated from the true value (Thurstone and Chave, 1929). Thus, experimental psychology was explicitly modeled after experimental practice in physics, in which the physicist tries to establish the true value of the temperature of boiling water by conducting a series of measurements in which each measurement individually deviates from the true value and from each other.

Kahneman employed the experimental psychological framework, but applied it differently. In Kahneman's work, the true value was known. The true value was an accurate prediction of a recruit's future leadership capacities, or the true value was not running through a traffic light when driving a car. The question Kahneman then raised was how, when, and why the cognitive machinery fails to act according to the true value. Kahneman used an experimental psychological framework, but applied it with the opposite purpose. He did not want to find out what the *true* value was, but how people *deviate* from the true value. In Kahneman's research, the true value was always clear and determined by the experimenter. Kahneman knew how the cognitive machinery ideally responds, and investigated whether it actually does do so. In Kahneman's understanding, the scientist thus completely determined in each experimental situation what the good, optimal, or rational behavior should be. This was in line with the scientific desire to eliminate all introspection because it assumed that the experimental subject cannot judge whether it is giving the correct response or not. In Kahneman's experiments, the experimenter determined how the subject should behave and determined how it did behave. All authority for judging behavior was placed in the hands of the scientist.

Because Kahneman has never provided an extensive theoretical exposition of the assumption that human beings often make cognitive errors, one could easily dismiss it as merely a nice way of illustrating theories that are perhaps not too exciting. But that would be a mistake. The key to understanding Kahneman's psychology lies in his conviction that human beings often make cognitive errors. In the example of the army psychologist at the beginning of the article, Kahneman and his colleagues really believed that through their extensive studies, they could accurately predict, or at least predict better than by mere chance, the future performance of different candidates for a job. The fact that they could not was for the young Kahneman a true cognitive illusion that he needed to correct for himself (Kahneman, 2002).

Another illustrative example recalled by Kahneman in his autobiography was the moment a flight instructor disagreed with the psychologists' theory that praise is more effective in developing skills than is punishment. The flight instructor reasoned that although he praised the good performance of his recruits, the next time the performance would almost always be worse. Similarly, he would always punish recruits who had done a poor job, and this would almost always improve performance the next time. To Kahneman, this was a clear cognitive illusion. A good performance is statistically more likely to be followed by a worse performance than by an equally good or even better performance, and vice versa. Also the truck or car driver described earlier who was engaged in a conversation and thus did not see a traffic light that he or she would otherwise not miss, really did make an error. His or her cognitive apparatus was tuned to noticing traffic lights, but it failed to do so.

To Kahneman, it was and is a given fact of life that human beings often make cognitive errors. However, science could help in two ways. First, scientists could set out what the correct way of behaving is for each situation. For the truck driver, it is obvious what the correct behavior is, but for the flight instructor, it may not be intuitively clear what the correct way of reasoning is. Scientists can therefore help to establish the correct way of reasoning. Second, scientists, and in particular psychologists, could help by investigating when, how and in what way human beings make cognitive errors and thus provide a basis for designing tools or education to help human beings correct these cognitive errors.

4. The Collaboration: Heuristics, Biases, and Prospect Theory

In 1969, Kahneman and Tversky started a collaboration that would result in twenty-one papers and two coedited books, including one published with Slovic. They continued to cooperate on different projects until Tversky's death in 1996, but the most productive and creative period was from 1969 to 1979, including the widely cited 1974 *Science* and 1979 *Econometrica* articles.[10] The cooperation was initiated by Kahneman, who was looking for new ways to experimentally test his intuition that an individual's cognitive apparatus systematically fails, and who tried to find a theory that might account for these cognitive errors. But the ensuing program stemmed as much from Tversky's growing doubts concerning Savage and Edwards's assumption that, generally speaking, individuals decide according to the normative rules of logic, Bayesian statistics, and expected utility theory (Savage, 1954; Edwards, 1954, 1961).

When Tversky returned to Hebrew University in 1969, Kahneman and Tversky gradually started to collaborate. Although their collaborative work constituted an important part of their research, especially in the 1970s, it was never the only project in which they were engaged. Kahneman continued to work on vision research, and Tversky kept working on measurement theory. The role that the collaborative work with Kahneman played in Tversky's life

---

[10]   Tversky and Kahneman (1974), "Judgment under Uncertainty: Heuristics and Biases" and Kahneman and Tversky (1979), "Prospect Theory: An Analysis of Decision under Risk."

is nicely illustrated in fifteen letters Tversky wrote to his close friend David Krantz (b. 1938) between 1967 and 1977.[11] His work with Kahneman is briefly mentioned for the first time in 1969, when Tversky, in an offhand remark, notes that "I am working a little bit with Danny, on the problem of statistical intuition, which helped to reinforce my prejudices concerning the importance of statistics."[12] A month later, the work with Kahneman seems to have taken off seriously, as one project among a number of different projects Tversky was working on:

> Danny and I got deeply involved in the problem of processing uncertainty: we are running a research seminar and a couple of studies on the topic . . . I am working now on the Chapters of our book [*Foundations of Measurement I*]. The editing apparently takes much more time than I realized, but is certainly worth doing. What has happened to our MDS paper submitted to JMP?[13]

When two years later he wrote about the reorganization of the psychology department at Hebrew University he and Kahneman were seeking to advance, Tversky briefly mentioned what would become the famous 1974 *Science* publication. "Danny and I are writing a sort of review paper on our work for someplace like Science, and I returned to Chapter 16 [of *Foundations of Measurement II*]."[14]

Kahneman and Tversky's joint work became a mix of their earlier individual research. Tversky's work on decision theory, with its distinction between the normative and descriptive realm, became coupled with Kahneman's psychology of mistakes. For their first article, Tversky posed a set of questions to eighty-four participants who attended the 1969 meetings of the American Psychological Association and the Mathematical Psychology Group that meant to capture Kahneman's personal experience of incorrect research planning and unsuccessful replications. "Suppose," Kahneman and Tversky asked,

> you have run an experiment on 20 Ss [subjects], and have obtained a significant result which confirms your theory ($z = 2.23$, $p < .05$, two-tailed). You now have cause to run an additional group of 10 Ss. What do you think the probability is

---

[11] I thank David Krantz for allowing me to access these letters. The letters do not form part of a generally accessible archive.

[12] Tversky's letter to Krantz, October 5, 1969, personal collection.

[13] Tversky's letter to Krantz, November 2, 1969, personal collection. "MDS paper" and JMP refers to Tversky and Krantz (1970) "The dimensional representation and the metric structure of similarity data," published in the *Journal of Mathematical Psychology* (JMP; e-mail Krantz to author, August 11, 2008).

[14] Tversky's letter to Krantz, November 14, 1971, personal collection.

that the results will be significant, by a one-tailed test, separately for this group? (Kahneman and Tversky, 1972, p. 433)

According to Kahneman and Tversky, the answer depends on the exact interpretation of the information provided. However, it should be below but close to 0.5, they argued. Nine of the eighty-four participants gave answers between 0.4 and 0.6, which Kahneman and Tversky interpreted as "reasonable." The other seventy-five, however, gave answers that exceeded 0.6. The median response of all participants was as high as 0.85. Thus, even those professionals who were trained and were explicitly asked to give the normatively correct answer failed to calculate it correctly. Kahneman and Tversky felt justified in inferring the strong and bold thesis "that people have strong intuitions about random sampling; that these intuitions are wrong in fundamental respects; that these intuitions are shared by naïve subjects and by trained scientists; and that they are applied with unfortunate consequences in the course of scientific inquiry" (Tversky and Kahneman, 1971, p. 105).

To the retrospective outsider, the question seems much too detailed for conference participants asked to fill out a questionnaire between conference sessions, even if they are professors of psychology. But although it is undoubtedly true that Kahneman and Tversky formulated the question such that the desired result would be likely to appear, the formulation of the question is also a testimony to the perceived superiority of scientific language. To Kahneman and Tversky, as to many of their contemporaries, human behavior had to be measured and judged against the yardstick of science. Therefore, the scientific wording could not be bended too far in the direction of imperfect human understanding. However, where many of their contemporaries took similar experimental falsifications of individuals' capacity to reason along scientific lines as proof that something had to be wrong with the science (e.g., Ellsberg, 1961; Allais and Hagen, 1979; Baumol, 1951, 1958; Simon, 1955, 1959; Slovic and Lichtenstein, 1971), Kahneman and Tversky took it as evidence of a cognitive failure of the individuals tested. They found it appalling and fundamentally disturbing to see that even trained professionals failed to behave according to the dictates of normative theory.

Why did the majority of them fail? Before his collaboration with Kahneman, Tversky's answer would have been either that there had been something wrong with the experiment or that the normative theory was wrong (e.g., Tversky, 1969, 1972; Slovic and Tversky, 1974). This time, however, Kahneman and Tversky took a different route. Taking an idea from the learning theory of Estes (1964), Kahneman and Tversky hypothesized that individuals have the tendency to suppose that a sample from a population must represent the population in its general characteristics. In other words, they implicitly accounted for their results by supposing that the biological makeup of human beings makes individuals ignore the possibility that a sample of a population may not be an accurate representation of that population. Kahneman and Tversky hypothesized that this provides individuals with the wrong intuition and that as a result they fail to give the right answer. However, Kahneman and Tversky took the research of Estes (1964) a step further by concluding that if individuals systematically consider a sample to be representative of its population, then it could be thought of as a "heuristic." They advanced the idea the human mind uses this heuristic to base decisions on.

The reason why the majority of scientists and laypersons systematically deviated from the norm answer that was given in Tversky and Kahneman's (1971) "Belief in the Law of Small Numbers" and further developed in Kahneman and Tversky's (1972), "Subjective Probability: A Judgment of Representativeness" was that human beings, in general, do not base their decisions on the normative laws of, in this case, probability theory and statistics, but instead use a "representative heuristic." Kahneman and Tversky described the representative heuristic as the phenomenon that "[t]he subjective probability of an event, or a sample, is determined by the degree to which it: (i) is similar in essential characteristics to its parent population; and (ii) reflects the salient features of the process by which it is generated" (Kahneman and Tversky, 1972, p. 430). In the example, the individuals interrogated supposed the draw to be a good representation of the population the experiment was meant to say something about, and focused on the salient feature of the test, namely, that it confirmed the theory significantly. As a result, of this representative heuristic, most of the professional psychologists estimated the probability requested to be much higher than it actually was (as said, the median estimate was 0.85).

Because human beings have much more faith in small samples than they should, Kahneman and Tversky half jokingly labeled this phenomenon the "belief in the law of small numbers," in reference to the law of large numbers. The analogy with faith and belief casted the issue in terms of subjective religion, prejudice and limited knowledge versus objective, value free science; it characterized the observation in terms of the incapable individual versus the rational, enlightened scientist. In other words, it expressed Kahneman and Tversky's view that an individual's erroneous behavior is the result of false beliefs for which the individual – including even the professor of psychology – cannot really be blamed. The "deviations of subjective from objective probability seem reliable, systematic, and difficult to eliminate" (Kahneman and Tversky, 1972, p. 431), and "[t]he true believer in the law of small numbers commits his multitude of sins against the logic of statistical inference in good faith. The representation hypothesis describes a cognitive or perceptual bias, which operates regardless of motivational factors" (Tversky and Kahneman, 1971, p. 109). In Kahneman and Tversky's framework, science, and, in particular, mathematics decision theory and economics, determined what the normatively correct decisions were in each decision situation. In this framework, normative was equated with rational and objective. The actual decision made by the individual was part of a "descriptive" or "subjective" realm, and could be either in accord or in disaccord with the normative or rational benchmark. If in disaccord, this implied the individual had made an "error," "mistake," or, in the language of behavioral economics from the early 1980s onward, an "ir-," "non-," "not fully," or "boundedly rational" decision.

Kahneman and Tversky's next experiment addressed not scientists, but individuals in general, and retained the formal, scientific wording. Assuming that the probability of a newborn to be a boy or a girl is 0.5, consider the following question:

All families of six children in a city were surveyed. In 72 families the *exact order* of births of boys and girls was G B G B B G.

What is your estimate of the number of families surveyed in which the *exact order* of births was B G B B B B? (Kahneman and Tversky, 1972, p. 432, emphasis in the original)

The normatively correct answer is seventy-two, as any sequence of boys and girls is equally probable. However, average estimates of the second sequence were systematically lower than the first. People, in other words, incorrectly believed the first sequence to be more probable than the second, from which Kahneman and Tversky concluded that "[p]eople view chance as unpredictable but essentially fair" (Kahneman and Tversky, 1972, p. 435). An alternative, but related explanation provided by Kahneman and Tversky was that people judged the first sequence to be more probable than the second because it better represented their image of a family with six children or that an image of a family with three boys and three girls was more readily available than an image of a family with five boys and one girl (Kahneman and Tversky, 1972).

From 1972 to 1974, based on these and similar examples, Kahneman and Tversky argued that the normative models worked descriptively far worse than had previously been thought. But instead of arguing that either the experiments were flawed or that the normative theory was wrong, the two options available in Tversky's research on human decision making in the 1960s, they now argued that the experimental results were perfectly valid and that there was nothing wrong with the normative theory. Instead, the new conclusion that was drawn was that when individuals (including scientists) make their decisions intuitively, they systematically deviate from the rational norm. The argument was thus directed explicitly against Tversky's former mentor and collaborator Edwards, as well as against the towering figure of Savage. With respect to Bayes's rule, Edwards and Savage had mistakenly assumed "that man, by and large, follows the correct Bayesian rule, but fails to appreciate the full impact of evidence, and is therefore conservative" (Kahneman and Tversky, 1972, p. 449). The mainstream representatives of signal detection theory were also criticized.[15] "Peterson and Beach (1967), for example, concluded that the normative model provides a good first approximation to the behavior of the Ss who are 'influenced by appropriate variables and in appropriate directions'" (Kahneman and Tversky, 1972, p. 449). Kahneman and Tversky had come to fundamentally disagree with them. "[In] his evaluation of evidence, man is apparently not a conservative Bayesian: he is not Bayesian at all" (Kahneman and Tversky, 1972, p. 450).

The alternative theory Kahneman and Tversky proposed was their Heuristics and Biases theory, first labeled as such in Tversky and Kahneman's (1974), "Judgment under Uncertainty: Heuristics and Biases." In this theory, people do not use the normative theories of probability and logic to make decisions under uncertainty, but instead rely on a number of heuristics, heuristics that sometimes lead to systematic deviations. In the often-quoted definition, heuristics and biases theory "shows that people rely on a limited number of heuristic principles which reduce the complex tasks of assessing probabilities and predicting values to simpler judgmental operations. In general, these heuristics are quite useful, but sometimes they lead to severe and systematic errors" (Tversky and Kahneman, 1974, p. 1124). Kahneman and Tversky emphasized the importance and functioning of a few heuristics, such as representativeness, availability, and anchoring. But by no means was the heuristics and biases theory meant to remain confined to these few heuristics. There was no limit to the number of heuristics that possibly could be discovered in humans' minds. The heuristics and biases

---

[15] Signal detection theory (SDT) is a branch of psychophysics that investigates the individual's ability to distinguish between signal and noise. In other words, it investigates decision making under noisy conditions. See e.g. Green and Swets (1966).

program summed up the many violations of the normative models Kahneman and Tversky had found, and provided a small, non-exhaustive list of explanations that might account for these violations.

The term *heuristic* appeared for the first time in 1971 without any precursors in either Kahneman's or Tversky's earlier work, and from the beginning was used without introduction as a natural term for an intuitive response. From the 1950s to the 1970s, Herbert Simon had used *heuristic* and similar terms in his uncompromising attack on – what he understood to be – the behavioral foundations of neoclassical economics, and the alternative he proposed in the form of human decision making based on heuristics (e.g., Simon, 1955, 1959, 1963, 1986). It is therefore tempting to conclude that Kahneman and Tversky's use of the term somehow derived from Simon. But that would be a mistake. As illustrated by Kahneman and Tversky's use of the term, *heuristic* "was just a word from the language."[16] Simon used the term in a different way and is moreover not mentioned in Kahneman and Tversky's research of the early 1970s.

It is useful to briefly set out the difference between the two. In Simon's view, individuals use rules of thumb or heuristics to make decisions. An example of a heuristic could be to set an aspiration price for the house one wishes to sell, and to go with the first offer that exceeds the aspiration price. Or, alternatively, the heuristic could be to accept the best among the first *n* offers (e.g., Simon, 1955). To Simon, such a heuristic was meant to optimize the decision made given all the constraints the individual faced in terms of information, cognitive capacity, and time. If the heuristic yielded a satisfactory outcome, it would be maintained; if not, it would be adjusted. Importantly, to Simon the heuristic's function was not to approximate the global optimum given all the possibly relevant information and computing capacity, but to achieve a satisfactory outcome given the information and capacity that one had.

In Kahneman and Tversky's approach, by contrast, the function of heuristics was to simplify and reorganize the decision problem in such a way that it was manageable for a not very sophisticated decision maker. The objectives of heuristics were to approximate the optimum given all relevant information and full knowledge of statistics, logic, and expected utility theory. The heuristics did not yield the decision, but reorganized the informational input in such a way that a decision-making process was possible. In the birth order problem, for instance, individuals, as said, commonly believe a family

---

[16] Kahneman, interview, 2009.

of G B G B B G instead of B G B B B B to be more likely because it better represents the individual's image of a family of six children (representativeness) or because it has such a family more readily available (availability). In other words, the availability heuristic links the incoming information to already present information about six-children families to simplify the decision. In this case, however, that organization of the information leads to the wrong conclusion. And because the heuristic is part of the biological makeup of the individual, it will not change. If the question is given more thought, the individual may opt for both options to be equally likely, particularly if the individual has just taken a course in logic and statistics. That is to say that the individual may override its own intuition using its capacity to reason. But the individual's initial intuitive response will always be the first option to be more likely.

Thus, in Kahneman and Tversky's account, the individual could not adjust his or her heuristics, as a person could in Simon's approach. The Simon individual might replace his or her initial aspiration price for selling the house with a lower aspiration price when no bids reach the aspiration level. For Kahneman and Tversky, on the contrary, the heuristics are part of a given, unchanging biological makeup of the individual. Availability, representativeness, and so on are seen as components belonging to the human information processing machinery that cannot be changed:

> What is perhaps surprising is the failure of people to infer from lifelong experience such fundamental statistical rules as regression toward the mean . . . Statistical principles are not learned from everyday experience. . . . people do not learn the relation between sample size and sampling variability, although the data for such learning are abundant. (Tversky and Kahneman, 1974, p. 1130)

To mathematical psychologists and behavioral decision researchers such as Coombs, Edwards, Luce, and Tversky, a human, when acting intuitively, was acting as a statistician. Also in Kahneman and Tversky's research, as in Tversky's other work "man is viewed as an intuitive statistician who acts in order to maximize some specified criteria while operating on the basis of probabilistic information" (Rapoport and Tversky, 1970, p. 118). In addition, the individual was viewed as an intuitive optimizer of utility, and an intuitive logician. The major difference was that to Kahneman and Tversky, the individual was an imperfect statistician, a logician, and an optimizer of utility. The individual behaved according to the normative models, but only after a set of fixed heuristics had reorganized the input. In many ways, this was a different theory than Simon's theory of bounded rationality.

In 1979, Kahneman and Tversky published their now famous article on "Prospect Theory: An Analysis of Decision under Risk" in *Econometrica*. The article marked a shift in emphasis away from probabilistic decision problems to an investigation of people's capacity to behave according to the normative theory of expected utility theory. It was the first attempt to produce a more complete descriptive theory of human decision making under uncertainty. Prospect theory has often been presented as being different from heuristics and biases (e.g., Kahneman, 2002), and it is certainly true that prospect theory brought the different heuristics into one overarching framework. But the foundation still was the idea that human beings rely on a set of heuristics for their decision making and that the use of these heuristics sometimes leads to systematic deviations from the normatively correct decision. In this regard, it should be noted that it took Kahneman and Tversky some five years to get the article published in *Econometrica* and that the last four of these five years were used to tweak a for the most part finished argument to fit an economic audience.[17]

This continuity between heuristics and biases and prospect theory is illustrated by the remarks made in Tversky's letter to Krantz, April 10, 1975. In this letter, Tversky, for the first time, devoted more than just one line to his scientific work with Kahneman, and he was clearly enthusiastic about the project. The letter illustrates that the basic argument of prospect theory had crystallized in the spring of 1975:

Danny and I are working primarily on decision making and we believe for the first time that we understand the basic principles governing choices between gambles. . . . The key elements in the theory we propose are: 1) an S-shaped utility function defined on differences from status quo rather than on total asset position and 2) uncertainty weights (not to be confused with subjective probability) by which the utilities are weighted. We are collecting empirical data which seem to provide very strong support for this model. . . . I will send you a draft of the paper in the very near future.[18]

In 1975, four years before prospect theory would be published, Kahneman and Tversky were in the middle of developing their heuristics and biases theory. Prospect theory, then, is best understood as an extended version of their heuristics and biases theory that focused on financial decisions and expected utility theory. Moreover, its rhetoric was specifically designed to convince not only readers of *Econometrica*, primarily economists, but also

---

[17] Kahneman (2002); and Kahneman, interview, 2009. Initially, the article submitted to *Econometrica* was known as "Value Theory" (Kahneman, 2002).

[18] Tversky's letter to Krantz, April 10, 1975, personal collection.

decision theorists, mathematical psychologists, and other mathematically oriented behavioral scientists. Kahneman and Tversky's attempt to broaden the scope of their approach during this period is also illustrated by a workshop Tversky co-organized with Daniel McFadden (b. 1937), econometrician and 2000 cowinner of the Nobel memorial prize in economics "for his development of theory and methods for analyzing discrete choice."[19] The workshop, held in October 1977 and titled "Cognition, Choice, and Economic Behavior," was supported by the Mathematical Social Science Board and the National Science Foundation and was intended to bring together psychologists and economists interested in cognition and choice theory.[20]

Kahneman and Tversky made the connection with their earlier work in the first few lines of the 1979 article, which set out the conception of expected utility theory as a normative theory that also makes descriptive claims:

Expected utility theory has dominated the analysis of decision making under risk. It has been generally accepted as a normative model of rational choice, and widely applied as a descriptive model of economic behavior. Thus it is assumed that all reasonable people would wish to obey the axioms of the theory and that most people actually do, most of the time. (Kahneman and Tversky, 1979, p. 263)

In a clever way, these opening sentences alluded to both the psychological and the economic framework. To psychologists, these sentences restated the well-known normative-descriptive framework and signaled a contribution to an established field of research. Positivist economists in the line of Friedman (1953), on the other hand, might have raised their eyebrows at the injunction of the "normative," but they would certainly have agreed that reasonable people wish to obey the axioms of expected utility theory and that they actually do so, or at least most of the time. Note, furthermore, that Kahneman and Tversky carefully avoided the term *rational* and used *reasonable* instead. Evoking the term *rational* might have suggested that this was an article in the line of critique of economics. The use of *rational* would certainly have induced some economists to think that these two psychologists had the same research program as Simon, who had won the Nobel memorial prize in economics the year before. From the start, prospect theory was carefully constructed to be able to broaden the scope to economists especially.

---

[19] "The Sveriges Riksbank Prize in Economic Sciences in Memory of Alfred Nobel 2000," *Nobelprize.org*, accessed April 27, 2010, http://www.nobelprize.org/nobel_prizes/economic-sciences/laureates/2000/.

[20] McFadden and Tversky's letter to Luce, June 20, 1977, R. Duncan Luce Papers, Unprocessed Archive, Harvard University Archives, Cambridge, MA.

The content of prospect theory is well known. As in heuristics and biases theory, Kahneman and Tversky based their argument on a series of hypothetical questions they had presented to experimental subjects, in this case psychology students at Hebrew University. The problems the subjects were presented with were decision problems, involving different material outcomes and different probabilities. Most of the questions were reformulations or variants of Allais's decision problems (Allais, 1953a, 1979; see also Chapter 2). One example of Kahneman and Tversky's use of an Allais-type approach is in the question in which subjects were asked to state which of the following lottery options they preferred:

A: (4,000, 0.80)   or   B: (3,000)

That is, they were asked whether they preferred 4,000 shekels with a probability of 0.8, or 3,000 shekels for certain.[21] Most of the subjects in this case chose B. This implied that they did not maximize the expected monetary outcome. However, opting for the choice B could be explained by assuming that the decision maker was risk averse. Subsequently, subjects were asked which of the following two lottery options they preferred:

C: (4,000, 0.20)   or   D: (3,000, 0.25)

In this case, most of the subjects chose C and hence maximized the expected monetary outcome. In combination with the first choice, this was problematic because it implied that subjects were sometimes risk averse but, on other occasions, maximized the expected monetary outcome and hence were not risk averse. Note that the second choice is equal to the first with probabilities divided by four. With these and similar examples, Kahneman and Tversky illustrated that despite its normative status, expected utility theory as a descriptive theory was invalidated. In specific circumstances people systematically deviated from the norms of expected utility theory. A new descriptive, "alternative account of individual decision making under risk," was therefore required. The alternative account was christened "prospect theory" (Kahneman and Tversky, 1979, p. 274).[22]

---

[21] At the time of the experiment, 4,000 shekels was about one-third of the modal monthly Israeli income.

[22] Kahneman (2002) recalls that they deliberately looked for a name that did not refer to any other theory or phenomenon in economics and psychology. Indeed, JSTOR yields only one, idiosyncratic counterexample. In 1977, Edmund W. Kitch of the University of Chicago developed a new economic theory for the patent system in the *Journal of Law and Economics*: "For expositional convenience, this view of the patent system will be called the prospect theory" (p. 266).

According to prospect theory, a human decision maker first employs a number of heuristics to make a decision problem manageable. This process was called the editing phase. Complicated decisions are broken down into different simpler decisions, different decisions are lumped together into one big decision, a benchmark is set with which the decision is compared, and so on. The purpose of this editing phase was to make the decision manageable. After this, the decision was evaluated in what was referred to as the evaluation phase. The evaluation phase had the same structure as the maximization of expected utility, but instead of the objective values of the material payoff and probability, it used the individual's subjective perception of the material payoff and probability. The subjective perception of the material payoff was referred to as value (denoted v) and the subjective perception of probability was referred to as decision weight (denoted π). In expected utility theory, a subject who is faced with a choice between outcome x that occurs with probability p and outcome y that occurs with probability q derives utility according to the following function:

$$U(x,p;y,q) = p \cdot u(x) + q \cdot u(y), \qquad (4.2)$$

in which utility u is a subjective valuation of the outcome according to the axioms of von Neumann and Morgenstern (2004 [1944]) and Savage (1954). In other words, it defines how an individual values an outcome given its preferences if it behaves according to the normative rules of rational decision making. Furthermore, in the expected utility theory of equation (4.2) the individual perceives the probabilities of the outcomes as what they objectively are. In prospect theory, by contrast, a subject that following the editing phase faces the exact same choice values this choice according to this function:

$$V(x,p;y,q) = \pi(p)v(x) + \pi(q)v(y), \qquad (4.3)$$

in which v is similar to u, but based on empirical observations in experiments rather than axiomatically defined utilities; constructed with respect to an individual reference point, rather than to an objectively defined benchmark; and with a risk-seeking character in the loss domain. The probabilities of the outcomes are similarly subject to a perception bias of the individual.[23]

---

[23] The experimentally induced subjective probability curve of Kahneman and Tversky (1979) suggested that the probabilities of one event space as perceived by the individual may not add up to 1 and hence violate Kolmogoroff's axioms (Kolmogoroff, 1933). Tversky and Kahneman (1992) offered solutions to this problem.

At first sight, it seems unnecessarily confusing to label the actual, descriptive valuation of the outcome of a choice by the individual "value," instead of utility. As such, it was part of a broader confusing use of concepts such as value and utility by psychologists and economists. Other examples include the discussions surrounding von Neumann and Morgenstern's use of the utility concept as discussed in Chapters 1 and 2, and Edwards's and other behavioral decision researchers' reinterpretation of this concept within their own Lewinian framework as discussed in Chapter 3. At the same time, it was a clever deviation from other meanings and definitions. By making "value" instead of "utility," the term that referred to the subjective attractiveness of a choice option, Kahneman and Tversky were able to design a framework that could be accepted by both psychologists and economists. To psychologists, the value framework matched the Lewinian valence framework; to economists, it preserved the traditional framework of expected valuation by the individual while at the same time allowing for the possibility that individual economic behavior deviates from the von Neumann-Morgenstern expected utility through the replacement of "utility" with "value." In addition, the term *value* was historically a central concept in economics that could be used very well to denote the pleasure an economic agent derives from choosing a specific option.

Prospect theory is related to what is essentially psychophysics, in a similar way as Allais (1953b, 1979), and more directly than either von Neumann and Morgenstern (2004 [1944]) or Savage (1954). Psychophysics, as briefly set out in Chapter 2 in the context of the Allais-Savage debate, is the originally nineteenth-century German tradition in psychology that investigates the human mind as a perceptual machinery that perceives an increasing energy of the stimulus with decreasing marginal sensitivity (Boring, 1929; Danizger, 1997; Heidelberger, 2004). Along psychophysical lines, Kahneman and Tversky argued that "[a]n essential feature of the present theory is that carriers of value are changes in wealth or welfare, rather than final states," and that "[t]his assumption is compatible with basic principles of perception and judgment." This basic principle was that

[o]ur perceptual apparatus is attuned to the evaluation of changes or differences rather than to the evaluation of absolute magnitude. When we respond to attributes such as brightness, loudness, or temperature, the past and present context of experience defines an adaptation level, or reference point, and stimuli are perceived in relation to this reference point. Thus, an object at a given temperature may be experienced as hot or cold to touch depending on the temperature to which one has adapted. (Kahneman and Tversky, 1979, p. 277)

Kahneman and Tversky extended this basic argument to other attributes: "The same principle applies to non-sensory attributes such as health, prestige, and wealth. The same level of wealth, for example, may imply abject poverty for one person and great riches for another – depending on their current assets" (Kahneman and Tversky, 1979, p. 277). Similar to Allais, Kahneman and Tversky argued that this principle of psychophysics was a fundamental aspect of all the behavioral sciences, including economics.

The use of heuristics and the framework of psychophysics allowed Kahneman and Tversky to construct a theory in which individuals try to make the best decision, and yet could often be observed as making decisions that systematically deviate from the normatively correct decision. The individual does its best, but because human beings apply heuristics to reconstruct decision problems to manageable proportions, and because they have a specific perceptual system that distorts the stimulus, their reasoned decisions may deviate from the normatively correct solution. Kahneman and Tversky had to cut the link between the normative and the descriptive theory in order to maintain the normative theory while at the same time allowing for the conclusion that people systematically and persistently deviate from the norm. Human beings, that is, normal healthy adults, who in Savage and Edwards's accounts were capable of normatively correct reasoning, could no longer be expected to behave according to the normative rules.

Ultimately, prospect theory was based on the authority of science, even if also scientists' first intuitive response could be mistaken. Prospect theory took the axioms of decision theory as the norm for behavior and developed the measurement framework so that the experimental observations would fit. Deviations from the axiomatic norms were understood as errors or mistakes, and they bore no implications for the norms. Because of the clear separation between the normative and the descriptive, it was now possible to construct a separate account of decision making in the descriptive domain, without implications for the normative theory. In prospect theory, human beings were understood as having a biased perception of the relevant input of probabilities and payoffs, just as they had a biased perception of sensory inputs such as temperature and weight.

5. Explaining the Success of the Kahneman-Tversky Perspective

Kahneman and Tversky's research is part of a vast literature encompassing psychology, economics, and mathematics, which seeks to criticize and/or elaborate the axiomatization of behavior as commenced by von Neumann and Morgenstern (2004 [1944]) (Gigerenzer and Murray, 1987; Goldstein and Hogarth, 1997; Hogarth and Reder, 1987; Guala, 2000; Fishburn, 1981). Some of these contributions have been more successful than others, but arguably, few, if any, have been as successful as have been Kahneman and Tversky – as exemplified by Kahneman's 2002 Nobel Memorial Prize in Economics and the number of times Kahneman and Tversky's work has been cited (e.g., Laibson and Zeckhauser, 1998). At the same time, Kahneman and Tversky's research has been met with substantial criticism, part of which can probably be explained by Kahneman and Tversky's success and influence itself.

The most-often-repeated criticism has been that Kahneman and Tversky believed people to be irrational. The argument was that if human beings can send people to the moon and return them safely, they cannot be that irrational. One of the most remarkable exponents of this view was Edwards, who wondered how it is possible that people are so poor at assessing uncertainties, as they were in Kahneman and Tversky's theory, and yet, at the same time, could be so skilled at driving their cars. Edwards never elaborated on his reservations with respect to the work of Tversky and Kahneman, perhaps from fear of losing the image of coherence of his program, yet it is no secret that he disagreed with their work (e.g., Phillips and von Winterfeldt, 2006).[24] The 1980s and 1990s gave rise to a whole surge of criticism regarding Kahneman and Tversky's approach to human decision behavior. The most prominent philosophical critique was provided by Cohen (1981). The most extensive criticisms from within experimental psychology came from Gerd Gigerenzer (b. 1947; see, e.g., Gigerenzer, 1991, 1993, 1996; Gigerenzer and Murray, 1987; Sedlmeier and Gigerenzer, 1997, 2000; Hertwig and Gigerenzer, 1999). Gigerenzer has been the only critic to whom Kahneman and Tversky have explicitly responded (Kahneman and Tversky, 1996). Other critics include Lopes (1991) and Cosmides and Tooby (1996). Thus, the most salient question pertaining to the work of the two psychologists is therefore why they were successful when others were less successful, despite the broad critique they received. In my opinion, three aspects stand out in particular.[25]

Friendly Criticism and the Normative-Descriptive Shuffle

Kahneman and Tversky's work is to be seen within the postwar understanding of science as the supreme and ultimate judge of rationality, impartiality, and open-mindedness (Amadae, 2003; Mendelsohn, 1989; Hollinger, 1995;

[24] Krantz, interview, 2008; and Dawes, interview, 2008.
[25] See Hands (2011) for further explanations.

Selcer, 2009). But there is something more to it as well. In nineteenth- and twentieth-century psychophysics and experimental psychology, the scientist was the ultimate expert regarding the objective value of the stimulus because the scientist determined the value of the stimulus (Boring, 1929; Danziger, 1997; Heidelberger, 2004). Experimental psychologists wanted to know how an individual perceived the different stages in the brightness of a lightbulb, and in these experiments, experimental psychologists naturally knew what the objective values of the different stages of brightness were because they themselves had set up the experiment. Edwards (1954, 1961) applied this experimental psychological program to decision making, but limited the superior knowledge of the scientist. Like Savage, Edwards emphasized that all normal healthy adults could evaluate the axioms of rational decision making, and assumed that everyone would agree with his axioms after some careful thought. Edwards, but also Tversky in his work of the 1960s, adopted Savage's framework and assumed that human beings in principle make their decisions in accordance with the axioms of rationality.

Kahneman and Tversky's research changed that, but without directly discrediting the earlier work of Savage and Edwards or that of the economists. In prospect theory, Kahneman and Tversky employed the standard normative-descriptive distinction of experimental psychology, behavioral decision research, and mathematical psychology and assumed that economists would employ the very same distinction. This partly reflected the standard understanding of economics in behavioral decision research and psychology. It should not be forgotten that Edwards understood economists' theories of individual human behavior as normative theories. One possible conclusion therefore is that Kahneman and Tversky were not familiar with economists' use of positive and normative and understood these terms to mean the same thing as the descriptive and normative of behavioral decision research. But Kahneman and Tversky's use of normative and descriptive can also be seen as a very clever way of trying to convince economists of the relevance of prospect theory for economics. Note, also, that in their earlier heuristics and biases theory, Kahneman and Tversky's use of normative and descriptive played an important role. In prospect theory, Kahneman and Tversky did not tell the economists that their theory was complete nonsense or useless. Instead, they claimed to understand economics as using one theory to cover both the normative and the descriptive realm. For the normative part, they fully agreed with economists, which fitted in neatly with practice in behavioral decision research. But, Kahneman and Tversky argued, economists had been mistaken in using that same theory in the descriptive domain.

Kahneman and Tversky's approach differed in a subtle but fundamental way from, for instance, Simon's, the well-known critic of economics. Just as Kahneman and Tversky, Simon understood economics to have both normative and descriptive ambitions, but unlike Kahneman and Tversky, he considered economics to have embarked on the wrong track entirely. To Simon, the (what he understood to be) normative theory of neoclassical economics was too rigid by not allowing improvements of optimal behavior. Using this static normative theory as a description of actual human decision behavior was plainly absurd (e.g., Simon, 1959, 1978, 1987; for overviews and discussions of Simon's position regarding economics, see Crowther-Heyck, 2005; Sent, 2005; Mirowski, 2002; Augier and March, 2004). Kahneman and Tversky were much less hostile. In fact, they were in favor of current practice in economics – after all, behavioral decision research and measurement theory were considered to be at least partly based on economics – and they only meant to suggest that a few adjustments be made to improve it. Thus, in the second sentence of the prospect theory article they argued that "[expected utility theory] has been generally accepted as a normative model of rational choice" (Kahneman and Tversky, 1979, p. 263) and left it undisputed in the rest of the article. Contrary to Simon, Kahneman and Tversky argued that there was nothing wrong with economists' theory of expected utility maximization. It was only that this was the normative theory, and not an accurate description of actually observed human behavior. Economists do not need to abandon the theory of expected utility maximization, but instead, they should seek a proper descriptive counterpart to this normative theory.

Thus, Kahneman and Tversky were not attempting to travel across the psychology-economics border to become economists and to contribute to economics. What they intended to do, was rather to shift the economics-psychology border in such a way that their work and economics would become part of the same behavioral science. Subsequently, they could then argue that their research had proved existing theories wrong and had provided a viable alternative. For their argument, it did not really matter whether one understood the move as shifting the border so that parts of economics became part of psychology and behavioral decision research or as shifting the border so that behavioral decision research became part of economics. The message would remain the same, namely, that behavioral decision researchers and economists were all part of the same scientific program and that although prospect theory showed that many economists had been partially mistaken, the problem had been solved. With prospect theory, Kahneman and Tversky made a claim of unification. A first explanation for Kahneman and Tversky's success among economists is that they provided a relatively friendly criticism that allowed expected utility theory a life under the rubric of the normative theory. Moreover, they offered an alternative for the descriptive realm in the form of prospect theory that closely resembled expected utility theory.

The Role of the New Type of Experiments

A second reason for the success of Kahneman and Tversky's perspective of human decision making were the type of experiments they employed. Their collaboration marked a departure from the experimental practices of each in the 1960s. For Kahneman, this is less surprising than for Tversky, because Kahneman's vision research was in a different field than his later work with Tversky and required experiments with lightbulbs and dots on screens in completely controlled laboratories. For Tversky, the difference is more striking as his research with Kahneman in many ways was a continuation of his earlier work and experiments.

Tversky's experiments between 1965 and 1970 were always done with a small number of subjects; seven or eight was a normal group size. Although this was not always explicitly indicated, it is furthermore clear that in the majority of cases, the experimenter and subject were previously acquainted because, for example, the subjects had participated in a university course the experimenter taught as their professor. The experiments were done in a traditional experimental psychological setting. The subjects were often assigned numbers, for instance one through seven, and referred to individually. When discussing the empirical results, the subjects were sometimes analyzed individually, which was typically exemplary for a perceived more general behavioral pattern. Thus, for instance, in an experiment published in 1969, the utility curve of subject 3 was discussed because of its peculiar shape, and in similar experiments conducted in 1966, statements of a post-experiment interview with subjects were compared with their performance during the experiment (Tversky and Edwards, 1966; Tversky, 1969). In this regard, Tversky's experimental work was an example of research from before the "inference revolution" of the mid-twentieth century (Gigerenzer and Murray, 1987, p. 182; see also Danziger, 1990). That is to say, the analyses did not calculate an average response over experimental subjects, but instead tried to find an explanation that would cover the observed behavior of the individual experimental subjects. In addition, the individual trials of the experiments were relatively long. For example, in one experiment (Rapoport and Tversky, 1970) subjects were asked to judge which of two lightbulbs was brighter 1,000 times in a row. The experiment consisted of a sequence of two or three trials of about one hour each. As a result, the experiment took quite some time. In this most time-intensive experiment done by Tversky, "[t]he subjects met five times a week for seven weeks. Each experimental session lasted about two hours" (Rapoport and Tversky, 1970, p. 108). In many ways, Tversky's experiments of the 1960s resembled the experimental methodology employed in Thurstone (1931).

In their collaborative research during the 1970s, Kahneman and Tversky conducted different kinds of experiments than the two had done individually in the 1960s. From the early 1970s onward, the experiments consisted of questionnaires with hypothetical questions that mainly students were asked to fill out. These questionnaires could be distributed anywhere, to participants at conferences, to students during a course at the university, and in a shopping mall on a Saturday afternoon. Laboratory experiments provided a setting in which all of the variables could be carefully monitored. However, Kahneman and Tversky's questionnaire experiments provided only copies of the questionnaires and pens to fill them out. No separate laboratory space was needed, and no payment of the experimental subjects was required; filling out the questionnaires took a few minutes at the most. In the 1979 prospect theory article, Kahneman and Tversky defended their new method of experimentation and contrasted it with two other methods of investigation. First, they distinguished the possibility of "field studies," which used "naturalistic or statistical observation" that could yield important insights when a new area of research was opened, but in the end could only provide "crude tests of qualitative predictions, because probabilities and utilities cannot be adequately measured" (Kahneman and Tversky, 1979, p. 265). Second, they recognized the method of laboratory experiments, which had the disadvantages that stakes could only be relatively small and that for financial reasons, it was difficult to conduct an experiment in which the subjects were asked to choose between, say, $300 for certain or a 0.8 chance at obtaining $400. The third method, which they argued proved to be the best for solving the problem they were investigating, was "the method of hypothetical choices." It solved the problem of the absence of control of field studies, while at the same time solving the external validity problem of laboratory experiments. It did, however, rely on the assumption that people "know how they would behave in actual situations of choice" and that they "have no special reason to disguise their true preferences" (Kahneman and Tversky, 1979, p. 265).

There is not a direct link among the heuristics and biases program, prospect theory, and the new, more relaxed standards of the experimental method. That is to say, heuristics and biases and prospect theory could, in principle, have been developed without the new means of conducting experiments. But the new standards of experimental control facilitated Kahneman and Tversky's research in fundamental ways. It is safe to say that, without the method of hypothetical questions, they could not have developed heuristics and biases and prospect theory. For instance, it would have been almost impossible to assemble eighty-four professional psychologists in a single laboratory in order to ask them what their opinions were on a statistical draw performed in front of them. Thus, although there is not a direct link between Kahneman and Tversky's heuristics and biases, prospect theory and their experimental method, it is difficult to see how they could have been tested and developed without this new method.[26] The success of Kahneman and Tversky's new program is, hence, in part explained by the new experimental methodology they employed.

Intuitively Appealing Examples

A third reason for Kahneman and Tversky's success in economics is their effective use of intuitively appealing examples. Typically, the argument in Kahneman and Tversky's research was made not so much by giving theoretical explanations for why such-and-such was a good theory or account of observed behavior, but by supplying examples of the experimental questions subjects had been asked which were meant to give the reader an intuitive understanding of the point they were trying to make. The appeal of the examples employed gradually developed over time. Already, the birth control example arguably was a clearer appeal to the reader's intuition than was the statistical test example of Tversky and Kahneman (1971). Subsequently, the appeal to the subjects' and readers' intuition about everyday decision making further developed. For instance, in another experiment, subjects were posed the following question:

A cab was involved in a hit-and-run accident at night. Two cab companies, the Green and the Blue, operate in the city. You are given the following data:

(i)   85% of the cabs in the city are Green and 15% are Blue.
(ii) A witness identified the cab as a Blue cab. The court tested his ability to identify cabs under the appropriate visibility conditions. When presented with a sample of cabs (half of which were Blue and half of which were Green)

---

[26] I do not discuss the question of whether different experimental methods yield different data and phenomena on which to construct theories here. Obviously, someone such as Savage considered the experimental method crucial, whereas Kahneman and Tversky, as indicated earlier, considered it to be of much less relevance.

the witness made correct identifications in 80% of the cases and erred in 20% of the cases

Question: What is the probability that the cab involved in the accident was Blue rather than Green? (Tversky and Kahneman, 1980, p. 62)

The majority responded 80 percent, which was probably based on how often the witness had identified the color correctly. However, again they failed to take into account the base-rate distribution. Using Bayes's theorem, the normatively correct answer is slightly more than 41 percent.

The best-known query among the many experimental questions of Kahneman and Tversky became the so-called Linda problem, no less because it was often used by Kahneman and Tversky's adversaries. The Linda problem runs as follows:

Linda is 31 years old, single, outspoken and very bright. She majored in philosophy. As a student, she was deeply concerned with issues of discrimination and social justice, and also participated in anti-nuclear demonstrations.

Which of the following two alternatives is more probable:

1) Linda is a bank teller.
2) Linda is a bank teller and active in the feminist movement.

(Tversky and Kahneman, 1983, summarized from pp. 297 and 299)

On average, there was a strong bias toward judging option (2) to be more probable than option (1), this despite the fact that option (2) is logically contained in option (1). Because this bias is an illustration of the failure to see that the probability of the conjunction of two or more events can never exceed the probability of one of the events, this bias was labeled the conjunction fallacy.

The appeal and intuition of these examples provide a third explanation for Kahneman and Tversky's success, because the readers of their articles could relate the examples to their own everyday decision making. It was also via these intuitive examples that Kahneman and Tversky received some strong opposition in the 1980s and 1990s. Kahneman and Tversky's adversaries typically proceeded by deconstructing their examples and illustrations, or by giving counterexamples. It was, for instance, shown that a different conclusion could be inferred from the observed behavior, or that responses to another set of hypothetical questions falsified Kahneman and Tversky's conclusions (e.g., Gigerenzer, 1991, 1993, 1996; Hertwig and Gigerenzer, 1999; Lopes, 1991).

6. Conclusion

The methodological tension Tversky was struggling with in the late 1960s, involved the question how to combine the introspective, or intuitive basis of von Neumann and Morgenstern (2004 [1944]) and Savage (1954), with experimental results that pointed in many directions, but only occasionally in the direction of the intuitive theory. As the axioms were understood as introspective or intuitive truths, they could only be proved wrong based on introspective or intuitive reasoning. Measurement theory and normative decision theory were simply not understood and employed as theories that could be proved wrong experimentally. At the same time, however, Tversky wanted to do justice to the experimental results he had obtained. Thus, Tversky was effectively caught between the intuitive truth of the axioms of measurement theory and decision theory and the behavioral deviations that surfaced in his experiments. He had to decide between taking his experiments seriously or accepting the axioms of measurement theory and decision theory.

In the early 1970s, Kahneman offered Tversky a solution that accepted the experimental behavioral deviations as valid while at the same time left intact the fundamentals of measurement theory and decision theory. Kahneman and Tversky's research introduced the idea that although rational individuals should adhere to the normative theories of logic, Bayesian updating and expected utility calculation in their decision making, individuals, in fact, systematically and predictably deviate from these norms.

With heuristics and biases, Kahneman and Tversky made their name in behavioral psychology, and in cognitive science generally. It maintained the framework of reasoning from a set of optimal or normative behavioral rules as commenced by von Neumann and Morgenstern (2004 [1944]) and Savage (1954), but rigorously separated the normative from the descriptive domain. Although Kahneman and Tversky thus departed from the approach taken by Edwards, it fully remained a program of human engineering that identified fallible human behavior with the explicit purpose of engineering solutions to improve human decision making. Prospect theory, and its publication in *Econometrica*, broadened Kahneman and Tversky's audience to economists. However, despite their clever rhetoric, their success among psychologists and their developing collaboration with some economists, it was not clear how the economic community at large would respond, if it would listen at all. The next chapter shows that there were essentially two very different responses to Kahneman and Tversky in the economic community.

Incorporating Psychological Experiments in Economics and the Construction of Behavioral Economics

1. Introduction

Daniel Kahneman and Amos Tversky's prospect theory was published in *Econometrica* – one of economics' most prestigious journals. Broadly speaking, two responses can be distinguished among the economists. Over the years, Richard Thaler (b. 1945) has been the most prominent in advancing Kahneman and Tversky's approach for economics in what would become behavioral economics. David Grether (b. 1939) and Charles Plott (b. 1938), by contrast, played a vital role in formulating an answer to the psychologists in line with Vernon Smith's (b. 1927) experimental economics. These two different interpretations of the same psychological experiments, constituted two different ways of looking at the economic world.

Smith pioneered the use of experiments in economics in the late 1950s and early 1960s – among others in his now famous "An Experimental Study of Competitive Market Behavior" (1962), published in the *Journal of Political Economy* – and was the driving force behind the gradual expansion of experimental economics in subsequent decades (Lee, 2004; Lee and Mirowski, 2008; Leonard and Fontaine, 2005). Because of the surge of experimental results behavioral decision research produced in the 1970s, Grether and Plott, two economists who had recently joined Smith's experimental program, felt compelled to stick out a position for the economic discipline regarding the experimental results from psychology. Much to their own surprise, their experiments corroborated the results of psychologists. This led Grether and Plott, and later Smith, to completely discard preference theory as a valid description of (what they would come to label as) initial human behavior. At the same time, the experimental results to their minds only confirmed the role of time in driving the market to higher degrees of rationality.

An initially diverse and unorganized group of financial and other economists, led more or less by Thaler, drew very different conclusions from these same experimental results. They saw them as proof for observed anomalies in financial markets, and hailed Kahneman and Tversky's prospect theory as the most important contestant for replacing the traditional microeconomic model of human behavior. An important catalyst for this new research program on the border of economics and psychology was the behavioral economics program of first the Alfred P. Sloan and later the Russell Sage Foundation.[1]

In the second section, I introduce the experimental program Smith created during the 1960s and 1970s. Based on this experimental program, Grether and Plott tested the experimental results of the psychologists and drew conclusions for economics. The third section shows how financial economists, and in particular Thaler, responded to the corroborated findings of the psychologists. Section 4 discusses the subsequent development of behavioral economics, including the crucial support of the Sloan-Sage behavioral economics program.

---

[1] Not everyone agrees with this interpretation. For instance, Guala (2005), Friedman and Sunder (1994), and Davis and Holt (1993) advance Kahneman and Tversky's 1979 *Prospect Theory* article as an important contribution to experimental economics. Similarly, Bowles (2004) molds all existing literature into one framework, which he labels *Microeconomics*, subtitled *Behavior, Institutions and Evolution*. Very roughly, the historical argument in this literature is that the behavioral type of research could emerge because of the preparing groundwork laid by experimental economics. The behavioral line is understood as adding a new line to the experimental program that focuses on individuals. Authors such as Smith (e.g., Smith 1989, 2008) and Plott (e.g., Grether and Plott 1979, 1982), on the other hand, consider the behavioral program historically unrelated to experimental economics. To these authors, it is a theory of psychology and hence not part of economics. In the same way, but from the behavioral perspective, Kahneman (2003), Loewenstein (1999b), and Camerer and Loewenstein (2004) consider behavioral economics to have arisen as a prominent program despite the confusing intermingling of experimental economists. Similarly, different readings of the 2002 Nobel Memorial Prize in Economics for Vernon Smith and Daniel Kahneman could be advanced. We could read this splitting of the most prestigious prize in economics as not assuming a position between two fundamentally opposed camps, or we could understand it as simply awarding the two most important researchers in a broad field of experimentalist economics. Of course, historical analysis will always emphasize one interpretation at the expense of others. That said, I think recognizing behavioral economics and experimental economics as two quite different programs provides the best taxonomy for understanding developments in the 1980s and 1990s.

2. Corroboration and Incorporation of Psychology's Behavioral Deviations in Smith's Experimental Economics

To comprehend what happened around the use of experiments in economics in the late 1970s and early 1980s, we need to start with Smith's experimental economics. During the 1950s to the 1970s, Smith gradually had come to the conclusion that economics needed to be altered (e.g., Lee, 2004, 2008; Smith, 1959, 1962, 1965, 1967, 1974). His experiments formed an important basis for this. Smith stressed that time was necessary for the market to reach equilibrium and argued that experiments should be used to investigate which factors determine to which equilibrium the market drives the economy over time. According to Smith, economics was too theoretical and failed to look seriously at actual behavior in the real-world economy. For instance, Smith complained that the standard references, Paul Samuelson's *Foundations of Economic Analysis* (1947) and Roy Allen's *Mathematical Analysis for Economists* (1938), only discussed "the purely formal properties of the theory" (Smith, 1959, p. 65) and were of little direct use when applied to real-world problems. He complained that these authors talked about the "inputs" of the production function without giving them any interpretation. When one did so, one immediately was forced to make a distinction between different kinds of inputs, Smith argued, and as a result, one ended up with mathematical results that were quite different. Smith insisted repeatedly that, as opposed to the standard theory, his position had implications "in a very real economic sense" (Smith, 1959, p. 67).

Smith's experimental results and his growing dissatisfaction with modern economics led him midway through the 1970s to what is probably his strongest denouncement of this framework. "I believe that the microeconomic theory of the pre-1960's is a dead end," Smith wrote, and immediately added an alternative: "The new microtheory will, and should, deal with economic foundations of organization and institution, and this will require us to have an economics of information and a more sophisticated treatment of the technology of transacting" (Smith, 1974, p. 321). However, Smith did not imply that pre-1960s microeconomics should be put aside but instead argued for a serious revision and extension of the theoretical framework. Experimental research in economics more generally arose from a brief period of postwar cooperation between operations researchers, computer scientists, mathematicians, economists, and psychologists between the mid-1940s and mid-1950s that also involved the discussion regarding von Neumann and Morgenstern's axioms as discussed in Chapter 2 (Dimand, 2005;

Weintraub, 1992; Lee, 2004). The perceived link remained close enough for Smith to participate in discussions on Savage and others' decision theory. In "Measuring Nonmonetary Utilities in Uncertain Choices: The Ellsberg Urn" (1969), Smith took a position in the ensuing debate on the violations of Savage's normative theory as presented by Maurice Allais, Daniel Ellsberg, and others. Ellsberg (1961) had employed a "hypothetical experiment," to falsify first and foremost Savage's "Sure-Thing Principle," or Independence axiom, which says that the preference of an individual between two states will not alter if the same event is added to both states; that, in other words, the preference is independent of whatever else might happen (Ellsberg, 1961; Savage, 1954, pp. 21–26). Ellsberg had concluded provocatively that the "Savage approach gives wrong predictions and . . . bad advice" (Ellsberg, 1961, p. 669).

Smith's response to the Ellsberg argument is important because it shows how Smith attempted to strike a balance between Savage's theory and its opponents, an attempt in which he tried to bridge the opposing theoretical and experimental sides. "I stand with those, like Savage, Raiffa, and Schlaifer, who say they would not want to violate the axioms consciously," Smith started his argument. Yet, he was unwilling to go all the way with Savage: "However, having stated this I am not prepared to assert that he who seriously and consciously violates the axioms, and in my judgment 'knows what he is doing,' is thereby simply making a 'mistake,' and should be given a little more conditioning and 'education'" (Smith, 1969, pp. 324–325).

Thus, Smith took a position that in a crucial way differed from the position taken by decision theorists such as Savage and behavioral decision researchers such as Edwards, Kahneman, and Tversky. People may have very good reasons for deviating from the axioms, Smith argued. For instance, they could take into account what other people, such as friends and colleagues, think of their decisions. Crucially, to Smith, deviations from Savage's axioms, even when they were systematic, were not problematic because over time the market would correct those mistakes. For Savage, Edwards, and Tversky, a decision was either normatively correct (rational) or normatively false (irrational; Savage, 1954; Edwards, 1954, 1961; Tversky, 1969). For Smith, rationality was a matter of content and degree. People might have reasons for initially deviating from the rational norms, but in a market context, the institution of the market would ensure that in due time they would adjust their behavior toward the rational behavior. Smith was of the opinion that "even if [Savage's] axioms are to be regarded as basically a normative theory, the theory can also do valuable service in helping us to understand actual behavior" (Smith, 1969, pp. 324–325). The normative theory shows where and when people deviate from the norm and, in this sense, guides the description of observed decision behavior. But it also serves as a description of human behavior in market equilibrium, and thus helps us to understand how decision behavior adjusts over time in markets.

Another way in which Smith's experimental work differed from that conducted by behavioral decision researchers is that his decision makers were not individual subjects but economic units. In one of his theoretical papers on investment and production planning, for instance, Smith started as follows: "We imagine individual decision making units, which we call 'firms'" (Smith, 1960, p. 198). The individual decision-making units of Smith's theories and experiments were not individual human beings, as in decision theory and the experiments of the psychologists, but they were individual economic units such as firms, consumers, and producers. Smith was not interested in the individual as an individual, but was interested in the individual in its role as a particular economic decision-making unit.

In fact, one could say that Smith was not even interested in the individual as an economic decision-making unit but in how the market institution influenced the unit's behavior over time. In "Experimental Studies of Discrimination Versus Competition in Sealed-Bid Auction Markets," Smith stated that the "primary purpose" of his experiments was "to study individual bidding behavior and price determination under two alternative forms of market organization: (1) price discrimination, . . . and (2) pure competition" (1967, p. 56). It was not the individual unit's behavior that should be investigated, but the market environment that affected its behavior. In mathematical psychology and behavioral decision research, the individual functioned as a measurement instrument for (average) individual psychological characteristics (see Chapter 3). In Smith's experiments, the individual functioned as a measurement instrument for characteristics of the market mechanism.

To sum up, because Smith's experiments have been connected to the experiments of the psychologists of behavioral decision research, and because Smith at different points actively engaged in discussions on decision theory, it might appear that experimental economics, decision theory, and behavioral decision research developed in tandem in the 1960s and 1970s. But Smith's experimental economics differed in at least two crucial ways from the experiments conducted by the psychologists. First, Smith did not investigate the individual human being but instead investigated economic decision-making units. Smith was only interested in individual human beings in their role as an economic decision-making unit. Second, Smith did not assume the static point of view in which it is believed that the individual that deviates from the normative theory has made a mistake. In contrast, Smith was interested in how decision behavior changes over time and in the environments that induce these changes. Smith took a stance that he at least once labeled "a crude macrobiological approach," in which the system, when not exogenously altered, tends toward a "stable equilibrium" (Smith, 1968, p. 410).

But Smith did not entirely dismiss the experimental results of behavioral decision research either. The stream of experimental results obtained by behavioral decision research in the 1970s that showed that individuals violate rational choice theory required experimental economists to assume a stance. Grether and Plott, who had joined Smith's experimental economic research in the 1970s, decided to subject the experimental results of the behavioral decision researchers to a test. Initially, they referred only to the experiments of Paul Slovic and Sarah Lichtenstein, but took these as representative of experimental results produced by psychologists generally, and thus referred to them as "psychological experiments" producing "psychological results." The reason that they could easily test the psychologists' results was that all the material and expertise were already available. The rise of experimental economics had created an environment in which the results of the psychologists could be tested without requiring economists to learn new methods or techniques. Checking as many possible explanations for the results obtained by the psychologists as they could think of, Grether and Plott (1979, 1982) sought to falsify the findings of the psychologists. Moreover, they set out to test the experimental findings based on the standards of (experimental) economics, which they considered more rigorous than those of the psychologists. The rise of the experimental method in economics had made experimental economists confident they could beat psychologists at their own game, or at least critically assess their work by using their own experimental method.

Grether and Plott (1979, 1982) focused on the alleged phenomena of "preference reversals," which occur when individuals change their preferences regarding the same choice when it is formulated differently, and "intransitivity," the related phenomenon showing that actual individual preferences are not always transitive.[2] Grether and Plott (1979) were very

---

[2]   Their references to behavioral decision research's experiments consisted of only a few articles, namely Slovic and Lichtenstein (1971, 1973). Slovic and Lichtenstein, however, were quick to remark in the *American Economic Review* that "there is a substantial body of research on preference reversals within the psychological literature that is being neglected here. Moreover, reversals should be seen not as an isolated phenomenon, but as one of a broad class of findings that demonstrates violations of preference models" (Slovic and Lichtenstein, 1983, p. 597).

suspicious of the empirical evidence produced by the psychologists, and aware that economists and psychologists did not always use rational choice theory for the same purpose. They emphasized that "[t]here is little doubt that psychologists have uncovered a systematic and interesting aspect of human choice behavior" (Grether and Plott, 1979, p. 624), but wondered whether (1) the phenomenon also held in more typical economic situations and (2) whether it could be explained by means of economic theory.

The main worry of Grether and Plott was that the experimental results were mere artifacts produced by the experimental setup of the psychologists. They produced thirteen (!) methodological and theoretical economic explanations for the falsifications: (1) no real money was used, and incentives may therefore have been misspecified; (2) different incomes of the subjects may have influenced some experiments; (3) in most of the psychological experiments, indifference between two options was not possible; (4) perhaps subjects did not give their true selling or bidding price but acted strategically; (5) subjectively perceived probabilities from the lotteries used may not be equal to the actual objective probabilities; (6) perhaps subjects chose lexicographically, as in Tversky's elimination-by-aspects theory (Tversky, 1972), which would account for a moderate form of preference reversals; (7) perhaps the magnitudes of the choices were too close, leading to apparent intransitivity, such as in Tversky (1969); (8) the cost of decision making could be too high compared to the expected payoff, leading subjects to not make an effort; (9) perhaps the choices subjects faced contained too much information for the subject to process within the time available; (10) subjects could have been confused or might have misunderstood the experiment; (11) perhaps the phenomena reported occurred only in a few subjects; (12) the subjects were relatively unsophisticated psychological undergraduates, whereas more sophisticated subjects might make more rational choices; and (13) the experimenters were psychologists, leading subjects to speculate about the true purpose of the experiments, and hence perhaps to change their behavior.[3]

This last explanation in particular illustrates that Grether and Plott went to great lengths to show that the findings of the psychologists had been mere artifacts. In their own words, "[t]his paper reports the results of a series of experiments designed to discredit the psychologists' works as applied to

---

[3] Although formulated in different times and with respect to different articles from psychology, the counterarguments and objections formulated by Grether and Plott are reminiscent of the objections raised by Wallis and Friedman (1942) against Thurstone (1931), as discussed in Chapter 1.

economics" (Grether and Plott, 1979, p. 623). Grether and Plott's message was that every possible explanation for the psychologists' findings needed to be controlled for, even the argument that the results should not be taken seriously for the sole reason that the experimenters had been psychologists. Grether and Plott set up two experiments in which they controlled for all thirteen possible explanations. They specified incentives, and they made the experiments very simple and assured that all subjects understood the choices they could make. Furthermore, they used undergraduates as well as graduates, made it clear that they were economists and not psychologists, and they took the two possible explanations of Tversky into consideration. But, much to their surprise, they obtained results that were similar to those of the psychologists. Consequently, they remained "as perplexed as the reader who has just been introduced to the problem" (Grether and Plott, 1979, p. 624).

The first Grether and Plott article was published in the same year as Kahneman and Tversky's prospect theory, but in Grether and Plott (1982), they recognized prospect theory as a prominent example of preference theory that adjusts a number of assumptions of rational choice theory in order to account for the empirical findings. However, Grether and Plott (1982) stressed that also prospect theory could not account for their experimental results: "We need to emphasize that the phenomenon causes problems for preference theory in general, and not for just the expected utility theory. Prospect theory as a special type of preference theory cannot account for the results" (Grether and Plott, 1982, p. 575).

The conclusions Grether and Plott derived from these results are important because they set the standard for experimental economists' responses to these and similar findings for the following quarter of a century. According to Grether and Plott (1979, 1982), the experimental results pointed to an inconsistency between actual behavior and rational choice theory that was "deeper than the mere lack of transitivity or even stochastic transitivity." The empirical results suggested "that *no optimization principles of any sort* lie behind even the simplest of human choices" (Grether and Plott, 1979, p. 623, emphasis added). Grether and Plott did not believe that the empirical results could be incorporated by making a relatively minor adjustment to rational choice theory, but drew the radical conclusion that utility maximization and rational choice should be completely abandoned as a description of and as an explanation for the decision-making behavior of individuals.

However, and this was equally crucial, Grether and Plott did not imply that utility maximization and rational choice as a description of market behavior were invalidated. With respect to market behavior the experimental results only showed that economic subjects, who in the final market equilibrium behave according to rational choice and utility maximization, initially behave according to a to-be-developed theory that is completely unlike utility maximization and rational choice. Because the disciplining, *rationalizing* institution of the market operates between individual behavior and market behavior, a falsification of individual rational optimization did not falsify rational choice as a description of equilibrium market behavior. Quite the contrary, the experimental results only emphasized the role of the market as the mechanism that over time rationalizes individual behavior. Grether and Plott's experimental work was inspired by Smith, and Smith, in turn, took over the conclusions derived by Grether and Plott (e.g., Smith, 1982, 1989, 1994, 2008).

Thus, two important aspects of experimental economists' use and reception of behavioral decision research in the early 1980s need to be stressed. First, experimental economists, and Grether and Plott first and foremost, corroborated the experimental findings of "the psychologists" for "the economists." After Grether and Plott, it was no longer possible to dismiss psychologists' findings merely on the ground that they were produced by psychologists. Second, Grether and Plott inferred their own, specific view of economic behavior of agents and the role of the market. The experimental results completely invalidated preference theory as describing decision making by economic agents when they are first presented with a choice but at the same time emphasized the role of the market in driving the economic agents to more rational behavior.

3. Thaler's Economic Anomalies and the Creation of Behavioral Finance

After the experimental results from psychology had been corroborated for economics by experimental economists Grether and Plott, economists were freed to employ the psychological findings to their own liking. Next to the experimental economists, a new generation of economists including Werner De Bondt, Lawrence Summers, Robert Shiller and Andrei Shleifer, started to apply the experimental results to financial markets (De Bondt and Thaler, 1985, 1990; Summers, 1986; Shleifer, 2000; Shiller, 1979, 1981, 1989, 2000). More established early contributors were Kenneth Arrow and Richard Roll (Arrow, 1982; Roll, 1981, 1983). But the most active and most influential economist in this group from the early 1980s onward was Richard Thaler – a business economist from the University of Rochester. What these economists had in common was a similar theoretical use of the experimental results of the psychologists. Like the experimental economists, they referred explicitly to the experimental results of Slovic, Lichtenstein, Kahneman, Tversky, and others as "psychological," and identified the producers of these results equally explicitly as "psychologists." But they inferred conclusions for economics from the "psychological" experimental results that were very different from those of the experimental economists.

To understand why and how, we first need to take a few steps back. Let me start with the rise of financial economics. In postwar neoclassical economics, the market had largely become an empty concept. Based on general equilibrium theory, a direct link was assumed between the behavior of individuals and the market; the market was nothing more than the sum of all the individual behaviors. In the 1960s and 1970s, a new field in economics appeared that used the neoclassical theory as a theoretical foundation for its empirical investigation of stock market behavior. Following research conducted during the 1950s and 1960s by Franco Modigliani, Merton Miller, and Harry Markowitz, financial economics, as the new field came to be called, gradually appeared as an accepted genuine subbranch of neoclassical economics in the second half of the 1960s and the 1970s (Jovanovic, 2008; Poitras and Jovanovic, 2007; MacKenzie, 2006; Mehrling, 2005, 2011). The empirical study of stock markets was among others linked to neoclassical economics through what came to be referred to as the efficient market hypothesis, which specified the theoretical position of neoclassical economics in the case of the stock market, and any market for that matter (Jovanovic, 2008). "A market in which prices always 'fully reflect' available information is called 'efficient'" (Fama, 1970, p. 383).

The central question for financial economists was whether stock markets indeed are efficient, as theory predicted, or inefficient, for which an explanation then would have to be found. In the second half of the 1960s and the 1970s, two opposing views developed. At the Massachusetts Institute of Technology (MIT), Paul Cootner, Hendrik Houthakker, and others, in part inspired by Benoit Mandelbrot, developed and defended the idea that the stock market was not efficient (Jovanovic, 2008; Mirowski, 1989, 1990; Sent 1998). "[P]rice changes are not purely random but follow certain longer run trends," Houthakker argued (quoted in Jovanovic, 2008, p. 228). Cootner, for his part, hesitantly endorsed Mandelbrot's work, remarking that "[i]f we have permitted ourselves to be fooled for as long as this into believing that the Gaussian is a workable one, is it not possible that [Mandelbrot's] revolution is similarly illusory?" (Cootner, 1964, p. 418), but was nevertheless convinced that "[t]he stock market is not a random walk" (Cootner, quoted in Jovanovic, 2008, p. 225).

The Chicago Graduate School of Business held and fiercely defended the opposite view: that the stock market is efficient and that stock prices over time will appear to be a random walk (Jovanovic, 2008). In Chicago, Eugene Fama, a student of Miller and Mandelbrot, arose as the main protagonist, defending the efficient market as an empirical and theoretical fact (e.g., Fama, 1970). Inspired indirectly by former Chicago mathematician Jimmie Savage, Fama distinguished between "sophisticated traders" who were experienced enough to determine the intrinsic value of securities and act accordingly and "other participants" who did not (yet) posses this skill and who produced the random noise around the intrinsic value. Sophisticated traders ensured that market prices remained or returned quickly to the underlying value of the stocks (Jovanovic, 2008; Fama, 1970).

Next to this rise of and debate about financial economics, a second, more general development in the 1960s and 1970s was a gradual reinterpretation of the behavioral principles or axioms on which economics was based. Chapter 2 extensively discussed the debate between Samuelson, Baumol, and Allais, on one hand, and Friedman and Savage, on the other hand, regarding the nature of the axioms of von Neumann and Morgenstern's *Theory of Games and Economic Behavior* (2004 [1944]). Where Samuelson, Baumol, and Allais took the axioms to be descriptive claims that might be refuted directly on the basis of empirical evidence, Friedman and Savage took the axioms to be characterizations that summarize behavior on a higher than purely descriptive level. In that regard, Friedman stood in a tradition of understanding the assumptions or principles on which economic theory is based that goes back at least to the mid-nineteenth century (Mill, 1844). In addition, Friedman advanced this understanding of economic principles as the basis of a positive economics that was to be strictly separated from ethical claims in the domain of normative economics (Friedman, 1953).

But a dispute between a few up-and-coming economists obviously is not necessarily representative of the view of the economic discipline at large. Instead, an indication of the views held by the broader economic community may be obtained by looking at leading textbooks of the time. Between the late 1940s and late 1970s, the most widely used undergraduate textbook by far in the United States was Samuelson's *Economics* – first published in 1948 – rivaled only by Campbell McConnell's *Economics* – first published in 1960 – and Richard Lipsey and Peter Steiner's *Economics* – first published in 1972 (Giraud, forthcoming; Elzinga, 1992). In the first few editions of the 1940s and 1950s, Samuelson's *Economics* did not employ the labels of positive and normative, but did start from the distinction between facts and values first introduced by David Hume. The textbook emphasized that "there is only one valid reality in a given economic situation, however hard it may be to recognize and isolate it. There is not one theory of economics for Republicans and one for Democrats, not one for workers and one for employers," and that "[b]asic questions concerning right and wrong goals to be pursued cannot be settled by economists as such. Each citizen must decide them for himself" (e.g., Samuelson, 1952, p. 5; 1952, p. 5).

At the same time, those first editions of Samuelson's *Economics* did not pay specific attention to the question on which evidence that "one valid reality" was based. McConnell's *Economics*, on the contrary, did. In its first edition, McConnell explained that

[t]he economist must first ascertain and gather facts which are relevant to consideration of a specific economic problem. This aspect of his job is sometimes called "descriptive economics." The economist then puts his collection of facts in order and summarizes them by "distilling out" a principle, that is, by generalizing about the way individuals and institutions actually behave. Deriving principles from facts is called "economic theory," or "economic analysis." Finally, the general knowledge of economic behavior which economic principles provide can then be used in formulating policies, that is, remedies or solutions, for correcting or avoiding the problem under scrutiny. This final aspect of the field is sometimes called "applied economics" or "policy economics." (McConnell, 1960, pp. 3–4)

. . .

Descriptive economics and economic theory are both concerned with facts; the former immediately and the latter once removed. Policy economics necessarily entails value judgments as to the desirability of certain events. When operating at this level, economists are no longer functioning as scientists, but rather as policy makers. They are dealing not only with facts, but also with values. (McConnell, 1960, p. 10)

Thus, the distinction between facts and values was considered a standard one in the economics discipline in the 1950s and 1960s, even if this was not usually translated into Friedman's (1953) positive and normative domain. Similarly, it seems that the understanding of economic theory as deriving from a set of characterizations of human behavior in the economy not only was held by Friedman, but was also the standard view among economists.

Then, roughly between 1970 and 1990, two important changes within the economic discipline surfaced in the introductory textbooks. First of all, the explicit distinction between the description of economic facts and the different procedure of deriving principles and theories from these facts, as so well set out in the quote from McConnell (1960), collapsed into one empirical domain of positive economics. At least as important, the empirical claims of this positive domain came to be understood as directly amenable to empirical refutation and verification. In addition, the political domain of reasoning based on values became more widely labeled as normative economics. A succinct summary of this new understanding of the economic discipline can, for instance, be found in the first (and subsequent) editions of Lipsey and Steiner's *Economics*:

> The positive concerns what *is, was,* or *will be,* and the normative statements concern what *ought to be*. Positive statements, assertions, or theories may be simple or very complex, but they are basically about what *is*. . .
>
> The statement "It is impossible to break up atoms" is a positive statement that can quite definitely be (and of course has been) refuted by empirical observations, while the statement "Scientists ought not to break up atoms" is a normative statement that involves ethical judgments. (Lipsey and Steiner, 1972, p. 15; 1981, pp. 17–18)

Also McConnell gradually adapted his exposition of economic theorizing. Although he maintained a condensed version of his earlier distinction between descriptive economics and the inference of economic principles and theories, the 1975 edition of his *Economics* for the first time emphasized that the "facts" of the descriptive domain meant "observable and verifiable behavior" (McConnell, 1975, p. 3). In the 1990 edition, McConnell (now together with Stanley Brue) continued to distinguish between facts and principles, but at the same time emphasized that both were directly refutable by empirical observations and hence part of positive economics. Likewise, in the 1985 edition of his *Economics*, Samuelson, now for the first time together with Nordhaus, remarked that "*Positive economics* describes the facts and behavior in the economy," and that "Normative economics involves ethics and value judgments" (Samuelson and Nordhaus, 1985, p. 7, emphasis in the original)

A second change that gradually surfaced in U.S. undergraduate textbooks in the 1970s and 1980s was the introduction of game theory and expected utility theory (see also Backhouse, 2008, 2010). These new theories were clearly intended as empirical claims about actual behavior of agents in the economy, even if some less sophisticated decision makers might make mistakes and thus produce some statistical noise around the rational mean, as in Fama's efficient market hypothesis. Thus, starting in the 1975 edition of his *Economics*, McConnell began to emphasize that "[t]he average consumer is a fairly rational fellow. He attempts to dispose of his money income in such a way as to derive the greatest amount of satisfaction, or utility, from it. . . . the typical consumer wants to get the most for his money" (McConnell, 1975, p. 488). Pindyck and Rubenfeld's *Microeconomics* (1995) provides another example of which many more are easily found: "The theory of consumer behavior begins with three basic assumptions regarding people's preferences for one market basket versus another. We believe that these assumptions hold for most people in most situations" (p. 63) – after which followed completeness, transitivity, and monotonicity. In short, in the 1970s and 1980s, economists came to understand their discipline as distinguishing between a positive and a normative realm, and more importantly understood the positive realm to be based on empirical claims about individual behavior in the economy that were directly subject to empirical verification and refutation. The key empirical claim was that the average individual in the economy was a fairly rational person.

Because of these general developments in economics, empirical evidence that showed the individual in the economy to not be a fairly rational person now implied a direct refutation of economic theory. All of a sudden, counterexamples such as produced by William Baumol, Maurice Allais, Daniel Ellsberg, and others became anomalies of economic theory. In the case of the MIT school in financial economics, this led to the conclusion that the idea of efficient markets and random walks – that is, the application of the neoclassical theory to finance – must be invalid. Yet, a solution was not immediately at hand. Mandelbrot forcefully argued that price variation does not follow the bell curve but instead has "fat tails," and that prices are not independent. Although Mandelbrot did not completely convince them, it set economists Cootner, Roll, Thomas Sargent, and others off in directions that substantially departed from the received view of neoclassical theory (Mandelbrot and Hudson, 2004; Cootner, 1964; Blattberg and Sargent, 1971; Roll, 1970). But the initial wave of enthusiasm died down when it turned out that Mandelbrot's theory was too difficult and impractical (Mirowski, 1989, 1990; Sent, 1998). Some ten years later, however, the corroboration of the experimental findings of the psychologists by Grether and Plott opened up a new realm of solutions to the neoclassical anomalies.

Kahneman, Thaler, and others interpreted the claims of the random walk school within the new understanding of the economic discipline as providing directly refutable empirical claims of human behavior under the rubric of positive economics. The experimental results of the psychologists, they argued, falsified the empirical claims of human behavior made by (financial) economists. An early and illustrative example of how neoclassical economists incorporated the psychology of Slovic, Lichtenstein, Kahneman, and Tversky into financial economics is Arrow's (1982) "Risk Perception in Psychology and Economics." As Arrow noted himself, he was not generally known as a scholar working on "securities and futures markets" (1982, p. 2). Yet he felt confident enough to share his thoughts on the matter as he had kept track of the field over the years as "someone interested in the extension of general equilibrium theory to transactions over time under conditions of uncertainty" (1982, p. 2). In the article, Arrow discussed a number of phenomena in the (stock) market that contradicted the "rationality hypothesis," such as individuals' unwillingness to accept government subsidized insurance below its actuarial value and observed irrationality in financial markets. Citing the "replication" of Slovic and Lichtenstein's preference reversals by Grether and Plott, Arrow suggested that "failures of the rationality hypothesis [in financial markets] are in fact compatible with some of the specific observations of cognitive psychologists" (1982, p. 5). Thus, Arrow, and this is a crucial step, drew a direct line from observations in the laboratories of the psychologists to contradictions observed in the market. Experimental results from psychology, which in themselves had nothing to do with the economy or with markets, were linked one-to-one with economics and were used as an explanation for the unsolved financial economic puzzles. In one sentence, Arrow linked two very different research practices: "an important class of intertemporal markets shows systematic deviations from individual rational behavior and . . . these deviations are consonant with evidence from very different sources collected by psychologists" (Arrow, 1982, p. 8). Systematic deviations from rational behavior by individuals in the laboratory could be an explanation for observed market deviations only when one understood the relation between individual and market behavior to be direct, as was now the case in economics.

Furthermore, Arrow recalled that "[a]ny argument seeking to establish the presence of irrational economic behavior always meets a standard counterargument: if most agents are irrational, then a rational individual can make a lot of money; eventually, therefore, the rational individual will take over all the wealth" (Arrow, 1982, p. 7). But, Arrow argued, arbitrage and related arguments could easily be countered: "(1) Not all arbitrage possibilities exist. . . . (2) More important, if everyone else is 'irrational,' it by no means follows that one can make money by being rational, at least in the short run" (Arrow, 1982, p. 7).

Attempts to incorporate the corroborated findings of the psychologists in financial economics such as Arrow (1982) appear scattered through the literature from 1980 onward. But Thaler was the first economist to draw economic implications from behavioral decision research findings systematically. Thaler's first behavioral finance–oriented paper "Toward a Positive Theory of Consumer Choice" appeared in 1980 in the *Journal of Economic Behavior and Organization*. In his articles, Thaler's constantly repeated mantra became that "many of the elements of prospect theory can be used in developing descriptive choice models in economics" (Thaler, 1980, p. 41). After that first article, extensive references to the work of Kahneman and Tversky occurred in almost every publication by Thaler. Thaler worked predominantly in financial economics in the 1980s, advancing the experimental results and the theoretical approach of Kahneman and Tversky as an explanation for the observed falsifications of the efficient market hypothesis, and thus disagreeing with the efficient market view. By 1991, Thaler had collected enough material to publish a book, titled *Quasi Rational Economics* and consisting of sixteen of his papers that critically assessed the traditional neoclassical economic models and offered alternatives. In 1993, Thaler edited another book titled *Advances in Behavioral Finance* for the Russell Sage Foundation, consisting mainly of papers from the latter half of the 1980s, which was followed by a second volume in 2005, with the same title. Kahneman and Tversky were the most important source of inspiration for behavioral economics, but Thaler was its earliest and strongest advocate.

Specifically, Thaler built on two lines of Kahneman and Tversky's research. Thaler systematically connected Kahneman and Tversky's biases of rational choice in experiments to the anomalies of rational choice theory found in financial economics, and he made this connection the cornerstone of a new research program. Sometimes explanations were offered based on prospect theory or by means of some other theory. Usually, however, these violations of economic theory were presented without any explanation to account for them, and Thaler simply stressed what they implied, that economic theory had been violated. In "Mental Accounting and Consumer Choice," for instance, Thaler (1985) presented the reader with four anecdotes that "illustrate a type of behavior" in which the "individual violate[s] a simple economic principle." The "standard economic theory," Thaler noted, "of course, is based on normative principles," and he offered prospect theory "as a substitute to the standard economic theory of the consumer" (Thaler, 1985, p. 200). All this made Thaler a great promoter of Kahneman and Tversky's work in economics and quickly turned him into a major recipient of, and influential voice in, the Alfred P. Sloan-Russell Sage behavioral economics program, which played a crucial role in establishing behavioral economics as a highly visible new subdiscipline in the 1980s and early 1990s.

4. Thaler, Kahneman, and the Sloan-Sage Behavioral Economics Program[4]

The first tentative efforts of collaboration between psychologists Kahneman and Tversky and economist Thaler in the early 1980s received a strong boost through the Alfred P. Sloan and later Russell Sage Foundation's behavioral economics program, which ran from 1984 through 1992. It is not possible to understand the rise of behavioral economics without assessing the role of the Sloan-Sage program. The primary contribution of the Sloan-Sage behavioral economics program was not the resources it provided, which were relatively modest. Instead, the program's contribution was to catalyze in the researchers it supported a sense of contributing to a new direction of the economic discipline. Partly this reflected the common strategy of U.S. foundations to pick an individual or small group of scientists and to stick with them until scientific success had been achieved (Jones and Rahman, 2009; Hauptmann, 2006). In addition, it reflected the good luck of being at the right place and at the right time. Moreover, it was a consequence of the careful management of the program's director Eric Wanner (b. 1942). The various actors involved in the behavioral economics program – Kahneman, Thaler, the advisory committee, and, particularly, Wanner – constructed a new behavioral subdiscipline in economics by, on one hand, tapping into existing missionary sentiments in the economic and psychological disciplines while, on the other hand, actively shaping this sense of mission.[5]

In 1960, psychologists Jerome Bruner (b. 1915) and George Miller (1920–2012) founded the Center for Cognitive Studies at Harvard University. The initiative sprang from their desire to formulate a nonbehaviorist, cognitive approach to psychology in which the mind's black box would be opened and decomposed into different interacting compartments. Cohen-Cole (2007) carefully illuminates how on its creation the center was conceived as an interdisciplinary institution that, through its organization and its separate location from the rest of the Harvard campus, would actively pursue cross-fertilization of different scientific disciplines related to

---

[4] A first major source of information for this section is two interviews with Eric Wanner at the Russell Sage Foundation, New York, on April 14, 2009, and on April 7, 2010. A second major source is the Russell Sage Archives at the Rockefeller Foundation Archives, Rockefeller Archive Center, Sleepy Hollow, New York. A third source is the annual reports of the Sloan Foundation of the 1970s and 1980s, made available by the Sloan Foundation.

[5] Although the behavioral economics program was loosely connected to Herbert Simon (1916–2001), it was, despite its name, not directly related to the short-lived Ford Foundation's Behavioral Sciences Program (1951–1957) or to George Katona's (1901–1981) Institute of Social Research at the University of Michigan, established in the late 1940s.

cognition, including psychology, linguistics, philosophy, biology, mathematics, anthropology, pediatrics, history, psychiatry, and psychoanalysis. The psychologists involved included, among others, Bärbel Inhelder (1913–1997) and Daniel Kahneman, participating linguists were, for instance, Noam Chomsky (b. 1928) and Jerry Fodor (b. 1935), whereas decision theory and industrial administration was represented by Herbert Simon.

The interdisciplinary focus of the center's founders also influenced their students. Wanner started his dissertation research as a psychologist in 1967 under the supervision of Miller, but when Miller left for Rockefeller University in 1969 before Wanner had finished writing, the supervision was transferred to psycholinguist Roger Brown (1925–1997). After completing his dissertation in 1969, Wanner was hired as an assistant professor at Harvard's Department of Psychology to teach the course Miller had left vacant after leaving Harvard. Wanner's career initially developed along common academic lines. He completed a partial revision of his dissertation in 1972 and further developed his experimental psycholinguistic research in a number of articles (e.g., Wanner, 1973; Wanner et al., 1975; Wanner and Shiner, 1976).

However, in the second half of the 1970s, Wanner gradually left the active practice of science. In 1976, Wanner joined Harvard University Press as an editor, where he initiated the Cognitive Science Series. The Cognitive Science Series aimed to provide up-to-date overviews of different subject areas within cognitive science. As such, its scope was similar to the scientific landscape the Center for Cognitive Studies had aimed to cover a decade earlier. The Cognitive Science Series ran from 1979 to 1989 and eventually consisted of nine volumes, many written by foremost cognitive scientists such as John R. Anderson (b. 1947) and Steven Pinker (b. 1954). As do many other scientific series, the Cognitive Science Series had an advisory board that invited, selected, and reviewed the books at their different stages of development, and a number of members were themselves authors of books in the series. Wanner managed to get many prominent cognitive scientists on the forty-six member advisory board, including Fodor, Anderson, Chomsky, Robert Abelson, Donald Davidson, Hilary Putnam, John Searle, his former supervisors Miller and Brown, and his former coauthors Gleitman and Kaplan.

The advisory board also included Kahneman and Tversky. Wanner had been aware of Kahneman's research from the time of his dissertation research onward, as Kahneman's research on attention and cognitive errors was more or less related to Wanner's own research on experimental psycholinguistics. Wanner, Kaplan and Shiner (1975), for instance, referred to Wright and

Table 5.1. *Total annual endowments and annual behavioural economic endowments of the Sloan Foundation and the Russell Sage Foundation*

Year	ASF total	ASF Beh Ec	RSF total	RSF Beh Ec
1984	$17,083,690	$36.000 (0.2%)		
1985	$19,234,455	$97,000 (0.5%)		
1986	$18,721,037	$430,500 (2.3%)	$878,874	$200,000 (22.8%)
1987	$20,758,106	$310,000 (1.5%)	$816,808	$398,200 (48.8%)
1988	$25,526,826	$217,000 (0.9%)	$916,112	$358,016 (39.1%)
1989	$17,227,448	$458,561 (2.7%)	$1,267,776	$342,190 (27.0%)
1990			$1,801,063	$96,827 (5.4%)
1991			$1,594,293	$180,680 (11.3%)
1992			$1,522,220	$293,500 (19.3%)
Total	**$118,551,562**	**$1,549,061 (1.3%)**	**$8,797,146**	**$1,869,413 (21.3%)**

Kahneman (1971). Moreover, as Wanner recalls, Kahneman and Tversky's collaborative research had been brought to his attention from the early 1970s onwards by colleagues at Harvard, so that by the late 1970s he was generally familiar with their work. Also the later famous prospect theory article in *Econometrica* was brought to Wanner's attention relatively early, in 1980 or 1981. Yet, it was only when Kahneman and Tversky agreed to be on the Cognitive Science Series advisory board that Wanner acquainted them personally. That is to say, as two members of a forty-six member advisory board. Wanner got to know them better after he had moved to the Sloan Foundation in 1982.

Both in the size of their funds and in their visibility private foundations are a twentieth century American phenomenon (Weaver, 1967, p. xv; Goodwin, 1998; Leonard, 1991; Grossman, 1982). The foundations were self-conscious in their support of economics, which had to serve the advancement of some larger social purpose such as the alleviation of poverty, maintenance of full employment, or protection of the environment. In other words, economics had to be useful (Pooley and Solovey, 2010; Crowther-Heyck, 2006). A major difference between the Sloan Foundation and the Russell Sage Foundation was the amount of annual funds available for grants. Table 5.1 shows that throughout the six years of its existence, the behavioral economics program was a relatively small program at the Sloan Foundation. By contrast, the Russell Sage Foundation's total annual endowments between 1986 and 1992 were much smaller than were those of the Sloan Foundation, and the share spent on the behavioral economics program was thus larger.

The behavioral economics program was created at the Sloan Foundation in 1984 under the presidency of Albert Rees (1921–1992). An accomplished labor economist, Rees obtained his PhD from the University of Chicago under the supervision of H. Gregg Lewis in 1950. Rees stayed at Chicago until 1966, serving as the editor of the *Journal of Political Economy* from 1954 to 1959 and as chair of the economics department from 1962 to 1966. In 1979, Rees became trustee and president of the Sloan Foundation, which at the time had $250 million in assets and gave $15 million in grants a year. Three years later, Rees managed to persuade Wanner to join the Sloan Foundation as a program officer to take care of Sloan's cognitive science program, impressed as Rees probably was by Wanner's Cognitive Science Series at Harvard University Press. The Sloan Foundation's cognitive science program had been running for some ten years, and during his years at Harvard, Wanner had been a researcher on one of the program's projects. However, managing the cognitive science program was not too interesting a job for the newly recruited program officer "because really all the big grants had been made and it was just a matter of tying everything up and writing reports to finish it off and so forth."[6]

Thus, Wanner proposed a new plan on the application of cognitive science to economics. The new plan gradually sharpened during 1982 and 1983. In early 1983, Wanner mentioned as "a possible area for investment" for the Sloan Foundation the theme of "what might be called the psychological foundations of economic behavior."[7] During a conversation between Wanner, Kahneman, and Tversky a few months later in which they explored the topic, the two star psychologists were not very optimistic, reasoning that to get economists' attention psychologists would have to be more economically sophisticated than they actually were, and advised Wanner not to spend too much money on the project, if anything at all (see also Kahneman, 2002). Nevertheless, over the course of 1983, "behavioral economics" which emerged as the name for the new program, and Wanner planned a few exploratory meetings with Kahneman and Tversky, and through them with Thaler. As a result, word was spread in the academic community that the Sloan Foundation was considering setting up a new program on behavioral economics, and during the second half of 1983, the first unsolicited grant requests started coming in. The only application that was considered and funded by Wanner and Rees in 1983 was a proposal by Thaler to spend a sabbatical with Kahneman at the University of British Columbia.

---

[6] Eric Wanner, interview with the author, Russell Sage Foundation, New York, April 14, 2009.
[7] Wanner's letter to Fischoff, January 26, 1983, Box 194, Folder 1427, Rockefeller Foundation Archives, Rockefeller Archive Center, Sleepy Hollow, New York.

However, after the program officially commenced the other early proposals were also reviewed and decided on. Throughout this whole process, Wanner worked closely with Rees on the new program, who as an empirically oriented Marshallian Chicago economist was skeptical but tolerant toward the idea that an empirically grounded psychology could be usefully employed in economics.

Rees and Wanner started by composing an advisory committee for the program that would review the incoming proposals and award the funds available. To avoid that one of the two groups that the program aimed to bring together would dominate the other and to ensure that it would be an interdisciplinary program, Wanner and Rees decided that there should be two psychologists and two economists on the advisory committee. Also the label "behavioral economics" was understood to be deliberately half psychology–half economics. The first person they picked for the advisory committee was Leon Festinger (1919–1989), a social psychologist and, among others, a colleague of Katona at the Institute of Social Research at the University of Michigan in the 1950s and a participant in the 1952 Santa Monica Seminar discussed in Chapter 2. In addition, Festinger had been involved with the Sloan Foundation's cognitive science program and was interested in economics. Second, Wanner approached economist Thomas Schelling (b. 1921), whom Wanner knew from Harvard and whose work on paradoxes and conflict strategies seemed related to the new program (e.g., Schelling, 1960, 1969). Rees recommended economist William Baumol (b. 1922), an organization theorist and early critic of von Neumann and Morgenstern's axiomatic approach to decision making, as set out in Chapter 2 (Baumol, 1951, 1958). The fourth member Wanner and Rees agreed on and who accepted was cognitive psychologist Abelson, a member of the advisory board of the Cognitive Science Series Wanner had initiated at Harvard University Press.

In mid-June 1984, the board of trustees of the Sloan Foundation officially installed the advisory committee and endowed it with $250,000 to fund a number of "seed projects" in subsequent years, to see if the program could work.[8] As is clear from Table 5.1, the amount of money spent on the behavioral economics by the Sloan Foundation was comparatively small and the board of trustees basically took Rees's word for it. As early as July 1984, Abelson expressed a view that seems to have been shared

---

[8] Wanner's notes on the advisory committee meeting, December 7, 1984, Box 194, Folder 1428, Rockefeller Foundation Archives, Rockefeller Archive Center, Sleepy Hollow, New York.

by the other advisory committee members as well as by Wanner, namely, that Kahneman and Thaler should be at the center of the new program: "Getting Thaler and Kahneman together is bound to produce progress. Their teamwork could be as seminal as the Tversky and Kahneman pairing, but more market oriented."[9] The first behavioral economics meeting was planned for December 7, 1984, at the Waldorf-Astoria Hotel, New York. In addition to the advisory committee and to Kahneman and Thaler, the following economists and psychologists were invited: Hillel Einhorn, Baruch Fischoff, Donald Hood, Thomas Juster, Charles Plott, Howard Kunreuther, Howard Raiffa, Oliver Williamson, Richard Zeckhauser, and Herbert Simon.[10]

Herbert Simon was considered one of the creators of the field of behavioral economics and in addition was the towering 1978 Nobel Memorial laureate. Hence, he was an obvious source of inspiration for the new Sloan-Sage program and from the start invited to participate. At the same time, he was not expected to be much involved because he was busy and because he had moved away from his earlier criticisms of neoclassical economics' behavioral assumptions.[11] Nevertheless, Simon attached "the highest importance to the exploratory program you [Wanner] are starting" and hoped to "be of some help to you [Wanner] in its further development."[12] Moreover, Simon stressed that "a major component in any program that is mounted in behavioral economics should be directed at securing training for doctoral students and young economists in the techniques of making field studies, getting information directly from executives in business firms, and possibly also running experiments," which had equally been recurring themes in Simon's criticisms of neoclassical economics in the 1950s and 1960s (Simon, 1955, 1959, 1962).

Thus, in its early stages, the new behavioral economics program was clearly understood as a further exploration and advancement of Simon's behavioral economics. Not only did Wanner, Kahneman, Thaler, and the

---

[9] Abelson's letter to Wanner, July 26, 1984, Box 202, Folder 1494, Rockefeller Foundation Archives, Rockefeller Archive Center, Sleepy Hollow, New York.

[10] It is not completely clear why Tversky was not invited. Because his advice was solicited from the start, the only possible explanation seems to be that for unknown reasons, he did not want get involved in the exploratory meetings.

[11] Something similar held for Arrow, but further in the background. Arrow was seen as ally, and it seems his support was actively sought. Yet Arrow chose not to become directly involved. Later on, in 1986, Arrow successfully applied for a $30,000 grant for a "Research Seminar on Behavioral Economics."

[12] Simon's letter to Wanner, December 5, 1984, Box 202, Folder 1494, Rockefeller Foundation Archives, Rockefeller Archive Center, Sleepy Hollow, New York.

others involved adopt Simon's label of "behavioral economics" without any apparent discussion; Simon's language and ideas are also clearly visible in the early program statements and objectives. For instance, in a letter to Sloan's board of trustees in mid 1985 the advisory committee remarked that

> progress in this new field will depend on moving beyond laboratory demonstrations of the inaccuracy of the behavioral assumptions employed in economics and toward efforts to develop and test more behaviorally sophisticated economic theory. Accordingly, the Committee recommends a funding program in 1986 offering support for research on behavioral economic models, for observational studies of economic decision making in real settings, and for simulated market experiments designed to examine the market consequences of individual psychological processes.[13]

But the new behavioral economics program was also understood to move beyond Simon's earlier criticisms of neoclassical economics, by focusing on the systematic distortions of Kahneman and Tversky rather than on the random limits of rational decision making of Simon. Thus, while initially the major source of inspiration was Simon, during 1985, Wanner, Kahneman, Thaler, and the advisory committee quickly developed their own focus and language. First of all, the new program was concentrated more specifically on "the potential contribution of psychology and other behavioral sciences to the study of financial markets,"[14] in particular because "financial markets are often considered the most efficient of markets and thus might be thought to be the most immune to non-rational factors."[15] Anomalies of rational behavior would hence have their strongest impact on theories of financial markets, and alternative behavioral theories that incorporate the "nonrational" behavior would be most visible there. To make this focus stand out more clearly, the label of "behavioral finance" was appropriated as one area of behavioral economic research.[16] Moreover, the program's organizers stressed that

---

[13] Advisory committee's letter to Sloan's board of trustees, n.d. (+/–1985), Box 194, Folder 1429, Rockefeller Foundation Archives, Rockefeller Archive Center, Sleepy Hollow, New York.

[14] Wanner's letter to "Everyone," n.d. (+/– early October 1985), Box 194, Folder 1429, Rockefeller Foundation Archives, Rockefeller Archive Center, Sleepy Hollow, New York.

[15] Ibid.

[16] Thaler recalls, "I am not sure how that name [behavioral finance] emerged but by the time I wrote my first finance paper in 1985 with De Bondt [De Bondt and Thaler, 1985], the term behavioral economics was being used for the kind of economics I and some others were doing so BF [behavioral finance] became the natural term for the application of these ideas to financial economics" (Richard Thaler, e-mail to author, January 14, 2009).

for the [October 11, 1985] meeting to be most productive, we cannot afford to get too bogged down in discussions of whether or not a particular empirical finding is or is not an anomaly, i.e. whether there exists some explanation within the rational, maximizing, economic paradigm. Rather, we should try to work toward an evaluation of competing explanations, and the evidence that might be used to discriminate between behavioral hypotheses.[17]

In other words, the program's organizers – Wanner, Kahneman, Thaler, and the advisory committee – actively tried to prevent a theoretical economic discussion of neoclassical economic theory and, in advance of the program, tried to steer the discussions toward behavioral terms.

Another important element in this collaborative effort was Thaler's anomalies columns for the *Journal of Economic Perspectives* (*JEP*). In 1986, the journal's founding editors, Joseph Stiglitz (b. 1943), Carl Shapiro (b. 1955), and Timothy Taylor (b. 1960) decided that one element of their new journal would be "features," a series of short papers around one theme of which one would appear in every issue of the journal. As Taylor recalls,

We started with three features: a "Recommendations for Further Reading" feature written by Bernard Saffran, an "Economic Puzzles" feature written by Barry Nalebuff, and the "Anomalies" feature written by Richard Thaler. My memory is that Joe and Carl had Thaler in mind pretty much from Day 1. They had talked with Dick, and he had a list of potential topics pretty much ready to go. . . .

Our original plan with the "Anomalies" column was that it would include a range of anomalies: micro, macro, even theory or econometrics. However, getting authors to write these kinds of columns in JEP style proved tricky, and Dick and his co-authors generated a lovely stream of behavioral topics for us.[18]

Thaler published two series of "anomalies" papers for the *Journal of Economic Perspectives* that had the sole purpose of proclaiming that economics had serious problems regarding its theory of economic behavior. Each paper had a length of about 4,000 words. The first series contained fourteen anomalies articles and appeared from the first issue of the journal in 1987 through to 1991.[19] The second series contained four publications and appeared between 1995 and 2001. Thaler's anomalies columns provided the core of the new Kahneman and Tversky–inspired behavioral economics with a highly visible platform, and arguable served as a strong catalyst for its development.

---

[17] Wanner's letter to "Everyone," n.d. (+/– early October 1985), Box 194, Folder 1429, Rockefeller Foundation Archives, Rockefeller Archive Center, Sleepy Hollow, New York.
[18] Timothy Taylor, e-mail to author, April 6, 2010.
[19] The anomalies of the first series have been collected in *The Winners Curse* (1992).

The first anomaly article in 1987 documented "the January effect." When the market for stocks is in efficient equilibrium, in the neoclassical world, the average monthly return should be equal for each month. There is no reason to expect that stocks would perform better just because it happens to be a certain month. However, this was exactly what was observed in the case of January. In particular, for smaller firms, stock returns were substantially higher in January compared with other months. How could this January effect be possible given the theory of efficient markets? The answer was that it was not possible, with the question left open how to solve this anomaly.

Loewenstein and Thaler (1989) showed that many similar anomalies existed in and outside the economy that have to do with intertemporal choice. For example, people prefer to pay too much tax in advance and to receive some back when the year is over instead of the reverse, even when the first option is subject to costs in terms of lost interest. Schoolteachers who can choose between being paid in nine months (September-June) or in twelve (September-August), choose the second option although from an economic perspective the first is more rational. But Loewenstein and Thaler also cited a dermatologist who lamented that her patients were unwilling to avoid the sun when she told them about the risks of sun cancer but who were quick to stay out of the sun when she told them about the risk of getting "large pores and blackheads." This example, Loewenstein and Thaler argued, was also a violation of economic theory because it showed myopia in patients they should not have if they acted rationally. The implicit reasoning was that economic theory could be applied to every aspect of our lives and that therefore violations of economic theory could also be drawn from every corner of life: "where there are testable predictions, there are anomalies" (Loewenstein and Thaler, 1989, p. 183). The recurring message of the anomalies articles was that there are serious problems with economic theory that cannot be easily dismissed and that need to be taken seriously.

In his anomalies columns, Thaler cited examples from finance that were clearly economic. The structure of the anomalies, however, was often similar to the biases produced by Kahneman and Tversky (e.g., Kahneman and Tversky, 1972, 1979; Tversky and Kahneman, 1974). One anomaly that Thaler frequently investigated and that became one of the principal anomalies of behavioral finance was the "endowment effect" (e.g., Thaler, 1980; Kahneman et al., 1990, 1991). The endowment effect was an application of the framing effect of Kahneman and Tversky that showed that individuals' preferences are subject to an initial framing process. In other words, individuals' preferences depend on the quantity of the means with which they are endowed. The experiment is as follows: Divide a group of subjects randomly into two subgroups and give one of the two subgroups a standard coffee mug. Subsequently, ask the members of the subgroup with the mug what price they would minimally want to sell the mug for. Also ask subjects of the subgroup without mugs what price they would maximally want to pay for the mug. Typically, the willingness to accept (WTA) is about twice the willingness to pay (WTP). Apparently, people reframe their preferences after receiving the mug. In economics, this endowment effect could serve as an explanation for the often observed fallacy of taking into account sunk costs (see, e.g., Thaler, 1980, 1987; Tversky and Kahneman, 1981). The endowment effect was furthermore understood to falsify the Coase theorem, which says that in order to attain the efficient market allocation, the initial endowment of the goods should be irrelevant. The Coase theorem depends on the assumption that for every individual WTA equals WTP, so that trading will continue until the goods are in the hands of those with the highest WTP. But given the demonstrated systematic difference between WTA and WTP, the Coase theorem no longer held true: "Contrary to the assumptions of standard economic theory that preferences are independent of entitlements, the evidence presented here indicates that people's preferences depend on their reference positions" (Kahneman et al., 1990, p. 1344).

The first real test of the new Sloan-Sage behavioral economics program was a conference on "The Behavioral Foundations of Economic Theory," June 10 through 15 , 1986, organized by Robyn Hogarth and Melvin Reder at the University of Chicago.[20] The conference did not go very well for the members of the Sloan behavioral economics program:

[Eric Wanner (EW):] In the old days people tried to kill [behavioral economics]. You talked about behavioral finance...I remember a conference that we ran in probably 1985 at the University of Chicago.

[Floris Heukelom (FH):] That's 1986. It's the...

[EW:] Good, you know all about it. Really the finance economists were out to kill them. People like Merton Miller...I'm trying to think...some of those papers are brutal. They're basically just efforts to ridicule behavioral finance, and to kind of laugh it out of existence. So in those days it really was a hard thing to do.[21]

In the meantime, the number of researchers invited to participate in the behavioral economics program had expanded to forty names in December 1985, including George Akerloff, Kenneth Arrow, Robert Frank,

---

[20] Late in 1984, Hogarth and Reder had applied for financial support at Sloan through the new program. The proposal was declined by the advisory committee because it had already decided to sponsor a similar conference at Princeton University in late 1984.

[21] Wanner, interview, April 14, 2009.

David Grether, Robyn Hogarth, George Loewenstein, Mark Machina, James March, Richard Nelson, Charles Plott, Howard Raiffa, Robert Shiller, Vernon Smith, Lawrence Summers, and Sidney Winter. All forty researchers were told that "[t]he Sloan Foundation has decided to develop a limited funding program in behavioral economics in 1986. The purpose of this letter is to describe the program briefly and to invite you to consider making an application."[22]

Simon was, of course, also on the list of the now forty invited economists and psychologists. Although Simon had been quite supportive of the new program in his first response to Wanner a year earlier, he now offered some critical remarks on the approach taken. According to Simon, Wanner's new program took "too seriously the premises of contemporary economic methodology that theories ('models') come first and empirical work afterwards."[23] In addition, Simon noted that following his own work of the late 1950s a "considerable body of empirical work"[24] had already been built. The problem was not that the empirical work was not there, but that economists had not noticed it, as "mainline economists continue to ignore vast bodies of relevant evidence in their preferred pursuit of armchair model building."[25] Therefore, Simon considered "rather insulting"[26] the behavioral economics program's first objective to "develop economic models on the basis of behavioral principles and to show that such models represent a clear improvement over traditional models, either in terms of accuracy or empirical coverage."[27] That said, Simon was "greatly mollified" by the list of people invited, which he considered to be "just the right people" who would not "be put off by the things I object to in your letter."[28] Out of courtesy,

---

[22] Wanner's letter to forty invited researchers, December 18, 1985, Box 194, Folder 1430, Rockefeller Foundation Archives, Rockefeller Archive Center, Sleepy Hollow, New York. To give an impression of the projects funded, the 1986 round provided Akerlof with $30,000 for a project on "Near Rational Behavior and its Market Consequences"; Einhorn and Hogarth with $63,000 for research on "A New Model of Decision under Uncertainty," Smith and Isaac with $50,000 for an experiment on "Market Anomalies, Computerized Matching Markets, and Public Goods Provisions"; and Thaler with $27,000 for a project on "Continued Research on the Economic Consequences of Beliefs about Fairness."

[23] Simon's letter to Wanner, January 6, 1986, Box 194, Folder 1430, Rockefeller Foundation Archives, Rockefeller Archive Center, Sleepy Hollow, New York.

[24] Ibid.

[25] Ibid.

[26] Ibid.

[27] Wanner's letter to forty invited researchers, December 18, 1985, Box 194, Folder 1430, Rockefeller Foundation Archives, Rockefeller Archive Center, Sleepy Hollow, New York.

[28] Simon's letter to Wanner, January 6, 1986, Box 194, Folder 1430, Rockefeller Foundation Archives, Rockefeller Archive Center, Sleepy Hollow, New York.

Wanner and the advisory committee decided to invite Simon for discussion and dinner after one of the advisory committee meetings. Following this meeting, Simon continued to be a background consultant to the program.

During the same period, Wanner stepped up his efforts to encourage researchers to send in a proposal or to collaborate with one another. For instance, following a short but cordial note from Stanford psychologist, former collaborator of Simon, and Russell Sage Foundation trustee James March – one of the new names on the list of researchers invited – Wanner responded by suggesting March could put together a proposal with fellow Stanford researchers Arrow and Tversky who seemed "interested in making a proposal for support for graduate or post doctoral students."[29] Quickly thereafter, March became involved with the behavioral economics program in another way as well. After being promoted to the position of vice-president of the Sloan Foundation in the summer of 1985, Wanner was appointed as a trustee and president of the Russell Sage Foundation in the summer of 1986. He started officially on October 1, 1986. Wanner realized that this would probably mean that "this program will not be continued at Sloan after I leave"[30] and organized a meeting with March to discuss the possibility of "transplanting some version of it [the behavioral economics program] to Russell Sage."[31] March quickly responded that he "was delighted that you [Wanner] started it [the behavioral economics program] and would be equally delighted if we continued it at the Russell Sage."[32]

Thus, after some negotiation, Wanner could report to the advisory committee that "the [Russell Sage Foundation] Board approved the idea of a joint program with the Sloan Foundation."[33] At the same time, however, the board of trustees of Russell Sage strongly suggested that one of its members, March, could be on the advisory committee. Wanner and the advisory committee were in favor but also feared that this would tip the balance too much to psychology.[34] Thus, in a letter dated February 17,

---

[29] Wanner's letter to March, January 10, 1986, Box 208, Folder 1554, Rockefeller Foundation Archives, Rockefeller Archive Center, Sleepy Hollow, New York.

[30] Wanner's letter to March, July 22, 1986, Box 208, Folder 1554, Rockefeller Foundation Archives, Rockefeller Archive Center, Sleepy Hollow, New York.

[31] Ibid.

[32] March's letter to Wanner, July 29, 1986, Box 208, Folder 1554, Rockefeller Foundation Archives, Rockefeller Archive Center, Sleepy Hollow, New York. Another program Wanner was working on during his early years at the Russell Sage Foundation was the "Persistence of Poverty" program.

[33] Wanner's letter to the advisory committee, February 18, 1987, Box 194, Folder 1432, Rockefeller Foundation Archives, Rockefeller Archive Center, Sleepy Hollow, New York.

[34] In addition, Wanner, March, and the advisory committee members saw some potential juridical problems in this arrangement, but were also sure these could be worked out, which they were.

1987 Wanner and Rees (still president of the Sloan Foundation) invited March to join the advisory committee, which invitation March accepted, while at the same time Rees, as a labor economist, was asked by the advisory committee to join its ranks. As a result, the advisory committee now consisted of six members, three psychologists, and three economists. It was headed by the president of the Russell Sage Foundation and had on its advisory committee both the president of the Sloan Foundation and a trustee of the Russell Sage Foundation.

Having Rees on the advisory committee in particular seems to have helped to ensure at least another few years of Sloan support for the program – thus positively defying Wanner's earlier fears of the end of the behavioral economics program at the Sloan Foundation as expressed in his letter to March. With the two new members on the advisory committee, the behavioral economics program proceeded.[35] From the start, however, the behavioral economics program had a different status at Russell Sage as compared to Sloan, and not only because Wanner was the president of Russell Sage. At Sloan, the board of trustees simply took President Rees's word for the small behavioral economics program. Table 5.1 shows that the amount of grants awarded to the behavioral economics program never exceeded 2.7 percent of the total amount of grants issued. At Russell Sage, the behavioral economics program consumed a much larger portion of annual spending, up to nearly 50 percent in 1987.

However, despite Wanner's presidency at Russell Sage and the heavy advisory committee, the future of the behavioral economics program was by no means self-evident. To give the program more focus, and to encourage the participating researchers to provide more concrete results, Wanner suggested the advisory committee to set up a few working groups at Russell Sage "which focus on a particular topic."[36] Eventually, three nonresidential working groups emerged over the course of 1987 and 1988, which would come to define the core of behavioral economics research that ascended to prominence in the economic discipline in the 1990s and 2000s. The working group on "Intertemporal Choice" was led by Loewenstein and Jon Elster, and, among others, resulted in Loewenstein and Elster's *Choice over Time* (1992).

---

[35] On top of the twelve grants from the Sloan Foundation in 1986 already mentioned, the behavioral economics program issued its first support from the Russell Sage Foundation in 1986 in the form of a $200,000 grant to Kahneman and Tversky for a new book on "Decisions: Rationality and Illusion in Judgment and Choice." Writing the book proved difficult, however. Eventually, a new collection of Kahneman and Tversky's papers titled *Choices, Values, and Frames* was published in 2000.

[36] Wanner's letter to the advisory committee, October 16, 1986, Box 194, Folder 1431, Rockefeller Foundation Archives, Rockefeller Archive Center, Sleepy Hollow, New York.

The working group on "Behavioral Approaches to Financial Markets" was headed by Thaler and Robert Shiller, and provided input for Shiller's *Market Volatility* (1989) and *Irrational Exuberance* (2000). The proposed working group on experimental economics, however, proved more difficult to organize. Initially, the idea was to have Smith or Plott lead or colead a working group on experimental economics together with a behavioral psychologist such as Kahneman or one of his associates. That, however, did not work out because of the different theoretical interests. Smith and Plott wanted to concentrate on the question how the market over time steers individual behavior toward the rational equilibrium, and to focus on what the equilibrium exactly looks like. Wanner, Kahneman, Thaler, and the advisory committee, on the other hand, were more interested in how initial individual behavior deviates from the theoretically defined equilibrium, irrespective of whether an equilibrium exists or not. In addition, Wanner, Kahneman, and Thaler questioned how often economic markets are allowed the time to mature toward equilibrium.

An immediately related difference that everyone knew was there, but that everyone also tried to avoid discussing in the open, was the respective political views. Smith was an outspoken free-market advocate who drew his inspiration from, among others, Friedrich von Hayek. Kahneman, Thaler, and Wanner, on the other hand, are best described as moderate liberals who questioned the assumed superiority of the market. Both sides tried to find common ground, Smith in an effort to obtain research funds from the Sloan-Sage program and Kahneman, Thaler and Wanner in order to maintain the image of a broad apolitical and scientific program. However, both sides failed, nevertheless, in part due to the ideological differences. Thus, the plan was abandoned, and Colin Camerer was put in charge of the working group on experimental economics. The episode also reveals that the advisory committee and, in particular, Kahneman, Thaler, and Wanner were closely monitoring the content and development of the behavioral economics program. The focus and inclusion of disciplines in the "portfolio" of grants was carefully managed, and Wanner was constantly looking for new researchers who might submit a proposal that could fit the program.

During 1988 and 1989, the behavioral economics program continued along the lines developed in the years 1983 through 1987 and was supported by two foundations. In 1989, Festinger, Rees, and March stepped down as advisory committee members and were replaced by Kahneman. The advisory committee now consisted of economists Baumol and Schelling and psychologists Abelson and Kahneman. Also in 1989, a program of visiting scholars was initiated under the heading of the behavioral economics program at the Russell Sage Foundation, through which researchers were invited to spend up to a year at the Russell Sage Foundation's office in New York to collaborate on projects with other visiting scholars or to finish a book. From 1989 to 1991, the visiting scholars program was given increasing importance by Wanner and the advisory committee. In addition, a Russell Sage Foundation Behavioral Economics books series began in 1991. The first book to be published in this series was Thaler's (1991) *Quasi Rational Economics*. Eventually, eleven books were published, among which were also Loewenstein and Elster's (1992) *Choice over Time* and Thaler's (1993) *Advances in Behavioral Finance.*

Compared to the stepping down of Festinger and March, the retirement of Rees, because of age and deteriorating health, from the Sloan presidency and from the advisory committee had by far the most impact. As anticipated, it implied the end of the Sloan Foundation's support of the behavioral economics program. Thus, as of 1990, the behavioral economics program would continue as only a Russell Sage program. Early in 1992, the Russell Sage board of trustees told Wanner that it planned to end the behavioral economics program toward the end of the year and to seek other purposes for the roughly 30 percent of the annual budget that the program was consuming. Although Wanner judged this a fair point, he explored the possibility to save a part of the program in one way or another. In a first step, he asked all researchers who had received grants or other support under the behavioral economics program between 1984 and 1992 to briefly express to the board of trustees "whatever effect the program may have had on your own research"[37] and to "offer an appraisal of the current state of behavioral research in economics."[38] Second, Wanner asked the recipients to address "the general prospects for future work in behavioral economics."[39] The letter was sent to some ninety economists and psychologists. About a third of the recipients responded; among them, of course, were those researchers most closely involved, such as Thaler, Kahneman, Loewenstein, and Camerer. It will be no surprise that their responses were positive. Others, however, were less positive. For instance, in a long a letter to Wanner, Vernon Smith severely criticized both the organization of the behavioral economics program and the research on which it had focused.[40]

---

[37] Wanner's letter to recipients, April 30, 1992, Box 196, Folder 1442, Rockefeller Foundation Archives, Rockefeller Archive Center, Sleepy Hollow, New York.

[38] Ibid.

[39] Ibid.

[40] Smith's letter to Wanner, May 15, 1992, Box 196, Folder 1442, Rockefeller Foundation Archives, Rockefeller Archive Center, Sleepy Hollow, New York.

In the summer of 1992, the behavioral economics program officially closed and the advisory committee was disbanded. Put together, however, the letters of the recipients convinced the board of trustees to agree to one last form of financial support through what would be the organizational novelty of a "Behavioral Economics Roundtable," composed of former recipients of behavioral economics grants and endowed with $100,000 annually. To the Russell Sage Foundation, the main advantage of this organizational novelty was that Russell Sage staff no longer would be involved in behavioral economics and that neither an advisory committee would be required. The first ten members installed on the Behavioral Economic Roundtable were Akerlof, Blinder, Camerer, Elster, Kahneman, Loewenstein, Schelling, Shiller, Thaler, and Tversky. Since its creation in 1992, the Behavioral Economic Roundtable has been an effective promoter of behavioral economics through its biannual summer institute and its support of young researchers through a small-grants program. The Behavioral Economics Roundtable still exists at the time of writing.

5. Distinguishing Experimental Economics from Behavioral Economics, 1980s through the 2000s

The difference between Kahneman and Thaler's behavioral economics and Smith's experimental economics was that Kahneman and Tversky's behavioral economics investigated individual behavior and that Smith's experimental economics investigated markets. In addition, they represented opposite sides of the political spectrum. The growing number of behavioral economic publications in the 1980s and, more generally, the influence of Kahneman and Tversky's work pressed Smith to distinguish his experimental economics more clearly from these psychologists and their economic offspring. In 1989, ten years after the first Grether and Plott article, Smith asked,

How do we close the ... gap, between the psychology of choice and agents' economic behavior in experimental exchange markets? ... I think we economists need to accept these replicable empirical results [of behavioral decision research] as providing meaningful measures of *how people think about economic questions*. For their part, psychologists need to accept the dominating message in experimental research on the performance of a wide variety of bidding, auctioning and customer (posted price) markets: markets quite often "work" in the sense that over time they converge to the predictions of the economists' paradigm. (Smith, 1989, p. 165, emphasis in original)

The conclusions drawn from the experimental results of Grether and Plott (1979, 1982) have been held by Smith, Grether, Plott, and other experimental economists from the late 1970s until the present. Over the years, experimental economists have struggled with how to formulate their approach and how to distinguish their ideas from Thaler's behavioral economics. Part of the difficulty was (and still is) that experimental economists and Kahneman and Tversky's prospect theory are seemingly very close. Experimental economists agreed that the psychologists' experimental findings indeed disprove rational choice of individual decision behavior, which easily led to the conclusion that they also agreed with the theoretical implications that were drawn by behavioral decision researchers and behavioral economists.

Another difficulty was that experimental economists conducted the same kind of experiments as the behavioral decision researchers and behavioral economists, but with a different purpose. Behavioralists conducted experiments with individual human subjects to investigate the decision-making characteristics of the individual. Experimental economists conducted experiments with individual human subjects to investigate the market. The two sides conducted the same experiments, but with a different question in mind. Experimental economists were not interested in the particular individuals in experiments or in the individual or in his or her characteristics in general. They needed the individuals to experiment on a phenomenon that was altogether different from the individual subjects of the experiment. Like the biologist who investigates a virus through its effect on laboratory mice, so too do experimental economists investigate the market through its effect on individual behavior. Nevertheless, experimental economists were easily understood as investigating human behavior. Frequently found statements in experimental economics of the sort "[i]n laboratory market experiments, we test the theory's assumptions about agent behavior" (Smith, 1989, p. 154) could understandably be misunderstood as statements about the psychology of human beings. As a result of this subtle distinction, experimental economists felt pressed to differentiate themselves more clearly from Kahneman and Thaler's behavioral economics.

An important difference between experimental economics and behavioral economics was their use of time. In experimental economics, the market required time to drive the economy to equilibrium. Because of their use of time, experimental economists could maintain that individuals' behavior initially deviated from the norms of preference theory while at the same time maintaining that the emerging market equilibrium was in line with it. This was the main reason why Smith had difficulties explaining experimental economics' position to behavioral economists. *"People have their own homegrown beliefs about how markets work, or should work,"* Smith carefully explained, and *"questionnaire responses reflect these beliefs, which are often couched in terms of "fairness" criteria."* As a consequence, "[people's] *initial behavior in a market may reflect these beliefs.*" However, when these individuals operate in a market over time their behavior "*adapts to the incentive properties of markets*" (Smith, 1989, p. 166, emphasis in the original).

Smith (1989) went on to conclude that in economics there were "two experimental research programs," both of which, he added, required considerable development. First there was the "economist's maximizing paradigm," which "often performs well in predicting the equilibrium reached over time in experimental markets." However, the economist's maximizing paradigm "is not generally able to account for short run dynamic behavior, such as the contract price paths from initial states to final steady states" (p. 166). Second, there was "the psychologist's 'reference frame' descriptive paradigm" (p. 166). That is, Kahneman and Tversky's prospect theory and the behavioral economics that emerged from it. This "psychological" program did well "in explaining subjects' introspective responses, and their short-run or initial decision behavior, but it provides no predictive theory of reference frame adjustment over time" (p. 166). Smith was quick to point out that a well-known paper from the psychological program agreed with this analysis. "In fact, the statement (Kahneman, Knetsch and Thaler, 1986, p. 731) 'that they (people) adapt their views of fairness to the norms of actual behavior' can be interpreted as a description of what is observed in experimental markets" (p. 166).

Another way in which Smith tried to distinguish experimental economics more clearly from behavioral decision research and behavioral economics was by abandoning the label "experimental game" as a description of his experiments. In the 1950s, the 1960s, and the early 1970s, game theory, the application of rational choice theory to situations of human interaction, had been an important source of inspiration for Smith's experiments (Lee, 2004; Weintraub, 1992; Dimand, 2005). But classical game theory, as a description and explanation of the interaction of rationally acting self-interested individuals, started from a description of individuals as optimizers of utility.[41] The experimental results showed that this had been a wrong assumption. Therefore, game theory became inappropriate for experimental economists as a description of individual behavior. The fact that during the 1970s, Smith explicitly discarded his use of the term *experimental games* to describe his experiments has been declared an unsolved puzzle (Lee, 2004). But in the light of the corroborations produced by Grether and

---

[41] I focus here on the interpretation of game theory in the 1950 to early 1970s. Later users often changed the interpretation of game theory (Bowles, 2004; Gintis, 2000; Camerer, 2003).

Plott (1979, 1982), Smith's reasons can be illuminated. Game theory still described and explained the behavior of individuals in the eventual market equilibrium, but it could not explain individuals' behavior when they were first presented with an economic decision. It could neither explain the process of adjustment to equilibrium. As a result, the term *experimental game* became inappropriate as a description of experiments that investigated the adjustment behavior of the individual agents in a market setting. The experiments were still considered a game in the sense that they mimicked the crucial aspects of the market, but they were no longer a game in the sense of describing fully rational interacting individuals.

Pressed to distinguish experimental economics more clearly from behavioral economics, Smith was led to cooperate with psychologist Gerd Gigerenzer in the 2000s, a longtime critic of Kahneman and Tversky and an admirer of the work of Herbert Simon (e.g., Gigerenzer, 1996; Gigerenzer et al., 1999). For instance, in 2008, Smith published a monograph titled *Rationality in Economics, Constructivist and Ecological Forms* in which he drew an explicit link between his own and Gigerenzer's work. In the *Handbook of Experimental Economic Results, Volume 1* (2008), edited by Plott and Smith, Gigerenzer participated by making no fewer than six contributions, and the third volume in Gigerenzer's Adaptive Behavior and Cognition (ABC)'s research group on bounded rationality in its title emphasizes the link with Smith: *Ecological Rationality: Intelligence in the Real World* (2011).

6. Conclusion

In the early 1980s, behavioral decision research became relevant for, and was incorporated into, economics. However, it was incorporated in two very different ways. The first to pick up on behavioral decision research's experimental results were experimental economists such as Grether, Plott, and Smith. Grether and Plott (1979, 1982) corroborated the experimental findings of psychology and drew the conclusion that preference theory as a description of individual human behavior should be entirely abandoned. At the same time, experimental economists concluded that preference theory as a description of efficient markets in equilibrium could be maintained and that the experimental results only emphasized the rationalizing forces of the market. Furthermore, experimental economics did not accept behavioral decision research's alternative accounts and explicitly denounced the most visible theory among them, Kahneman and Tversky's prospect theory.

An unexpected result of experimental economists' corroboration of behavioral decision research's experimental results was that it paved the way for behavioral decision researchers to enter economics. Thaler and others understood the psychological findings to shed light on the irrationality of individual choices and drew a direct link from the irrationality of individual choices to irrational features of the behavior of (financial) markets. They immediately recognized Kahneman and Tversky's research, and especially Kahneman and Tversky (1979), as an important new and improved theory of individual decision behavior. The different responses of Smith's experimental economics and of Thaler's financial economics to the experimental results and to prospect theory's alternative can be explained in terms of the different notion of the market in experimental economics and financial economics. To Smith, the market was a rationalizing mechanism that requires time to drive the economy toward equilibrium. For financial economists such as Thaler, time was not an element of the market. Their different theoretical views regarding the economy, correlated with their opposing political views. Thaler was a liberal; Smith, a libertarian.

In other words, experimental economics and behavioral economics were both closely related and fundamentally different. They were closely related because they used the same set of psychological experiments to make an argument for changing the dominant neoclassical theory in economics. Furthermore, although asking different questions, they basically conducted the same experiments. They were, however, fundamentally different in the conclusions they inferred from the experimental results produced by the psychologists, in the way they wanted to extend the neoclassical theory, and in the way, they considered the neoclassical theory still valuable.

The primary contribution of the Sloan-Sage behavioral economics program, then, was to support and encourage one of the two economic responses to the psychology of Kahneman, Tversky, and others. With the retrospective wisdom of the scientific achievement of Kahneman, Thaler, and behavioral economics, it is tempting to conclude that behavioral economics would have developed anyway, with or without the support of the Sloan Foundation and the Russell Sage Foundation. But that would gloss over the efforts of Rees, Wanner, and the advisory committee to bring economists and psychologists together and to support the research that the more regular research funding institutes were unwilling to support. The careful balance between psychologists and economists Wanner maintained both in the advisory committee, in the list of researchers invited, and in the proposals granted ensured that neither one nor the other would feel dominated. Helped in part by his background in the interdisciplinary cognitive research at Harvard University in the 1960s and helped by his management of the Cognitive Science Series at Harvard University Press, Wanner created the conditions in which the interdisciplinary program of economists and psychologists could thrive.

After behavioral economics had been launched successfully as a visible new interdisciplinary program in the 1980s, behavioral economists began to define themselves more clearly in the 1990s, not only with respect to the neoclassical mainstream but also with regard to experimental economics and psychology. This is the topic of the final chapter.

Building and Defining Behavioral Economics

1. Introduction

A defining characteristic of Thaler's behavioral economics was that it adopted Kahneman and Tversky's understanding of normative and descriptive. In Kahneman and Tversky's framework, the normative constituted a number of rules for rational decision making, such as expected utility theory, logic, and Bayesian updating. As a result, it was ultimately the experts, that is, the scientists, who decided whether a particular decision was normatively correct or false. The descriptive part in Kahneman and Tversky's framework was the description of actual human decision making – which they found often deviated systematically and predictably from the normative benchmark. In addition, Thaler accepted Kahneman and Tversky's understanding of the positive realm of economics as covering both the normative and the descriptive domain. Thaler's introduction of Kahneman and Tversky's meaning of normative and positive could not but lead to confusion. Thaler equated Kahneman and Tversky's descriptive domain with economists' positive and used normative both in Kahneman and Tversky's meaning and in the economists' meaning (e.g., Friedman, 1953). Thaler (1980, p. 39) expressed it as follows:

Economists rarely draw the distinction between normative models of consumer choice and descriptive or positive models. Although the theory is normatively based (it describes what rational consumers *should* do), economists argue that it also serves well as a descriptive theory (it predicts what consumers in fact do). This paper argues that exclusive reliance on the normative theory leads economists to make systematic, predictable errors in describing or forecasting consumer choices. (emphasis in the original)

In line with Kahneman and Tversky, Thaler argued that further theoretical advancement of the normative theory was perfectly fine, but that because economists had ignored the fact that real-world behavior of individuals does not agree with this theory, they should also pay more attention to building a descriptive theory of economic behavior. Thus, Thaler not only accepted the empirical evidence presented by Kahneman and Tversky; he also accepted their accompanying methodological distinction. Essentially, Thaler accepted Kahneman and Tversky's attempt to re-create economics as a behavioral science. Prospect theory claimed that behavioral decision research and economics were part of the same program and that the approach of behavioral decision research was better than that of the economists. Therefore, the economists should adopt prospect theory and its methodological distinctions. Thaler accepted this reasoning entirely and provided Kahneman and Tversky's approach with more economic content.

The conceptual redefinition of economics that Thaler took over from Kahneman and Tversky determined the boundaries within which behavioral economics would develop in the 1990s and 2000s. The next section describes the most salient developments within behavioral economics of the 1990s and 2000s. More specifically, it discusses the development of behavioral economics by means of the research on intertemporal choice and the dual system approach, the endogeneity of preferences research, and the new welfare economics of libertarian paternalism. Section 3 then shows how this rapid growth of behavioral economics led behavioral economists to seek a closer affiliation with the economic mainstream and to seek a clearer distinction from experimental economics and psychology.

2. Defining and Distinguishing Behavioral Economics in the 1990s and 2000s

During the 1990s and 2000s Thaler, Kahneman, and other (former) participants of the Sloan-Sage program expanded behavioral economics from a small research program focused on violations of the neoclassical theory in financial economics, into a dominant new research program that looked for inspiration beyond behavioral decision research to a range of scientific disciplines and methods and that began to define behavioral economics more explicitly in opposition to neighboring fields such as experimental economics and psychology. These developments helped to expand behavioral economics into a broad and stable economic research program in which the influence of Kahneman and Tversky relatively declined. The two psychologists remained the iconic founding fathers, but the omnipresent influence they had achieved in Thaler's behavioral finance in the 1980s no longer existed. Kahneman and Tversky's normative-descriptive distinction remained the methodological basis of behavioral economics, but the labels were changed into full rationality versus less-than-fully, quasi, or, eventually, bounded rationality.

At the same time, however, behavioral economists remained faithful and always came back to the normative-descriptive framework originally introduced by Kahneman and Tversky. This conceptual core determined how behavioral economists understood the economic world, it determined the welfare implications they drew, and finally, it determined how they pulled back when their explorations diverged too far from this conceptual core. The new terminology of rationality lay the foundation for discussing behavioral economists' new paternalistic stance on economic policy advice that developed from the early 2000s.

Intertemporal Choice and the Dual System Approach

Behavioral economic research on intertemporal choice started in the early 1990s and culminated in the behavioral economic research based on the two-systems approach. The intertemporal choice and two-systems approach literature is illustrative for a number of reasons. It was chronologically one of the first major themes on which behavioral economists focused, and to this day, it continues to be an important topic in behavioral economics; witness, for instance, Kahneman's (2011) best-selling *Thinking Fast and Slow*. Second, it illustrates how behavioral economists incorporated Kahneman and Tversky's work. Finally, it shows how behavioral economists developed a theoretical framework that could be applied to any economic problem and was compatible with important developments in neuroscience and the cognitive sciences in general.

Two prominent behavioral economists who have worked on intertemporal choice have been George Loewenstein and David Laibson. Loewenstein completed his PhD at Yale University in 1985 and published his first article in 1987. From his first publication onward, he has been a strong proponent of more psychology in economics, but initially he was hardly influenced by the work of Kahneman and Tversky. Instead, an important theoretical influence came from the work of Jon Elster, with whom he wrote several articles and edited a book for the Russell Sage Foundation called *Choice over Time* (1992).[1] Loewenstein has published a number of articles on the history of psychological and economic explanations of intertemporal choice and utility, revealing an extensive knowledge of the history of economic thought (e.g., Loewenstein, 1992; Elster and Loewenstein, 1992; Frederick

---

[1] For a discussion on Elster's work on decision making, see, for example, Davis (2003).

et al., 2002; Angner and Loewenstein, 2012). Laibson completed his PhD at MIT in 1994 and started his academic career at Harvard University that same year. At MIT and Harvard, he has focused on violations of the traditional economic idea of exponential discounting. His articles are a mixture of experimentally corroborating this phenomenon, building mathematical economic models that account for the observed systematic deviations, and investigating the psychological and neurobiological substrates of the observed behavior.

For Loewenstein, the problem of the well-known exponential discounting utility (DU) model was not just that individuals discount hyperbolically; it also goes further. For instance, individuals can be shown to sometimes use a negative discount rate (Loewenstein and Prelec, 1991). If individuals prefer an increasing real-wage over a constant real-wage, even when the present value of the latter is higher than the former, they effectively employ a negative discount rate. Perhaps even more challenging for received economic theory was that individuals' intertemporal choices could be shown to be fundamentally inconsistent (e.g., Prelec and Loewenstein, 1997).[2] People who prefer *A now* over *B now* also prefer *A in one month* over *B in two months*. However, at the same time, they also prefer *B in one month and A in two months* over *A in one month and B in two months*. In other words, when faced with an intertemporal choice, individuals like to save the best for last, which is in fundamental disagreement with economic theory. Another well-known descriptive falsification of the DU model is the research on New York City cab drivers who judge their income "one day at a time" (Camerer, et al., 1997).

The DU model fails not only descriptively, but also normatively, Loewenstein argued. For instance, there does not seem to be a good reason to suppose that somebody who is indifferent toward oranges and apples today should also be indifferent toward (1) apples today, oranges tomorrow, and apples the day after and (2) apples three days in a row. Loewenstein argued that there is little normative and descriptive reason for holding on to the DU model, despite its aesthetic merits of mathematical simplicity and consistency. This conclusion produced a tension in Loewenstein's work. On one hand, he was an early recruit of Thaler and Kahneman's behavioral economics, and an important recipient of financial support through the Sloan-Sage program. But, on the other hand, he concluded that economic theory might also be problematic as a normative benchmark.

---

[2] Here, Loewenstein referred to Friedman and Savage (1948, 1952) who faced an analogous problem in explaining both gambling and insurance behavior.

Not surprisingly, then, Loewenstein was ambivalent about how to proceed. A number of publications show fundamental problems with the DU model both descriptively and normatively (e.g., Loewenstein, 1992, 1999a; Loewenstein and Prelec, 1991; Prelec and Loewenstein, 1997). But on other occasions, Loewenstein tried to extend the DU model as a descriptive theory while maintaining the normative benchmark. For instance, he built a mathematical model that could accommodate observed behavior and employed the normative benchmark as a limiting case (see, e.g., Loewenstein and Prelec, 1992). In this model, the discount factor was generalized to $1/(1 + at)$, where a can be exogenously given or determined by another function. Loewenstein also turned his attention to neuroscience as a possible means to a solution (see, e.g., McClure et al., 2004).

Loewenstein's explorations led him to doubt the normative-descriptive distinction of behavioral economics in the 1990s, but after a while, he pulled back from contesting the normative benchmark and made his work compatible with Kahneman and Tversky's approach. In the 2000s, Loewenstein acknowledged that his work had been stimulated "by the existence of a strong normative benchmark, expected utility theory" that behavioral theory in economics and psychology had advanced (Loewenstein et al., 2001, p. 367). Moreover, he added that in this area the "convergence in the theoretical perspectives of psychologists and economists . . . has been greater than for any other topic of mutual interest in the two disciplines (Loewenstein et al., 2001, p. 367).

A similar tension can be observed in the work of Laibson. In Laibson (1997), "Golden Eggs and Hyperbolic Discounting," he built a mathematical model of agents with hyperbolic discount functions that could explain a myriad of dynamically inconsistent individual preferences observed in experiments. "Golden Eggs" referred to the traditional rational economic individual decision model. In Laibson's model, the individual was faced with an "imperfect commitment technology," such as a retirement plan, which required that it be initiated one period before it started to work. Together with the hyperbolic discount function, this model "predicted" that individuals' consumption would closely track the progress of their income, but that with the "imperfect commitment technology" individuals were capable of correcting their hyperbolic discount functions by committing themselves in advance to their desired savings behavior. Because the imperfect commitment technology required individuals to commit themselves in advance, the far-sighted, rational planner effectively constrained the temptation to be immediately gratified once the money actually arrived.

Ipso facto, the model predicted that with "financial innovation" savings rates would go down because commitment technology no longer needed to be started up a period in advance. According to Laibson, this provided an explanation for the ongoing decline in U.S. saving rates. "Financial innovation" should be interpreted broadly here. It not only comprised new saving plans at banks, but also changes in "social commitment devices" such as marriage, work, and friendship. They allowed individuals' short-term hyperbolic discount functions to override their long-term rational discount functions. Under certain conditions, from a rational, long-term perspective, the result may be a reduction in welfare.

Laibson's "Golden Eggs" article is a typical 1990s contribution to behavioral economics. It made productive use of Kahneman and Tversky's distinction between the normative and the descriptive by reinterpreting this in terms of a "far-sighted" and a "myopic" planner. Laibson also added something to this framework, namely, the idea that in the economy, individuals might have the possibility of controlling their deviating behavior by means of commitment technologies. This idea of commitment technologies extended the Kahneman and Tversky framework. It suggested that individuals might be both deviating from the normative benchmark while at the same time helping to explain how they deviate from the norm. Further, it suggested that it is not so much the scientists that need to find ways to correct individuals' deviating behavior, but the individuals themselves.

In addition, whereas in the 1980s Thaler would have used accessible language and would have referred to psychology to explain and solve the problem, Laibson presented the problem in a formalistic economic jargon and did not reference psychology. Another example is Harris and Laibson (2001), "Dynamic Choices of Hyperbolic Consumers," which further elaborated on the idea of hyperbolic discounting. It tried to link the short-term hyperbolic discounting with the long-term (rational) exponential discounting and showed how individuals act who try to prevent their own future overconsumption. The paper started with the traditional discounting function for individuals, and replaced the constant discount factor δ with an "effective discount factor." This effective discount factor consisted of the sum of two components, the "long-run discount factor δ" and the "short-run discount factor $\beta\delta$," where hyperbolic discounting implied $\beta < 1$. The traditional discount factor was hence explicitly decomposed into a long-run, exponential component and a short-run, hyperbolic component. The assumption was that individuals, faced with "stochastic income" and a "borrowing constraint," anticipate their future inclination to hyperbolically discount (and thus to overconsume) and that they want to act against it. Hyperbolic discounting was thus explained as resulting from a strategic game with future selves:

> Since $\beta < 1$, the effective discount factor is negatively related to the future marginal propensity to consume (MPC). To gain intuition for this effect, consider a consumer at time 0 who is thinking about saving a marginal dollar for the future. We assume that this consumer acts strategically in an *intra*personal game where the players are temporally situated "selves." The consumer at time zero – "self 0" – expects future selves to overconsume relative to the consumption rate that self 0 prefers those future selves to implement. Hence, on the equilibrium path, self 0 values marginal saving more than marginal consumption at any future time period. From self 0's perspective therefore, it matters how a marginal unit of wealth at time period 1 will be divided between savings and consumption by self 1. Self 1's MPC determines this division. Since self 0 values marginal saving more than marginal consumption at time period 1, self 0 values the future less the higher the expected MPC at time period 1. (Harris and Laibson, 2001, p. 936, emphasis in the original)

In other words, because individuals knew they would discount hyperbolically in the future, they would also discount hyperbolically now. At the same time, Harris and Laibson (2001) demonstrate how Laibson retreated from the idea that individuals can influence their own behavior through commitment, and returned to the core of behavioral economics as provided by Kahneman, Tversky, and Thaler. The behavior displayed was merely the result of conflicting selves, none of whom could be controlled by the other.

Thus, the behavioral economists' way of dealing with intertemporal choice began to describe human behavior as the outcome of two systems or processes striving for dominance. Different labels appeared in the behavioral economic literature for these two systems: reasoning versus intuition (e.g., Kahneman, 2003, 2011), rationality versus emotion (e.g., Shefrin and Thaler, 1988; van Winden, 2007; Ben-Shakar et al., 2007), and cognitive versus affective (e.g., Camerer et al., 2005) were the most prominent. To be sure, understanding human behavior as the outcome of a conflict between different motives has a long and rich history, going back to the philosophy of Plato and Aristotle and to Homer's Ulysses tying himself to the mast so he could hear the Sirens sing (Davis, 2003, pp. 63–80). Behavioral economists' re-creation of neoclassical economics' understanding of individual behavior in terms of two souls inhabiting one body was therefore a recent development in a long history.

Some behavioral economists linked this dual-system solution to research in neuroscience and neurobiology, thus contributing to the creation of a new subfield called neuroeconomics.[3] This literature maintained the normative-descriptive distinction, but nevertheless, it slightly reinterpreted the distinction by supposing that the two sides of the distinction represent two sides of human behavior. In other words, the normative was reduced from something external to the individual to one of two faculties innate to human nature that strive for dominance. An illustrative example is McClure, Laibson, Loewenstein, and Cohen's (2004), "Separate Neural Systems Value Immediate and Delayed Monetary Rewards." The research described in the article sought and found evidence for neurobiological substrates for the two components of the effective discount factor as described earlier. When faced with delayed monetary rewards while lying in an magnetic resonance imaging scanner, subjects' brains showed peaks of activity in the parts of the brain associated with rational behavior (the lateral prefrontal cortex and the posterior parietal cortex); when faced with immediate rewards, the limbic system associated with the midbrain dopamine center was especially active.

The authors took their findings as evidence for the postulated difference between the short-term hyperbolic discounting, and the long-term rational exponential discounting. The normative long-run rational system strives for dominance with the short-term affective system. When the short-run system is affecting the outcome, the resulting behavior will be observed and classified as systematically deviating from the norm. As such, the neuroeconomic research conducted by behavioral economists at once maintained the link with the normative-descriptive core of Kahneman and Tversky's work while at the same time constructing a link with neuroscience.

Based on this and other research, in the 2000s, behavioral economists increasingly argued that the neuroscientific framework should be adopted as a basis for investigating individual (economic) behavior. The recurring argument in the neuroeconomic research was that in economic decision making, the individual's rational system tries to make the rational decision but, alas, is often overridden by a strong and dominant affective system. Intertemporal choice provided a good example. When people need to plan how to divide their income between consumption and spending at some point in the future, their affective system is not very much involved, and the rational system will decide on a rational division between the two. However, when the future becomes the present, the affective system kicks in, seeking immediate gratification and thereby seeking to override

---

[3] In the 1990s and 2000s, the label neuroeconomics was used by at least two groups of scientists (see, e.g., Vromen, 2007; Ross, 2008).

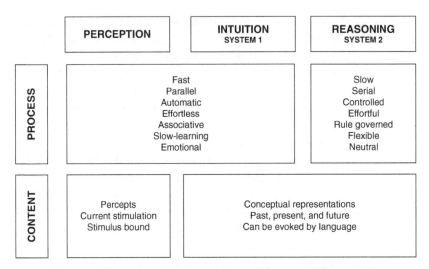

Figure 6.1. Three Cognitive System. *Source:* Kahneman (2003, p. 1451).

the rational system. In other words, the systematic deviations from rational decision making were understood as having resulted from a failed attempt by the individual's rational system to control its affective system. Within this general neuroeconomic approach behavioral economists proposed different frameworks for the two systems. Let me give two prominent examples.

In the paper that derived from his Nobel lecture (Kahneman, 2003; see also Kahneman, 2011), Kahneman argued for and employed the framework as depicted in Figure 6.1. Kahneman's framework is an intriguing mix of psychophysics, neuroscience, and the desire to accommodate a distinction between two decision-making processes. On the bottom row, we see a distinction between two kinds of input for decision making: current external stimulation and information already present in the mind. These two sources of information form the input for two cognitive systems as described in the middle row: an intuitive system (also more neutrally labeled system 1), and a reasoning system (more neutrally called system 2). The distinction between the two systems is mainly made in terms of the effort it costs to operate them. The reasoning system requires much effort and is relatively slow. The intuitive system operates much more quickly and is relatively effortless. Another distinction between the two is that between nonvoluntary impressions in system 1 and voluntary judgments in system 2. The top row further distinguishes between perception and the intuitive information processing of system 1. The distinction between the two information

	Cognitive	Affective
Controlled Processes ▪ serial ▪ effortful ▪ evoked deliberately ▪ good introspective access	I	II
Automatic Processes ▪ parallel ▪ effortless ▪ reflexive ▪ no introspective access	III	IV

Figure 6.2. Two Dimensions of Neural Functioning. *Source*: Camerer et al. (2005, p. 16).

processing systems and perception is made in terms of automaticity and accessibility. On the left, we find decision making that is fully automatic and inaccessible. One example is the perception/decision regarding which of two rooms has a higher temperature, a perception/decision that is made automatically and without the individual having access to its process. At the other end of the spectrum, we find decisions that are not made automatically and to which a large degree of accessibility is possible. An example is the decision regarding which of two houses is preferred and hence will be bought. The intuitive system is the middle ground between these two and reflects decision making that often proceeds automatically, but that can also be accessed and altered, such as the decision between €3,000 for certain and a 0.8 chance at €4,000. Using this framework, Kahneman thus brought together the automatic perceptual system investigated by psychophysics and behavioral economics' use of neuroscience, while at the same time allowing for the possibility of deviations from rational economic decision making.

Another prominent framework, extensively discussed in what may safely be considered as one of the canonical articles in neuroeconomics of the 2000s, Camerer, Loewenstein, and Prelec (2005), "Neuroeconomics: How Neuroscience Can Inform Economics" is Figure 6.2. In this representation, the two systems are either controlled or automatic. Examples of automatic, cognitive processes, quadrant III, are judgments of relative temperature and shapes of objects. The automatic affective system, quadrant IV, depicts the pleasure and pain system that, based on the information provided by quadrant III and based on information of past experiences, attaches a value to the object. Quadrants I and II constitute the cognitive and affective part of the decision making process that can be controlled. A decision maker may very much like to buy a car, but in quadrant I, reason determines that he or she cannot afford it. The individual may not be hungry at all, whereas in quadrant II, not wanting to disappoint his or her friend's cooking efforts, taking a bite nevertheless. Thus, in behavioral economics and its neuroeconomics research, descriptive real-world decision making should be seen as a struggle between a cognitive system that seeks a rational solution and an affective system that disregards the optimal decision in favor of immediate gratification.[4]

Are Preferences Innate to Human Nature or Do They Emerge through Interaction with the Environment?

The incorporation of the distinction made between the rational norm and its imperfect realization in the economic agent considerably broadened the scope of behavioral economics. However, there seemed to be limits to broadening the scope as well. This can be illustrated by behavioral economists' cooperation with anthropologists on the subject of the emergence of preference. This brief collaboration shows how behavioral economists, after an initial enthusiasm, retreated when it turned out that this collaboration resulted in research that was at odds with the fundamental behavioral economic assumption of a fixed, universal benchmark of full rationality. As in the case of intertemporal choice, behavioral economists were unwilling to give up this benchmark of full rationality. The research was a large-scale interdisciplinary study of the ultimatum game in fifteen small-scale societies. It was published in a number of journals. The most extensive discussion can be found in the book devoted to it: Joseph Henrich, Robert Boyd, Samuel Bowles, Colin Camerer, Ernst Fehr, and Herbert Gintis's *Foundations of Human Sociality* (2004). A reflection on the research summarized by Henrich can be found in Gigerenzer and Selten (2001).[5]

The motivation for this large interdisciplinary study was that the ultimatum game had been played all over the world and had always led to the result that individuals do not play the rational optimum but instead

---

[4] In that respect, the dual system approach of behavioral economics in the 1990s and 2000s was different from the approach taken by many other neuroscientists and social scientists, who did not see the cognitive system as superior to the intuitive, emotional, or affective system. Examples of the latter include the work of Damasio (e.g. Damasio, 2003), research descending from Simon (e.g., Gigerenzer et al., 1999, Gigerenzer and Selten, 2001), and evolutionary theory inspired science (e.g., Barkow et al., 1992).

[5] The research was funded through the MacArthur Foundation's research network The Nature and Origin of Preference. The network, "headed by Robert Boyd and Herbert Gintis received two grants: $2.55 million in 1997 and $1.8 million in 2002" (Stephen Richards, e-mail to author, December 4, 2008).

typically divide the money about in half.[6] However, the experiments had only been done with university students in advanced capitalist economies. The question was thus whether the results would hold up when tested in other environments.

The surprising result was not so much that the average proposed and accepted divisions in the small-scale societies differed from those of university students, but in how they differed. Roughly, the average proposed and accepted divisions went from 80 percent/20 percent to 40 percent/60 percent. Individuals in different societies thus showed a remarkable difference in the division they proposed and accepted. Henrich and his fellow researchers correlated these differences with two economic characteristics of small-scale societies. First, they documented how much a group's (normally the family) economic welfare depended on cooperation with other groups within a small-scale society. In this respect, the societies differed greatly from almost none to almost completely. Second, the researchers investigated how much the group's economic welfare depended on market exchange. There was also a divergence in the level of market integration. The researchers concluded that differences found in the behavior of individuals belonging to the various societies in the game should be attributed to differences in the environment in which they lived. As a consequence, preferences were not exogenous, but were determined by the environment. Henrich and his collaborators stated this explicitly in a brief summary of their research in the *The American Economic Review*:

preferences over economic choices are not exogenous as the canonical model would have it, but rather are shaped by the economic and social interactions of everyday life. This result implies that judgments in welfare economics that assume exogenous preferences are questionable, as are predictions of the effects of changing economic policies and institutions that fail to take account of behavioral change. (Henrich et al., 2001, p. 77)

Giving up the exogeneity of preferences would have far-reaching implications. It would mean that behavioral economists had to give up a fundamental tenet of economics, namely, that preferences are given. In turn, that would have far-reaching consequences for the theory of decision making itself. It would draw behavioral economists closer to cultural anthropologists, such as Boyd and Henrich, who conceived of culture in evolutionary

---

[6] The ultimatum game is the following: Player 1 proposes a division of a fixed sum of money, which player 2 either accepts (the money is divided according to the proposed division) or rejects (both players receive nothing). If both players are rational, player 1 proposes to player 2 the smallest amount possible and player 2 accepts.

or ecological terms. Taking this approach and the results of the experiments seriously would imply not only that to a large extent, individual preferences are determined by the environment and by learning, but it would also undermine the notion of fixed norms in behavioral decision research and well-defined rationality in economics. It is probably due to these extensive implications that behavioral economists involved in the project, such as Colin Camerer and Ernst Fehr, substantially reduced their involvement with the network.

Understanding Behavioral Economics in Terms of Rationality

When behavioral economics expanded, behavioral economists were both faithful to the Kahneman and Tversky legacy while at the same time they sought to broaden its scope. Problematic in this regard were the labels of normative and descriptive, which were considered confusing in an economic context that already had created its own understanding of these concepts (e.g., Friedman, 1953). As a consequence, behavioral economists in the 1990s and 2000s reinterpreted the normative-descriptive distinction in terms of rationality. Thaler was well aware of the fact that the reinterpretation of economics in terms of normative versus descriptive raised the question concerning the definition of the descriptive theory when the normative theory is about rational behavior. However, Thaler was not very specific, or at least he did not offer a conclusive answer. Thaler referred to behavior that deviates from the normative solution on a number of occasions as "irrational" or "nonrational." Furthermore, he noted that he "would not want to call such choices rational" (Thaler, 2000, p. 138). On other occasions, Thaler referred to the normative-descriptive distinction as rational versus emotional (see, e.g., Shefrin and Thaler, 1988, p. 611).

But the main interpretation Thaler used in the 1980s and 1990s was the term *quasi rationality*, most prominently as the title of a collection of articles, *Quasi Rational Economics* (1991). Quasi rationality suggests a category of behavior somewhere between the full rationality of the normative decision and irrational behavior. Regularly used in the 1980s and 1990s quasi rationality is perhaps best understood as the failed attempt of people to be rational, which is exemplified by the one suggested definition of the term that Thaler provided: "quasi rational, meaning trying hard but subject to systematic error" (Thaler, 2000, p. 136). On another occasion, it was characterized as "less than fully rational" (Thaler, 1991, p. xviii).

From the early 2000s onward, the term increasingly favored by behavioral economists was *bounded rationality*. The distinction that was made was that between the fully rational decision and the decision actually made that was deemed boundedly rational when deviating from the rational decision. Full rationality in behavioral economics was defined as follows:

The standard approach in economics assumes "full rationality." While disagreement exists as to what exactly full rationality encompasses, most economists would agree on the following basic components. First people have well-defined preferences (or goals) and make decisions to maximize those preferences. Second, those preferences accurately reflect (to the best of the person's knowledge) the true costs and benefits of the available options. Third, in situations that involve uncertainty, people have well-formed beliefs about how uncertainty will resolve itself, and when new information becomes available, they update their beliefs using Bayes's law – the presumed ability to update probabilistic assessments in light of new information. (Camerer et al., 2003, pp. 1214–1215)

Using the distinction between full and bounded rationality naturally entailed making references to the work of Herbert Simon. In one clear sweep, Kahneman and Tversky's distinction between the concepts of normative-descriptive were replaced by concepts more appropriate in an economic context, and at the same time, Simon was reappropriated as an authoritative source for the use of these concepts. As with the Sloan-Sage program of the 1980s and early 1990s, Simon's research provided behavioral economics with the fitting language and offered it the necessary authority. This is further exemplified by Kahneman in the *American Economic Review* article based on his Nobel lecture titled "Maps of Bounded Rationality: Psychology for Behavioral Economics" (2003). In the opening passage, Kahneman used the term *bounded rationality* and referred to Simon but, at the same time, subtly but clearly distinguished his and Tversky's work from Simon's:

The work cited by the Nobel committee was done jointly with Amos Tversky (1937–1996) during a long and unusually close collaboration. Together, we explored the psychology of intuitive beliefs and choices and examined their bounded rationality. Herbert A. Simon (1955, 1979) had proposed much earlier that decision makers should be viewed as boundedly rational, and had offered a model in which utility maximization was replaced by satisficing. Our research attempted to obtain a map of bounded rationality, by exploring the systematic biases that separate the beliefs that people have and the choices they make from the optimal beliefs and choices assumed in rational-agent models. (Kahneman, 2003, p. 1449)

In a clever way, Kahneman invoked Simon to construct authority for the behavioral economic program, while at the same time interpreting the concept of bounded rationality in such a way that it would become fully compatible with his and Tversky's approach and that of the behavioral economists.

Welfare Economics as a Form of Paternalism

The re-interpretation of Kahneman and Tversky's distinction between the normative and the descriptive in terms of a conflict within the economic decision maker had important consequences for welfare economics. Following Friedman (1953), and many others, most mainstream economists in the 1990s and 2000s associated welfare economics in one way or another with the term *normative* (see also Chapters 2 and 5). That was one reason why Kahneman and Tversky's labels of normative and descriptive invoked confusion when inserted into the economics discourse. The reinterpretation of normative versus descriptive in terms of full rationality versus bounded rationality solved this confusion and in turn allowed behavioral economists to develop their own position on welfare economics.

For instance, behavioral economics had discovered that people often save much less for their pensions than they should and that when they do save, they do not diversify their portfolios optimally. Following on these results, programs were set up to investigate how people can be induced to save more for retirement and to better diversify their stock portfolios (e.g., Cronqvist and Thaler, 2004; Thaler and Benartzi, 2004). Another example concerns the use of medication. It had often been found that people who need to take drugs on a regular basis are very lax at doing so. Even when the risks are substantial and potential costs in terms of health very great, such as in the case of medication that reduces the chance of having a second stroke, people are very lax at taking their medication properly. To solve this problem, programs were set up that investigate how insights from behavioral economics can be used to design incentive mechanisms that induce people to take their medication (e.g., Badger et al., 2007). Finally, behavioral economists have turned their attention to development economics, with the purpose of using insights from behavioral economics to improve the functioning of development programs (see, e.g., Mullainathan, 2007; and Betrand et al., forthcoming).

Well known is Thaler and Sunstein's (2003) "Libertarian Paternalism," later popularized in Thaler and Sunstein's (2008) *Nudge*. Libertarian paternalism can be understood as a paternalism that does not restrict individual freedom of choice. Thaler and Sunstein distinguished themselves explicitly from Paul Samuelson's revealed preference stance toward welfare issues:

We clearly do not always equate revealed preference with welfare. That is, we emphasize the possibility that in some cases individuals make inferior choices, choices that they would change if they had complete information, unlimited cognitive abilities, and no lack of willpower. (Thaler and Sunstein, 2003, p. 175)

In other words, the justification for paternalistic policies was the fact that decisions people actually make, their "revealed preferences," do not always match with their "true" preferences. Behavioral economists thus constructed a distinction between "revealed" and "true" preferences. This did not mean that preferences were considered context dependent. Rather, it meant that it depended on the context, whether the true preferences can and will be revealed appropriately. A source that was sometimes relied on in this regard was John C. Harsanyi who had argued that "in deciding what is good and what is bad for an individual, the ultimate criterion can only be his own wants and his own preferences," where the individual's "own preferences" were his "true" preferences: "the preferences he would have if he had all the relevant factual information, always reasoned with the greatest possible care, and was in a state of mind most conducive to rational choice" (quoted in Angner and Loewenstein, 2012, p. 679).

A more detailed and elaborate explication and defense of this new branch of behavioral economics can be found in Camerer et al. (2003) "Regulation for Conservatives: Behavioral Economics and the Case for 'Asymmetric Paternalism.'" In this article, the five authors (Camerer, Issacharoff, Loewenstein, O'Donoghue, and Rabin) made a case for what they labeled "asymmetric paternalism," where "[a] regulation is asymmetrically paternalistic if it creates large benefits for those who make errors, while imposing little or no harm on those who are fully rational" (Camerer et al., 2003, p. 1212). Behavioral economics, then, "describes ways people sometimes fail to behave in their own best interests" (Camerer et al., 2003, p. 1217). These "apparent violations of rationality . . . can justify the need for paternalistic policies to help people make better decisions and come closer to behaving in their own best interests" (Camerer et al., 2003, p. 1218).

Thaler and Sunstein (2003) countered possible aversions to paternalism by economists and others by linking paternalism to libertarianism. Camerer et al. (2003), on the other hand, founded their defense of paternalistic policies on the need for asymmetry in the paternalistic policy. The definition of asymmetric paternalism resembled the Paretean improvement argument: "a policy is *asymmetrically paternalistic* if it creates large benefits for those people who are boundedly rational . . . while imposing little or no harm on those who are fully rational (Camerer et al., 2003, p. 1219, emphasis in the original). Or, in other words, "asymmetric paternalism helps those whose rationality is bounded from making a costly mistake and harms more rational folks very little" (Camerer et al., 2003, p. 1254). Another way of putting it, Camerer et al. (2003) argued, is to see the limitedly rational individual as imposing negative externalities on his or her own demand curve.

"When consumers make errors, it is as if they are imposing externalities on themselves because the decisions they make as reflected by their demand do not accurately reflect the benefits they derive" (Camerer et al., 2003, p. 1221). Hence, there was a need for a policy maker who could remove the externalities and redirect behavior in such a way that the externalities disappeared. Furthermore, Camerer et al. (2003) noted that firms could either consciously or unconsciously use the irrationality of individuals to gain more profit.

Based on these results, behavioral economists argued that economists are morally obliged to act against the violations of full rationality:

> As economists, how should we respond to the seemingly self-destructive side of human behavior? We can deny it, and assume as an axiom of faith that people can be relied upon to do what's best for themselves. We can assume that families paying an average of $1,000 per year financing credit card debt are making a rational tradeoff of present and future utility, that liquidity constraints prevent investing in employer-matched 401k plans, that employees prefer investing in their own company's stock instead of a diversified portfolio... that people are obese because they have calculated that the pleasures from the extra food, or the pain of the foregone exercise, is sufficient to compensate for the negative consequences of obesity. (Loewenstein and Haisley, 2008, p. 213)

According to behavioral economists, economics was particularly suited for solving the violations of full rationality because it possessed the knowledge of how to "steer human behavior in more beneficial directions while minimizing coercion, maximizing individual autonomy, and maximizing autonomy to the greatest extent possible" (Loewenstein and Haisley, 2008, p. 215). In this regard, the role of the economist could be seen as analogous to the psychoanalytical therapist. "Just as the therapist endeavors to correct for cognitive and emotional disturbances that detract from the well-being of the patient, such as anxiety, depression, or psychosis, the economist/therapist endeavors to counteract cognitive and emotional barriers to the pursuit of genuine self-interest" (Loewenstein and Haisley, 2008, p. 216). In other words, the role of the (behavioral) economist thus advanced was quite similar to the role of (behavioral) psychology newly constructed during the Second World War, as discussed in Chapter 3.

Behavioral economists attempted to solve humankind's limited rationality problem by using phenomena similar to those that formed the basis for behavioral economics to begin with. The most important phenomenon in this regard was what was most commonly known in behavioral economics as framing. One of the central findings of Kahneman and Tversky's behavioral decision research and behavioral economics was that people are susceptible to the way in which a choice is presented to them. Depending on the "reference point," in Kahneman and Tversky's terms, or "frame," the term Thaler favored for behavioral economics, people change their preferences. The example taken from Thaler and Sunstein (2003) is of the cafeteria manager who can either place the desserts before the fruits or vice versa. If he or she frames this decision as fruits before desserts, the fruit will be chosen more often. Thus, framing is used to influence people's behavior without affecting their freedom to choose in any significant way. Changing the default option from not participating to participating in pension saving schemes is another often-quoted example.

By exploring how policies can be designed to solve the bounded rationality of individuals, behavioral economists took the full-rationality versus bounded rationality framework and the experimental results of psychologists and economists to their ultimate consequences. Behavioral economic paternalism was very much an economics solution to bounded rationality, emphasizing incentive mechanisms and monetary rewards. And despite the link it drew with libertarianism, it was, of course, very much a liberal program of helping the (cognitively) poor, and hence in a different corner of the political spectrum than Vernon Smith's libertarian advocacy of the free market.

3. Distinguishing Behavioral Economics from Experimental Economics

During the 1990s and 2000s, behavioral economists in addition came to define themselves across disciplinary lines. In particular, they gradually began to distinguish behavioral economics from the discipline of psychology and from the subdiscipline of experimental economics. In the case of psychology, the reason was that behavioral economists wanted to be accepted by the economic mainstream. To achieve this, they had to comply with the mainstream economic view that economics and psychology are separate disciplines and that economics is superior to psychology when it comes to rigor and formal modeling. Some aspects regarding the attempts made by behavioral economists to distinguish themselves from psychology have been hinted at earlier in the discussion concerning Laibson's way of incorporating psychological insights. More specifically, behavioral economists employed the following arguments to distinguish behavioral economics from the discipline of psychology.

First, behavioral economics was defined as economics based on its use of mathematical modeling. This argument remained largely implicit, as in the case of Laibson, but it was nevertheless clear that behavioral economists considered their use of mathematics superior to that of the psychologists and saw it as a defining characteristic of economics. Another illustrative example in this regard is the work of Matthew Rabin (e.g., Rabin, 1993, 1994, 1998). Rabin incorporated experimental results from psychology into economics, but combined this with advanced economic mathematical modeling. He argued that "none of the broad-stroke arguments for inattention to psychological research are compelling," but at the same time cautioned that "not all psychological research will be . . . proven to be of great economic importance." The reason was that because they come from psychology, these psychological results had not yet been subjected to "the same rigorous standards that our discipline, at its best, applies elsewhere" (Rabin, 1998, p. 41). That is, ultimately it required the mathematics of economics to judge how useful the insights from psychology were. This use of mathematics was something that defined behavioral economics as economics and therefore as different from psychology.

Second, behavioral economists distinguished themselves from psychology based on their use of the experimental method. For instance, in a methodological comment on sharing data or experiment instructions with other researchers, Camerer noted that "[i]f you asked a psychologist for data or instructions he or she might be insulted, because the convention in that field is to give the writer the benefit of the doubt" (Camerer, 2003, pp. 34–35).[7] Another example concerned the use of deception. A common experimental procedure in psychology was (and is) to tell the experimental subjects the experiment is about one thing when it is, in fact, about something else. Behavioral economists and experimental economists had resisted this method of deception ever since experiments had been used in economics. For instance, the reason that Grether and Plott (1979) in their replication of experiments reported in Slovic and Lichtenstein (1971) controlled for the fact that the experimenters had been psychologists was that they suspected that because the subjects knew they might be misled in a psychological experiment they would behave differently. In the 2000s, the explicit denouncement by economists of the method of deception led to extensive discussion between economists and psychologists (e.g., Hertwig and Ortmann, 2008; Ortmann and Hertwig, 2002; Jamisona et al., 2008).

The motivation for explicitly drawing a border between behavioral and experimental economics was different. Both research programs were part

---

[7] In this regard, it is interesting that Camerer holds a PhD (defended in 1981) in behavioral decision research, not in economics. His supervisor at the University of Chicago was Robyn Hogarth.

of the same economic science, and to define behavioral economics as economics, it was not necessary to distinguish between behavioral and experimental economics. However, following, for instance, the discussion between Kahneman, Thaler, Wanner, and Smith in the Sloan-Sage program surrounding the creation of an experimental economics working group (Chapter 5), it seems behavioral economists had become acutely aware of the theoretical and ideological differences between their own program and that of Smith and his associates. Thus, the two had to be distinguished, but preferably without suggesting in print that economic theory was influenced by political ideology and without emphasizing possibly conflicting theoretical views. Thus, the distinction was drawn in terms of methodology.

The different views of experimental economics by behavioral economists were grouped together in Loewenstein (1999b) "Experimental Economics from the Vantage-Point of Behavioural Economics." Loewenstein (1999b) positioned behavioral economics explicitly in opposition to experimental economics, and formulated his critique in terms of the "psychological distinction" of external versus internal validity. Under the heading of external validity, Loewenstein saw four problems with experimental economics. First, experimental economics put great emphasis on the use of auctions in its experiments. As people in reality hardly ever found themselves in an auction situation, it was doubtful that these experiments could tell us very much about economic behavior in the real world. Second, Loewenstein disagreed with experimental economists' use of repetition in what has been called the Groundhog Day argument. In reality, Loewenstein argued, people never make the exact same decision forty times in a row. Real-world behavior is much more like the first few rounds of an experiment than the last two or three rounds. Third, Loewenstein criticized experimental economists for their tendency to reduce real-world content to the absolute minimum possible. Apart from the fact that a context-free experiment is an illusion, Loewenstein argued that it also greatly reduced the external validity of the experiments.[8] Instead, economists should, just as Loewenstein himself, make the experimental situation as congruent with reality as possible; hence make the experiment "context rich." Fourth, according to Loewenstein experimental economists wrongly assumed that monetary rewards result in strict control over incentives. It had been shown in numerous experiments that this is not the case, said Loewenstein. Even with monetary incentives, subjects were likely to be also driven by other motives besides profit maximization. Finally, one problem concerning internal validity that

[8] Loewenstein both used "context" and "content."

Loewenstein observed was that experimental economists had been far too careless in not using randomization and in comparing the experimental results that had been obtained under different circumstances.

4. Conclusion

During the 1990s and 2000s, Thaler, Kahneman, and other (former) participants of the Sloan-Sage program expanded behavioral economics from a small research program focused on violations of the neoclassical theory in financial economics into a dominant new research program that looked for inspiration beyond behavioral decision research to a range of scientific disciplines and methods and that began to define behavioral economics more explicitly in opposition to neighboring fields such as experimental economics and psychology. At the same time, this rapid growth was bounded by the conceptual redefinition of economics Thaler had taken over from Kahneman and Tversky when he first began to collaborate with Kahneman in the early 1980s. However, the labels of normative and descriptive proved confusing in an economic context that already had created its own understanding of positive and normative. But that matter could be solved relatively easily. The concept of bounded rationality was taken from Simon and together with the concept of full rationality employed to rephrase Kahneman and Tversky's normative-descriptive distinction.

The intertemporal choice and two-systems approach illustrates how behavioral economists incorporated Kahneman and Tversky's work into economics. During this process, behavioral economists sometimes would venture so far as to also question the normative benchmark, but in the end, they always pulled back to this conceptual foundation. In addition, however, the intertemporal choice and dual systems approach literature illustrates that in building behavioral economics, behavioral economists came to see the normative not as something external to the individual, but as a rational system side by side an affective system, with which it strives for dominance. The incorporation of the distinction between the rational norm and its imperfect realization in the economic agent considerably broadened the scope of behavioral economics. But there seemed to be limits to broadening the scope as well. The brief collaboration between behavioral economists and anthropologists shows how behavioral economists, after an initial enthusiasm, retreated when it turned out that this collaboration resulted in research that was at odds with the fundamental behavioral economic assumption of a fixed universal benchmark of full rationality.

The reinterpretation of Kahneman and Tversky's distinction between normative/full-rationality and descriptive/bounded rationality in terms of a conflict within the economic decision maker had important consequences for welfare economics. By exploring how policies could be designed to solve the bounded rationality of individuals, behavioral economists took the full-rationality versus bounded rationality framework to their ultimate consequences. As such, behavioral economic paternalism was very much an economic solution to bounded rationality, emphasizing incentive mechanisms and monetary rewards. Moreover, it was program of helping the (cognitively) poor that is best seen as a liberal program adapted to the U.S. political context of the 2000s.

Finally, behavioral economists came to define themselves across (sub)-disciplinary lines in the 1990s and 2000s. First, behavioral economics became defined as economics on the basis of its use of mathematical modeling. The often implicit argument was that it required the mathematics of economics to judge how useful the insights from psychology were. This use of mathematics was something that defined behavioral economics as economics, and therefore as different from psychology. Second, behavioral economists distinguished themselves from psychology based on their use of the experimental method, in which they, for instance, argued against the use of deception by the psychologists. The motivation for explicitly drawing a border between behavioral economics and experimental economics was that behavioral economists had become aware of the theoretical and ideological differences between their own program and that of Smith and his associates. Thus, the two had to be distinguished, but preferably without suggesting in print that economic theory was influenced by political ideology and without emphasizing possibly conflicting theoretical views. Thus, the distinction was drawn in terms of methodology.

Those were the background and developments that produced the highly visible new economic subdiscipline of behavioral economics in the 2000s. Among others, behavioral economics became an important source of inspiration for a number of advisors and bureaucrats in the new Obama administration that came to power in January 2009 (Grunwald, 2009). An exposition of behavioral economics' travels from there will be left for another occasion.

Epilogue

On the surface, behavioral economics seems to simply add a new chapter to economists' research into the imperfections of the market. The exclusion of social costs such as environmental degradation, or the failure to produce certain public goods, were established nuances of the market's ability to reach an equilibrium that maximizes utility for society as a whole. Behavioral economics added that the market in addition may fail to reach a global optimum due to systematic bounded rationality in the economy's actors – and in consumers in particular. But however true such a first level of situating behavioral economics is, deeper down behavioral economics was a consequence of, and contributed to a much more fundamental shift of the economic discipline. From the late 1970s onward, the epistemology of economics gradually changed from being grounded in generalized characterizations of, among others, human behavior, to being based on empirical claims of economic behavior that could be refuted and verified directly by experimental and statistical observation. This shift was represented most saliently by a transition from economists' distinction between positive facts and normative value judgments, to a normative-descriptive dyad taken over from psychology. Through the work of Kahneman, Thaler, and others, economics became a behavioral science, in which the economist's principal objective is to engineer individuals' behavior to more rational expressions of their preferences.

To appreciate this underlying revision of economics it has been useful to start with John Stuart Mill's influential essay "On the Definition of Political Economy" (1844). In this essay, economics was understood as starting from a few principles of human behavior that could be obtained and verified through a combination of introspection and empirical observation. Examples include the pursuit of wealth and an aversion to labor. The link between these principles of individual behavior and empirical observation was never one-to-one in the sense that empirical observations could directly refute or verify the principles. Only a sufficient amount of introspective and empirical arguments could. The principles were about what the economy is, which were to be distinguished from value judgments of how things ought to be in the economy (Hands, 2001). In the language of John Neville Keynes and later Milton Friedman, these "characterizations" or "assumptions" of economic behavior and the theories and models that derived from them, constituted a domain of "positive" economic science, as opposed to a "normative" domain of ethical claims. In positive economics, one showed, say, how taxation and price elasticities are related; in normative economics, one expressed one's ethical objections against, say, taxing primary goods such as bread and housing.

By contrast, the psychological framework in which an individual's decision or response is compared with a correct decision or stimulus as set by the scientist stems from experimental psychology as first developed by Gustav Fechner and Wilhelm Wundt in the second half of the nineteenth century. In this experimental psychological framework individuals had to decide which of two lightbulbs was the brighter, which of two weights was the heavier, or which of two pictures was the farther away. In addition, in social psychology and psychometrics, as they developed in the first half of the twentieth century in the United States, the correct answer could be determined by the average of a group. Thus, psychologist Louis Leon Thurstone's well-known laboratory experiment of economic indifference curves (Thurstone, 1931) and its rebuttal by economists Allen Wallis and Milton Friedman (1942) illustrates the very different ways of investigating human behavior by psychologist Thurstone and economist Friedman, and shows how Friedman tried to uphold the Millian definition amid the logical positivist sway and its accompanying language. As the Millian definition said that economists can reason from plausible principles of human behavior in the economy by and large independently from psychological research of human behavior, it in addition provides one explanation for Friedman's strict distinction between economics and psychology.

In the 1940s, John von Neumann and Oskar Morgenstern's *Theory of Games and Economic Behavior* (2004 [1944]) added a new dimension. To von Neumann and Morgenstern the behavioral axioms on which their game theory was based, were generalized descriptions of the rational behavior the consumer, the producer, and other economic actors *intend* to achieve. These axioms left out the vast majority of empirical reality related to rational economic behavior and only summarized a few of its main characteristics. Moreover, if actors in the economy intended to behave rationally but failed to do so, the behavioral axioms were, of course, not descriptive of their actual behavior. The other side of this coin was that if actors want to behave rationally, but are unsure how to do so, they could consult the behavioral axioms and use them as a guide. In that sense, von Neumann and Morgenstern's axioms were normative.

Von Neumann and Morgenstern's game theory and the subtle epistemology of the behavioral axioms on which it was based resulted in some ten years of heated debate among psychologists and economists on how to integrate the new theory and its axioms in existing theories and methodologies. Jimmie Savage understood the axioms in the mathematical tradition of von Neumann as summarizing rational behavior on a level higher than purely descriptive. Friedman understood the axioms in the Millian tradition as characterizations of economics behavior. Because of the similarity between these two epistemologies, Savage and Friedman could collaborate on a further application of the von Neumann-Morgenstern approach to economics. Like von Neumann and Morgenstern (2004 [1944]), the purpose of Friedman and Savage (1948, 1952) was to "rationalize" a part of human behavior in the economy, namely individuals' responses towards risk. Paul Samuelson and in particular William Baumol, on the other hand, took the von Neumann-Morgenstern axioms to be descriptive claims about the measurement of utility that might be refuted directly by empirical observations. Between 1952 and 1954, the discussion between Baumol/Samuelson and Friedman/Savage was repeated in less conciliatory tones by Savage and Maurice Allais, which, among others, produced the famous Allais paradox. Others, including economists Kenneth Arrow and Jacob Marschak, tried to bridge the different views, with little success.

After their two publications in 1948 and 1952, Friedman and Savage developed their collaborative work in different directions. Savage went back to the mathematical foundations of statistics and to the interpretation of the behavioral axioms as advanced by von Neumann. Allais's criticisms did, however, lead Savage to insert in his almost-finished *The Foundations of Statistics* (1954) a distinction between a normative and an empirical interpretation of the axioms. In the normative domain, rational human beings investigated how decision making under uncertainty should be conducted, and established rational principles for this behavior. In other words, Savage's normative domain was the von Neumann-Morgenstern position. In the empirical domain, scientists investigated whether people in everyday life behave according to the principles of the normative theory. Savage's division between a normative and an empirical interpretation did not recognize Allais's criticism, but did acknowledge that there may be more than only the mathematical investigation of decision behavior.

Subsequently, psychologists reinterpreted Savage's normative-empirical distinction in terms of the traditional experimental distinction between a normative and a descriptive realm. Decision theory was understood as providing a theoretical framework for the objective stimuli that the subject is presented with in the case of decision making under uncertainty. The self-assigned task of psychologists, then, was to measure experimentally which decisions subjects make with respect to this objective stimuli.

In "The Methodology of Positive Economics," Friedman (1953), for his part, developed the epistemology of generalized characterizations into an argument regarding the "realism" of economic "assumptions" and rein-stated a conception of positive and normative science among economists that sharply contrasted with Savage's normative-empirical interpretation and with the psychologists' normative-descriptive understanding of deci-sion theory. To Friedman, "normative" meant ethical and thus nonscien-tific; positive, first of all, meant nonethical, not normative, and, hence, scientific.

Around 1953 and 1954, the discussion of von Neuman and Morgenstern and Savage's axioms settled into interpretations along disciplinary lines. Behavioral psychologists interpreted the behavioral axioms in terms of the experimental psychological normative-descriptive distinction. Economists, came to understand the behavioral axioms as assumptions within Fried-man's (1953) opposites of positive scientific claims and nonscientific normative value judgments. Choice or decision theory, as based on von Neumann and Morgenstern's axioms, was nonethical, scientific, and, hence, part of positive economics. Initially, the dominant interpretation of ratio-nal choice/decision theory was as generalized characterizations of economic behavior.

In postwar psychology, the normative and descriptive realms of ratio-nal human decision making were, in addition, integrated in a program of human engineering. In this program, measurement and rational decision making were two sides of the same coin, of which the rational individual served as a measurement instrument for its own subjective perception of the values and probabilities of the different decision options. This human engi-neering project in psychology underwent a significant change in the 1960s and 1970s when Daniel Kahneman and Amos Tversky's research introduced the idea that although rational individuals should adhere to the normative theories of logic, Bayesian updating, and expected utility calculation in their decision making, individuals in fact systematically and predictably deviate from these norms. Kahneman and Tversky's heuristics and biases program maintained the framework of reasoning from a set of optimal or normative behavioral rules, but rigorously separated the normative from the descriptive domain. However, although Kahneman and Tversky thus departed from the approach taken by the previous generation of behavioral psychologists, it fully remained a program of human engineering that identified fallible human behavior with the explicit purpose of engineering solutions to improve human decision making.

One consequence of detaching the normative from the descriptive was that normal healthy adults were no longer qualified judges of the axioms of the normative theory in decision making. The only person still qualified to judge whether a specific decision was normatively correct or not was the scientist who possessed a thorough training in logic, statistics, and decision theory. The main question in Kahneman and Tversky's work became what was the best description of actually observed decision behavior by individuals. The initial summary of their experimental findings as heuristics and biases eventually resulted in prospect theory, the first attempt to provide an all-encompassing account of human decision behavior observed in laboratories and questionnaire responses.

In economics, a number of things also changed in the 1970s. Gradually, the principles on which the economic discipline was based in the realm of positive economics came to be understood as empirical claims that were directly amenable to empirical refutation and verification. A second change was the adoption of game theory and expected utility theory in the economic discipline at large. Both theories were intended as empirical claims about actual behavior of agents in the economy, even if some less-sophisticated decision makers could make mistakes and thus produce some statistical noise around the rational mean. The key empirical claim was that the average individual in the economy was a fairly rational person. Psychologists Kahneman and Tversky took this to mean that according to economists, individuals not only should behave according to the rules of expected utility theory and other norms of rational behavior, but that individuals in their everyday lives also do so, or at least most of the time.

Kahneman and Tversky's (1979) prospect theory was published in *Econometrica* – one of economics' most prestigious journals. The first to pick up on behavioral decision research's experimental results were experimental economists such as David Grether, Charles Plott, and Vernon Smith. Grether and Plott (1979, 1982) corroborated the experimental findings of psychology and drew the conclusion that preference theory as a description of individual human behavior should be entirely abandoned. At the same time, they concluded that preference theory as a description of efficient markets in equilibrium could be maintained because the results only emphasized the rationalizing forces of the market. However, an unexpected result of experimental economists' corroboration of behavioral decision research's experimental results was that it paved the way for behavioral decision researchers to enter economics. Richard Thaler and other financial economists understood the psychological findings to shed light on the irrationality of individual choices, and drew a direct link from the irrationality of individual choices to irrational features of the behavior of markets. They immediately recognized Kahneman and Tversky's research, and especially prospect theory, as an important new and improved theory of individual decision behavior.

In other words, experimental economics and behavioral economics were both closely related and fundamentally different. They were closely related because they derived their experimental inspiration from psychology and because they used the same set of psychological experiments to make an argument for changing the dominant neoclassical theory in economics. Furthermore, although asking different questions, they basically conducted the same kind of experiments. They were, however, fundamentally different in the conclusions they inferred from the experimental results produced by the psychologists, in the way they wanted to extend the neoclassical theory, and in the way they considered the neoclassical theory still valuable. Their different theoretical views regarding the economy, correlated with their opposing political views. Thaler was a liberal; Smith, a libertarian.

The primary contribution of the Sloan-Sage behavioral economics program (1984–1992) was to bring economists and psychologists together and to support the research that the more-regular research funding institutes were unwilling to support. The careful balance between psychologists and economists Eric Wanner maintained both in the advisory committee, in the list of researchers invited and in the proposals granted ensured that neither one nor the other would feel dominated. In line with Kahneman and Tversky, Thaler, and other behavioral economists argued that further theoretical advancement of the normative theories of rational economic decision making was perfectly fine but that because economists had ignored the fact that real-world behavior of individuals does not agree with this theory, they should also pay more attention to building a descriptive theory of economic behavior. Thus, Thaler not only accepted the empirical evidence presented by Kahneman and Tversky, he also accepted their accompanying methodological distinction. Essentially, Thaler accepted Kahneman and Tversky's attempt to redefine economics as a behavioral science. This conceptual redefinition of economics determined the boundaries within which behavioral economics would develop. At the same time, Kahneman and Tversky's labels of normative and descriptive proved confusing in an economic context that already had created its own understanding of these concepts (e.g., Friedman, 1953). But the matter was solved relatively easily. The concept of bounded rationality was taken from Simon and together with the concept of full rationality employed to rephrase Kahneman and Tversky's normative-descriptive distinction. In one clear sweep, Kahneman and Tversky's distinction between the concepts of normative-descriptive was replaced by concepts more in line with economic jargon, while at the same time Simon was reappropriated as an authoritative source for the use of these concepts.

During the 1990s and 2000s, behavioral economics was expanded from a small research program focused on violations of the neoclassical theory in financial economics into a dominant new research program that looked beyond behavioral decision research to a range of scientific disciplines and methods. In addition, behavioral economists began to define behavioral economics more explicitly in opposition to neighboring fields such as experimental economics and psychology. Behavioral economists' intertemporal choice and two-systems research of the 1980s through 2000s illustrates how behavioral economists incorporated Kahneman and Tversky's work into economics. During this process, behavioral economists sometimes would venture so far as to also question the normative benchmark, but in the end, they always pulled back to this conceptual foundation. In addition, the intertemporal choice and dual systems approach literature illustrates that in building behavioral economics, behavioral economists came to see the normative not as something external to the individual, but as a rational system inside the individual side by side an affective system, with which it strives for dominance.

Moreover, the reinterpretation of Kahneman and Tversky's distinction in terms of a conflict within the economic decision maker had important repercussions for welfare economics. By exploring how policies could be designed to solve the bounded rationality of individuals, behavioral economists took the full-rationality versus bounded rationality framework to their ultimate consequences. An uncomfortable implication of the psychological framework in that regard was the suggestion that individuals do not choose what they prefer and that it was the scientist who had the ultimate authority of what the individual should prefer and, hence, choose. That did not sit well with the fundamental starting point of individual liberty and autonomy of U.S. economics or with the fundamental economic principle that the individual knows best what it prefers.

The problem was solved by making a distinction between true and revealed preferences. True preferences were the preferences the individual wants to act on and that he or she would reveal in the proper context. But because individuals often act only boundedly rational based on their true preferences, their revealed preferences would also often deviate from their true preferences. A popular example was pension saving. When asked how much they would want to save, individuals indicate to prefer to save percentages of their monthly income that will ensure a stable income after retirement. However, because of limited willpower, limited cognitive capacities, and other reasons of bounded rationality, they will fail to do so. Behavioral economic paternalism was very much an economic solution to bounded rationality, emphasizing incentive mechanisms and monetary rewards. Moreover, it was a program of helping the (cognitively) poor that is best seen as a liberal program adapted to the U.S. political context of the 2000s.

In other ways, behavioral economists also came to define themselves along disciplinary lines in the 1990s and 2000s. First, behavioral economics came to be defined more explicitly as economics based on its use of mathematical modeling. The argument was that it required the mathematics of economics to judge how useful the insights from psychology were. Second, behavioral economists began to distinguish themselves from psychology based on their use of the experimental method, in which they, for instance, argued against the use of deception by the psychologists.

Thus, behavioral economists have steered economics into an entirely new direction. Instead of reasoning from a few intuitively clear principles of human behavior, behavioral economists now start from descriptions of human behavior that can only be inferred from direct empirical observation in experiments and in statistics. And instead of arguing that as scientists economists should first of all refrain from discussing toward which ideal policy makers should direct the economy, behavioral economists have given economists a moral obligation to use their knowledge of the normative theories of rational human behavior to help individuals act more rationally on their preferences.

References

Non-Published Sources

Alfred P. Sloan Foundation annual reports 1980–2000, Alfred P. Sloan Foundation, New York City.

William Baumol Papers, Duke University Rare Book, Manuscript, and Special Collections Library, Duke University.

William Baumol, e-mail to author, October 18, 2011.

Clyde Coombs Papers, Bentley Historical Library, University of Michigan.

Robyn Dawes, interview with the author, Carnegie Mellon University, Pittsburgh, June 23, 2008.

Gerd Gigerenzer, e-mail to author, July 12, 2008.

Lyle V. Jones, e-mail to author, January 31, 2011.

Daniel Kahneman, interview with the author, Princeton University, Princeton, New Jersey, April 16, 2009.

David Krantz, e-mail to author, August 11, 2008.

David Krantz, interview with the author, Columbia University, New York City, June 20, 2008.

David Krantz, personal archive, Columbia University – not generally accessible.

George Loewenstein, e-mail to author, June 16, 2008.

R. Duncan Luce Papers, Harvard University Archives.

James March, e-mail to the author, 4 April, 2010.

Robert Pachella, interview with the author, University of Michigan, Ann Arbor, April 8, 2009.

Psychology Department archives, Bentley Historical Library, University of Michigan.

Albert Rees Papers, Duke University Rare Book, Manuscript, and Special Collections Library, Duke University.

Stephen Richards, e-mail to author, December 4, 2008.

Russell Sage Archives, Rockefeller Foundation Archives, Rockefeller Archive Center, Sleepy Hollow, New York.

Jimmie Savage Papers, Yale University Library.

Timothy Taylor, e-mail to the author, April 6, 2010.

Richard Thaler, e-mail to author, January 14, 2009.

Eric Wanner, interview with the author, Russell Sage Foundation, New York City, April 14, 2009.

Eric Wanner, interview with the author, Russell Sage Foundation, New York City, April 7, 2010.

Published Sources

Allais, M. (1953a). "Fondements d'une Théorie Positive des Choix Comportant un Risque et Critique des Postulats et Axioms de L'Ecole Americaine." *Econometrie* XL: 257–332.

Allais, M. (1953b). "Le comportement de l'homme Rationnel devant de le risque: critique des postulats et axioms de l'école americainne." *Econometrica* 21: 503–546.

Allais, M. (1953c). "La Psychologie De L'homme Rationnel Devant Le Risque: La Théorie Et L'experience." *Journal de la société statistique de Paris* 94: 47–73.

Allais, M. (1979 [1952]). The Foundations of a Positive Theory of Choice Involving Risk and a Criticism of the Postulates and Axioms of the American School. *Expected Utility Hypotheses and the Allais Paradox*. M. Allais and O. Hagen. Dordrecht, D. Reidel Publishing Company: 27–148.

Allais, M. and O. Hagen, Eds. (1979). *Expected Utility Hypotheses and the Allais Paradox*. London, D. Reidel Publishing Company.

Allen, R. G. D. (1938). *Mathematical Analysis for Economists*. London, Macmillan.

Amadae, S. M. (2003). *Rationalizing Capitalist Democracy, The Cold War Origins of Rational Choice Liberalism*. Chicago, University of Chicago Press.

Angner, E. and G. Loewenstein (2012). Behavioral economics. *Handbook of the Philosophy of Science Volume 13 Philosophy of Economics*. U. Maki. Amsterdam, Elsevier: 641–690.

Archibald, G. C., et al. (1963). "Discussion." *The American Economic Review* 53(2): 227–236.

Arrow, K. (1951a). "Alternative Approaches to the Theory of Choice in Risk-Taking Situations." *Econometrica* 19: 404–437.

Arrow, K. J. (1951b). *Social Choice and Individual Values*. New York, Wiley.

Arrow, K. J. (1982). "Risk Perception in Psychology and Economics." *Economic Inquiry* 20: 1–9.

Arrow, K. J. and F. H. Hahn (1971). *General Competitive Analysis*. San Francisco, Holden-Day.

Augier, M. and J. G. March, Eds. (2004). *Models of a Man: Essays in Memory of Herbert A. Simon*. Cambridge, MA, MIT Press.

Backhouse, R. (2008). Economics in the United States after 1945. *The New Palgrave Dictionary of Economics*. L. Blume and S. Durlauf. London, Palgrave: 8: 522–533.

Backhouse, R. (2010). *The Puzzle of Modern Economics*. Cambridge, Cambridge University Press.

Badger, G. J., et al. (2007). "Altered states: The Impact of Immediate Craving on the Valuation of Current and Future Opioids." *Journal of Health Economics* 26: 865–876.

Barkow, J. H., et al. (1992). *The Adapted Mind, Evolutionary Psychology and the Generation of Culture*. Oxford, Oxford University Press.

Basili, M. and C. Zappia (2010). "Ambiguity and Uncertainty in Ellsberg and Shackle." *Cambridge Journal of Economics* 34: 449–474.

Basset, G. W. (1987). "The St. Petersburg Paradox and Bounded Utility." *History of Political Economy* 19(4): 517–523.

Baumol, W. J. (1951). "The Neumann-Morgenstern Utility Index – An Ordinalist View." *The Journal of Political Economy* 59(1): 61–66.

Baumol, W. J. (1958). "The Cardinal Utility which Is Ordinal." *Economic Journal* 68: 665–672.

Ben-Shakar, G., et al. (2007). "Reciprocity and Emotions in Bargaining: Using Physiological and Self-Report Measures." *Journal of Economic Psychology* 28(3): 314–323.

Berelson, B. (1968). Behavioral Sciences. *International Encyclopedia of the Social Sciences.* D. L. Sills and R. K. Merton. New York, Macmillan: 41–45.

Bernoulli, D. (1954 [1738]). "Exposition of a New Theory on the Measurement of Risk." *Econometrica* 22(1): 23–36.

Bertrand, M., et al. (forthcoming). "Behavioral Economics and Marketing in Aid of Decision-Making among the Poor." *Journal of Public Policy and Marketing.*

Blattberg, R. and T. J. Sargent (1971). "Regression with Non-Gaussian Stable Disturbances: Some Sampling Results." *Econometrica* 39(3): 501–510.

Blaug, M. (1980). *The Methodology of Economics: Or How Economists Explain.* Cambridge, Cambridge University Press.

Boring, E. C. (1929). *A History of Experimental Psychology.* New York, The Century Co.

Boumans, M. J. (2005). *How Economists Model the World into Numbers.* London, Routledge.

Boumans, M. J., Ed. (2007). *Measurement in Economics: A Handbook.* London, Academic Press.

Bowles, S. (2004). *Microeconomics: Behavior, Institutions, and Evolution.* Princeton, NJ, Princeton University Press.

Bridgman, P. W. (1927). *The Logic of Modern Physics.* Toronto, Macmillan.

Bulmer, M. (2001). History of Social Survey. *International Encyclopedia of the Social and Behavioral Sciences.* N. J. Smelser and P. B. Baltes. Oxford, Elsevier: 14469–14473.

Burns, A. F. and W. C. Mitchell (1946). *Measuring Business Cycles.* New York, National Bureau of Economic Research.

Camerer, C. (2003). *Behavioral Game Theory: Experiments in Strategic Interaction.* Princeton, NJ, Princeton University Press.

Camerer, C., et al. (1997). "Labor Supply of New York City Cabdrivers: One Day at a Time." *Quarterly Journal of Economics* 112(2): 407–441.

Camerer, C., S. Issacharoff, et al. (2003). "Regulation for Conservatives: Behavioral Economics and the Case for 'Asymmetric Paternalism.'" *University of Pennsylvania Law Review* 151: 1211–1254.

Camerer, C. and G. Loewenstein (2004). Behavioral Economics: Past, Present, Future. *Advances in Behavioral Economics.* C. F. Camerer, G. Loewenstein and M. Rabin. Princeton, NJ, Princeton University Press: 3–52.

Camerer, C., et al. (2005). "Neuroeconomics: How Neuroscience Can Inform Economics." *Journal of Economic Literature* 43: 9–64.

Campbell, N. R. (1957). *Foundations of Science: The Philosophy of Theory and Experiment.* New York, Dover Publications.

Capshew, J. H. (1999). *Psychologists on the March, Science, Practice, and Professional Identity in America, 1929–1969.* Cambridge, Cambridge University Press.

Carnap, R. (1950). *Logical Foundations of Probability*. Chicago, University of Chicago Press.

Cattel, M. (1930). "Psychology in America." *Psychological Review*. Ninth International Congress of Psychology, Proceedings and Papers: 12–32.

Chapanis, A., et al. (1949). *Applied Experimental Psychology, Human Factors in Engineering Design*. New York, John Wiley & Sons.

Chomsky, N. A. (1957). *Syntactic Structures*. The Hague, Mouton.

Cohen, L. J. (1981). "Can Human Irrationality Be Experimentally Demonstrated?" *The Behavioral and Brain Sciences* 4: 317–370.

Cohen-Cole, J. (2007). "Instituting the Science of Mind: Intellectual Economies and Disciplinary Exchange at Harvard's Center for Cognitive Studies." *British Journal for the History of Science* 40(4): 567–597.

Coombs, C. H. (1983). *Psychology and Mathematics: An Essay on Theory*. Ann Arbor, University of Michigan Press.

Coombs, C. H., et al. (1970). *Mathematical Psychology: An Elementary Introduction*, CITY, Englewood Cliffs, Prentice Hall.

Coombs, C. H. and S. S. Komorita (1958). "Measuring Utility of Money through Decisions." *American Journal of Psychology* 71: 383–389.

Cootner, P. H. (1964). Comments on the Variation of Certain Speculative Prices. *The Random Character of Stock Market Prices*. P. H. Cootner. London, Risk Books: 413–418.

Cordeschi, R. (2002). *The Discovery of the Artificial: Behavior, Mind, and Machines before and beyond Cybernetics*. Dordrecht, Kluwer Academic Publications.

Cosmides, L. and J. Tooby (1996). "Are Humans Good Intuitive Statisticians after All? Rethinking Some Conclusions from the Literature on Judgment under Uncertainty." *Cognition* 58: 1–73.

Cronqvist, H. and R. Thaler (2004). "Design Choices in Privatized Social-Security Systems: Learning from the Swedish Experience." *American Economic Review, papers and proceedings* 94(2): 424–428.

Crowther-Heyck, H. (2005). *Herbert A. Simon: The Bounds of Reason in Modern America*. Baltimore, Johns Hopkins University Press.

Crowther-Heyck, H. (2006). "Patrons of the Revolution, Ideals and Institutions in Postwar Behavioral Science." *Isis* 97: 420–446.

Damasio, A. (2003). *Looking for Spinoza – Joy, Sorrow, and the Feeling Brain*. New York, Harcourt Books.

Danziger, K. (1990). *Constructing the Subject, Historical Origins of Psychological Research*. New York, Cambridge University Press.

Danziger, K. (1997). *Naming the Mind, How Psychology Found its Language*. London, Sage.

Daston, L. (1988). *Classical Probability in the Enlightenment*. Princeton, NJ, Princeton University Press.

Daston, L. and P. Galison (2007). *Objectivity*. New York, Zone Books.

Davis, D. D. and C. A. Holt (1993). *Experimental Economics*. Princeton, NJ, Princeton University Press.

Davis, J. B. (2003). *The Theory of the Individual in Economics*. New York, Routledge.

Davis, R. L. (1954). Introduction. *Decision Processes*. R. M. Thrall, C. H. Coombs, and R. L. Davis. New York, John Wiley & Sons: 1–18.

De Bondt, W. F. M. and R. Thaler (1985). "Does the Stock Market Overreact?" *The Journal of Finance* 40(3): 793–805.

De Bondt, W. F. M. and R. Thaler (1990). "Do Security Analysts Overreact?" *The American Economic Review* 80(2): 52–57.

de Finetti, B. (1937). "La prévision: ses lois logiques, ses sources subjective." *Annales de l'Institut Henri Poincaré* 7: 1–68.

de Finetti, B. (1949). "Le vrai et le probable." *Dialectica* 3: 78–93.

de Finetti, B. (1951). Recent Suggestions for the Reconciliation of Theories of Probability *Proceedings of the Second [1950] Berkeley Symposium on Mathematical Statistics and Probability*. J. Neyman. Berkeley, University of California Press: 217–226.

Debreu, G. (1954). Representation of Preference Ordering by a Numerical Function. *Decision Processes*. R. M. Thrall, C. H. Coombs, and R. L. Davis. New York, Wiley: 159–165.

Debreu, G. (1958). "Stochastic Choice and Cardinal Utility." *Econometrica* 26: 440–444.

Debreu, G. (1959a). "Cardinal Utility for Even-chance Mixtures of Pairs of Sure Prospects." *Review of economic studies* 71: 174–177.

Debreu, G. (1959b). *Theory of Value: An Axiomatic Analysis of Economic Equilibrium*. New York, Wiley.

Debreu, G. (1960). Topological Methods in Cardinal Utility Theory. *Mathematical Methods in the Social Science, 1959*. K. Arrow, S. Karlin, and P. Suppes. Stanford, CA, Stanford University Press: 16–26.

Diamond, P. A. and M. Rothschild, Eds. (1978).*Uncertainty in Economics: Readings and Exercises* San Diego, Academic Press.

Dimand, M. A. and R. W. Dimand, Eds. (1997). *The Foundations of Game Theory*. Cheltenham, UK, Edward Elgar.

Dimand, R. W. (2005). Experimental Economic Games: The Early Years. *The Experiment in the History of Economics*. P. Fontaine and R. Leonard. New York, Routledge: 5–24.

Dodge, R. (1919). "Mental Engineering during the War." *American Review of Reviews* 59: 504–508.

Dowie, M. (2001). *American Foundations: An Investigative History*. Cambrdige. The MIT Press.

Duderstadt, J. D. (1994). "Foreword." *The Making of the University of Michigan 1817–1992*. M. L. Steneck and N. H. Steneck. Ann Arbor, University of Michigan Press: V.

Dunlap, J. W. (1942). "The Psychometric Society – Roots and Powers." *Psychometrika* 7(1): 1–8.

Dupuy, J.-P. (2009). *On the Origins of Cognitive Science, The Mechanization of the Mind*. Cambridge, The MIT Press.

Edwards, W. (1954). "The Theory of Decision Making." *Psychological Bulletin* 51: 380–417.

Edwards, W. (1961). "Behavioral Decision Theory." *Annual Review of Psychology*(12): 473–498.

Edwards, W. and A. Tversky, Eds. (1967). *Decision Making*. Penguin Modern Psychology Readings. Baltimore, Penguin Books.

Ellsberg, D. (1961). "Ambiguity, and the Savage Axioms." *The Quarterly Journal of Economics* 75(4): 643–669.

Elster, J. and G. Loewenstein (1992). Utility from Memory and Anticipation. *Choice over Time*. G. Loewenstein and J. Elster. New York, Russell Sage Foundation: 213–234.

Elzinga, K. G. (1992). "The Eleven Principles of Economics." *Southern Economic Journal* 58(4): 861–879.

Erickson, P. (2010). "Mathematical Models, Rational Choice, and the Search for Cold War Culture." *Isis* 101(2): 386–392.

Eriksson, L. and A. Hajek (2007). "What Are Degrees of Belief?" *Studia Logica* 86(2): 185–215.

Estes, W. K. (1964). Probability Learning. *Categories of Human Learning.* A. W. Melton. New York, Academic Press: 89–128.

Fama, E. (1970). "Efficient Capital Markets: A Review of Theory and Empirical Work." *The Journal of Finance* 25(2): 383–417.

Fechner, G. T. (1964 [1860]). *Elemente der Psychophysiek.* Amsterdam, Bonset.

Festinger, L. and D. Katz, Eds. (1953). *Research Methods in the Behavioral Sciences.* Fort Worth, Dryden Press.

Fishburn, P. C. (1964). *Decision and Value Theory.* New York, Wiley.

Fishburn, P. C. (1981). "Subjective Expected Utility: A Review of Normative Theories." *Theory and Decision* 13: 139–199.

Fishburn, P. C. (1989). "Retrospective on the Utility Theory of von Neumann and Morgenstern." *Journal of Risk and Uncertainty* 2: 127–158.

Flom, M. C., F. W. Weymouth, et al. (1963). "Visual Resolution and Contour Interaction." *Journal of the Optical Society of America* 53(9): 1026–1032.

Fontaine, P. and R. Backhouse, Eds. (2010). *The Unsocial Social Science? Economics and Neighboring Disciplines since 1945.* Durham, NC, and London, Duke University Press.

Forman, P. (1987). "Behind Quantum Electronics: National Security as Basis for Physical Research in the United States, 1940–1960." *Historical Studies in the Physical and Biological Sciences* 18: 149–229.

Fourcade, M. (2009). *Economists and Societies, Discipline and Profession in the United States, Britain, & France, 1890s to 1990s.* Princeton, NJ, Princeton University Press.

Frantilla, A. (1998). *Social Science in the Public Interest: A fiftieth-year history of the Institute of Social Research.* Ann Arbor, Bentley Historical Library, University of Michigan.

Frederick, S., G. Loewenstein, et al. (2002). "Time Discounting and Time Preference A Critical Review." *Journal of Economic Literature* 40: 351–401.

Frederiksen, N. and H. Gulliksen, Eds. (1964). *Contributions to Mathematical Psychology.* London, Holt, Rinehart and Winston.

Friedman, J., Ed. (1996). *The Rational Choice Controversy: Economic Models of Politics Reconsidered.* New Haven, Yale University Press.

Friedman, M. (1953). The Methodology of Positive Economics. *Essays in Positive Economics.* Chicago, Chicago University Press: 3–43.

Friedman, M. and L. Savage (1948). "The Utility Analysis of Choice Involving Risk." *Journal of Political Economy* LVI (4): 279–304.

Friedman, M. and L. Savage (1952). "The Expected-utility Hypothesis and the Measurability of Utility." *Journal of Political Economy* LX (6): 463–474.

Friedman, D. and S. Sunder (1994). *Experimental Methods: A Primer for Economists* New York, Cambridge University Press.

Frijda, N. H. (1986). *The Emotions.* Cambridge, Cambridge University Press.

Fryback, D. (2005). "Ward Edwards: Father of Behavioral Decision Theory." *Medical Decision Making* 25: 468–470.

Gigerenzer, G. (1987a). The Probabilistic Revolution in Psychology – an Overview. *The Probabilistic Revolution 2*. L. Krüger, G. Gigerenzer and M. S. Morgan. Cambridge, MIT Press: 7–10.

Gigerenzer, G. (1987b). Survival of the Fittest Probabilist: Brunswik, Thurstone, and the Two Disciplines of Psychology. *The Probabilistic Revolution 2*. L. Krüger, G. Gigerenzer and M. S. Morgan. Cambridge, MIT Press: 49–72.

Gigerenzer, G. (1991). "How to Make Cognitive Illusions Disappear: Beyond 'Heuristics and Biases.'" *European Review of Social Psychology* 2: 83–115.

Gigerenzer, G. (1993). "From Metaphysics to Psychophysics and Statistics." *The Behavioral and Brain Sciences* 16(1): 139–140.

Gigerenzer, G. (1996). "On Narrow Norms and Vague Heuristics: A Reply to Kahneman and Tversky (1996)." *Psychological Review* 103(3): 592–596.

Gigerenzer, G. and D. J. Murray (1987). *Cognition as Intuitive Statistics*. Hillsdale, NJ, Lawrence Erlbaum.

Gigerenzer, G. and R. Selten (2001). *Bounded Rationality, The Adaptive Toolbox*. Cambridge, MIT Press.

Gigerenzer, G., P. M. Todd, et al., Eds. (1999). *Simple Heuristics That Make Us Smart*. New York, Oxford University Press.

Gintis, H. (2000). *Game Theory Evolving: A Problem-Centered Introduction to Modeling Strategic Behavior*. Princeton, NJ, Princeton University Press.

Giocoli, N. (2013). "From Wald to Savage: Homo Economicus becomes a Baysian Statistician." *Journal of the History of the Behavioral Sciences* 49(1): 63–95.

Giraud, Y. (forthcoming). The Political Economy of Textbook Writing: Paul Samuelson and the making of the First Ten Editions of *Ecoomics* (1945–1976).

Goldstein, W. M. and R. M. Hogarth, Eds. (1997). *Research on Judgement and Decision Making: Currents, Connections, and Controversies*. Cambridge, Cambridge University Press.

Goodwin, C. D. (1998). "The Patrons of Economic in a Time of Transformation." *History of Political Economy* Annual supplement: 53–81.

Green, D. and I. Shapiro (1994). *Pathologies of Rational Choice Thoery: A Critique of Applications in Political Science*. New Haven, CT, Yale University Press.

Green, D. M. and J. A. Swets (1966). *Signal Detection Theory and Psychophysics*. New York, Wiley.

Grether, D. and C. R. Plott (1979). "Economic Theory of Choice and the Preference Reversal Phenomenon." *The American Economic Review* 69(4): 623–638.

Grether, D. M. and C. R. Plott (1982). "Economic Theory of Choice and the Preference Reversal Phenomenon: Reply." *American Economic Review* 72(3): 575.

Grossman, D. M. (1982). "American Foundations and the Support of Economic Research, 1913–1929." *Minerva* 20(1–2): 59–82.

Grunwald, M. (2009). How Obama Is Using the Science of Change. *Time*. New York. April 2.

Guala, F. (2000). "The Logic of Normative Falsification: Rationality and Experiments in Decision Theory." *Journal of Economic Methodology* 7(1): 59–93.

Guala, F. (2005). *The Methodology of Experimental Economics*. Cambridge, Cambridge University Press.

Guilford, J. P. (1954). *Psychometric Methods*. New York, McGraw-Hill.

Hacking, I. (1975). *The Emergence of Probability: A Philosophical Study of Early Ideas about Probability, Induction and Statistical Inference.* London, New York, Cambridge University Press.

Hájek, Alan, "Interpretations of Probability," *The Stanford Encyclopedia of Philosophy* (Winter 2012 Edition), Edward N. Zalta (ed.), URL = <http://plato.stanford.edu/archives/win2012/entries/probability-interpret/>.

Hands, D. W. (2001). *Reflection without Rules, Economic Methodology and Contemporary Science Theory.* Cambridge, Cambridge University Press.

Hands, D. W. (2013). Normative Rational Choice Theory: Past, Present, and Future (July 9). Available at SSRN: http://ssrn.com/abstract=1738671 or http://dx.doi.org/10.2139/ssrn.1738671.

Hands, D. W. (2010). "Economics, Psychology, and the History of Consumer Choice Theory." *Cambridge Journal of Economics* 34: 633–648.

Hands, D. W. and P. Mirowski (1998). Harold Hoteling and the Neoclassical Dream. *Economics and Methodology: Crossing Boundaries.* R. Backhouse, D. Hausman, U. Mäki and A. Salanti. London, Macmillan: 322–397.

Harris, C. and D. Laibson (2001). "Dynamic Choices of Hyperbolic Consumers." *Econometrica* 69(4): 935–957.

Hauptmann, E. (2006). "From Opposition to Accommodation: How Rockefeller Foundation Grants Redefined Relations between Political Theory and Social Science in the 1950s." *American Political Science Review* 100(4): 643–649.

Hausman, D. M. (1992). *The Inexact and Separate Science of Economics.* Cambridge, Cambridge University Press.

Heidelberger, M. (1993). "Fechner's Impact for Measurement Theory (Comment on Murray, D. J. 'A Perspective for Viewing the History of Psychophysics')." *Behavioral and Brain Sciences* 16: 146–148.

Heidelberger, M. (2004). *Nature from Within, Gustav Theodor Fechner and His Psychophysical Worldview.* Pittsburgh, University of Pittsburgh Press.

Heise, D. R. (1970). The Semantic Differential and Attitude Research. *Attitude Measurement.* G. F. Summers. Chicago, Rand McNally: 235–253.

Henrich, J. (2001). Group Report: What Is the Role of Culture in Bounded Rationality? *Bounded Rationality, The Adaptive Toolbox.* G. Gigerenzer and R. Selten. Cambridge USA, MIT Press: 343–359.

Henrich, J., et al. (2001). "In Search of Homo Economicus: Behavioral Experiments in 15 Small-Scale Societies." *The American Economic Review* 91(2): 73–78.

Henrich, J., et al. (2004). *Foundations of Human Sociality: Economic Experiments and Ethnographic Evidence from Fifteen Small-scale Societies* Oxford, Oxford University Press.

Hertwig, R. and G. Gigerenzer (1999). "The 'Conjunction Fallacy' Revisited: How Intelligent Inferences Look Like Reasoning Errors." *Journal of Behavioral Decision Making* 12: 275–305.

Hertwig, R. and A. Ortmann (2008). "Deception in Experiments: Revisiting the Arguments in its Defense." *Ethics & Behavior* 18(1): 59–92.

Heukelom, F. (2011). "How Validity Travelled to Economic Experimenting." *Journal of Economic Methodology* 18(1): 13–28.

Hicks, J. R. and R. G. D. Allen (1934a). "A Reconsideration of the Theory of Value." *Economica* 1(1): 52–76.

Hicks, J. R. and R. G. D. Allen (1934b). "A Reconsideration of the Theory of Value. Part II. A Mathematical Theory of Individual Demand Functions " *Economica* 1(2): 196–219.

Hogarth, R. M. and M. W. Reder, Eds. (1987). *Rational Choice: The Contrast between Economics and Psychology.* Chicago, University of Chicago Press.

Hollinger, D. A. (1989). Academic Culture at Michigan, 1938–1988: The Apotheosis of Pluralism. *Intellectual History and Academic Culture at the University of Michigan: Fresh Explorations.* M. A. Lourie. Ann Arbor, H. Rackham School of Graduate Studies: 58–101.

Hollinger, D. A. (1995). "Science as a Weapon in Kulturkampfe in the United States during and after World War II." *Isis* 86(3): 440–454.

House, J. S., et al., Eds. (2004). *A Telescope on Society, Survey Research & Social Science at the University of Michigan & Beyond.* Ann Arbor, University of Michigan Press.

Hughes, T. P. (1998). *Rescuing Prometheus.* New York, Pantheon.

Hughes, T. P. and A. C. Hughes, Eds. (2000). *Systems, Experts, and Computers: teh Systems Approach in Management and Engineering, World War II and After.* Cambridge, MA, The MIT Press.

Hunter, W. S. (1946). "Psychology in the War." *American Psychologist* 1: 479–492.

Hyman, H. H. (1991). *Taking Society's Measure.* New York, Russell Sage.

Ingrao, B. and G. Israel (1990). *The Invisible Hand.* Cambridge, MIT Press.

Jallais, S. and P.-C. Pradier (2005). The Random Character of Stock Market Prices. *The Experiment in the History of Economics.* P. Fontaine and R. Leonard. New York, Routledge: 25–49.

Jallais, S., P. C. Pradier, and D. Teira et al. (2008). "Facts, Norms and Expected Utility Functions." *History of the Human Sciences* 21(2): 45–62.

Jamisona, J., et al. (2008). "To Deceive or Not To Deceive: The Effect of Deception on Behavior in Future Laboratory Experiments." *Jounral of Economic Behavior & Organization* 68(3–4): 477–488.

Jones, E. and S. Rahman (2009). "The Maudsley Hospital and the Rockefeller Foundation: The Impact of Philanthropy on Research and Training." *Journal of the History of Medicine and Allied Sciences* 64(3): 273–299.

Jones, L. V. (1959). "Prediction of Consumer Purchase and the Utility of Money." *Journal of Applied Psychology* 43: 334–337.

Jordan, J. M. (1994). *Machine-Age Ideology: Social Engineering and American Liberalism, 1911–1939.* Chapel Hill, University of North Carolina.

Jorland, G. (1987). The Saint Petersburg Paradox 1713–1937. *The Probabilistic Revolution 1.* L. Kruger, L. J. Daston, and M. Heidelberger. Cambridge, MIT Press: 157–190.

Jovanovic, F. (2008). "The Construction of the Canonical History of Financial Economics." *History of Political Economy* 40(2): 213–242.

Juster, F. T. (2004). The Behavioral Study of Economics. *A Telescope on Society, Survey Research & Social Science at the University of Michigan & Beyond.* J. S. House, F. T. Juster, R. L. Kahn, H. Schuman, and E. Singer. Ann Arbor, The University of Michigan Press: 119–130.

Kahneman, D. (1963). "The Semantic Differential and the Structure of Inferences among Attributes." *American Journal of Psychology* 76: 554–567.

Kahneman, D. (1964). "Temporal Summation in an Acuity Task at Different Energy Levels – a Study of the Determinants of Summation." *Vision Research* 4: 557–566.

Kahneman, D. (1965a). "Control of Spurious Association and the Reliability of the Controlled Variable." *Psychological Bulletin* 64(5): 326–329.

Kahneman, D. (1965b). "Exposure Duration and Effective Figure-ground Contrast." *Quarterly Journal of Experimental Psychology* 17: 308–314.

Kahneman, D. (1966a). "Time-intensity Reciprocity in Acuity as a Function of Luminance and Figure-ground Contrast." *Vision Research* 6: 207–215.

Kahneman, D. (1966b). "Time-intensity Reciprocity under Various Conditions of Adaptation and Backward Masking." *Journal of Experimental Psychology* 71: 543–549.

Kahneman, D. (1967). Temporal Effects in the Perception of Light and Form. *Models for the Perception of Speech and Visual Form.* W. Wathen-Dunn. Cambridge, M.I.T. Press: 157–170.

Kahneman, D. (1973). *Attention and Effort.* Englewoods Cliffs, CA, Prentice Hall.

Kahneman, D. (2002). "Autobiography," from http://nobelprize.org/economics/laureates/2002/kahneman-autobio.html.

Kahneman, D. (2003). "Maps of Bounded Rationality: Psychology for Behavioral Economics." *The American Economic Review* 93(5): 1449–1475.

Kahneman, D. (2011). *Thinking, Fast and Slow.* New York, Farrar, Straus and Giroux.

Kahneman, D. and D. Beatty (1966). "Pupil Diameter and Load on Memory." *Science* 154: 1583–1585.

Kahneman, D. and D. Beatty (1967). "Pupillary Responses in a Pitch-discrimination Task." *Perception and Psychophysics* 2: 101–105.

Kahneman, D., et al. (1967). "Perceptual Deficit during a Mental Task." *Science* 157: 218–219.

Kahneman, D. and E. E. Ghiselli (1962). "Validity and Nonlinear Heteroscedastic Models." *Personnel Psychology* 15: 1–12.

Kahneman, D., et al. (1990). "Experimental Tests of the Endowment Effect and the Coase Theorem." *The Journal of Political Economy* 98(6): 1325–1348.

Kahneman, D., et al. (1991). "Anomalies: The Endowment Effect, Loss Aversion, and Status Quo Bias." *The Journal of Economic Perspectives* 5(1): 193–206.

Kahneman, D. and J. Norman (1964). "The Time-intensity Relation in Visual Perception as a Function of Observer's Task." *Journal of Experimental Psychology* 68: 215–220.

Kahneman, D. and W. S. Peavler (1969). "Incentive Effects and Pupillary Changes in Association Learning." *Journal of Experimental Psychology* 79(2): 312–318.

Kahneman, D., et al. (1968). "Effect of Verbalization and Incentive on the Pupil Response to Mental Activity." *Canadian Journal of Psychology* 22(3): 186–196.

Kahneman, D. and A. Tversky (1972). "Subjective Probability: A Judgment of Representativeness." *Cognitive Psychology* 3: 430–454.

Kahneman, D. and A. Tversky (1979). "Prospect Theory: An Analysis of Decision under Risk." *Econometrica* 47: 313–327.

Kahneman, D. and A. Tversky (1996). "On the Reality of Cognitive Illusions." *Psychological Review* 103(3): 582–591.

Kahneman, D. and A. Tversky, Eds. (2000). *Choices, Values and Frames.* New York, Cambridge University Press.

Kalish, G. K., et al. (1954). Some Experimental N-person Games. *Decision Processes.* R. M. Thrall, C. H. Coombs, and R. L. Davis. New York, John Wiley & Sons: 301–327.

Katona, G. (1975). *Psychological Economics.* Amsterdam, Elsevier.

Keynes, J. M. (1921). *Treatise on Probability.* London, Macmillan & Co.

Kiddler, L. M. (1981). *Research Methods in Social Relations.* New York, Holt, Rinehart & Winston.

Kitch, E. W. (1977). "The Nature and Function of the Patent System." *Journal of Law and Economics* 20(2): 265–290.

Klein, J. L. (forthcoming). *Protocols of War.*

Kolmogoroff, A. (1933). *Grundbegriffe der Wahrscheinlichkeitsrechnung.* Berlin, Julius Springer.

Krantz, D. H., et al. (1971). *Foundations of Measurement I.* New York, Academic Press.

Krüger, L., et al., Eds. (1987). *The Probabilistic Revolution Volume 1: Ideas in History.* Cambridge, MIT Press.

Krüger, L., et al., Eds. (1987). *The Probabilistic Revolution Volume 2: Ideas in Science.* Cambridge, MIT Press.

Laibson, D. (1997). "Golden Eggs and Hyperbolic Discounting." *The Quarterly Journal of Economics* 112(2): 443–477.

Laibson, D. and R. Zeckhauser (1998). "Amos Tversky and the Ascent of Behavioral Economics." *Journal of Risk and Uncertainty* 16: 7–47.

Laming, D. (1973). *Mathematical Psychology.* London, Academic Press.

Lee, K. S. (2004). Rationality, Minds, and Machines in the Laboratory: A Thematic History of Vernon Smith's Experimental Economics. Notre Dame, University of Notre Dame. PhD: 300.

Lee, K. S. and P. Mirowski (2008). "The Energy Behind Vernon Smith's Experimental Economics." *Cambridge Journal of Economics* 32: 257–271.

Lemov, R. (2005). *World as Laboratory, Experiments with Mice, Mazes, and Men.* New York, Hill and Wang.

Lenfant, J.-S. (2012). "Indifference Curves and the Ordinalist Revolution." *History of Political Economy* 44(1): 113–155.

Leonard, R. (1991). Essays in the History of Economic Thought: Theory and Institutions in the Mid-Twentieth-Century Economics. *Economics.* Duke, Duke University. PhD.

Leonard, R. (2010). *Von Neumann, Morgenstern, and the Creation of Game Theory, From Chess to Social Science, 1900–1960.* Cambridge, Cambridge University Press.

Leonard, R. and P. Fontaine (2005). Introduction. *The Experiment in the History of Economics.* P. Fontaine and R. Leonard. New York, Routledge: 1–4.

Lewin, S. (1996). "Economics and Psychology: Lessons for Our Own Day From the Early Twentieth Century." *Journal of Economic Literature* 34(3): 1293–1323.

Lichtenstein, S. and P. Slovic, Eds. (2006). *The Construction of Preference.* Cambridge, Cambridge University Press.

Lipsey, R. G. and P. O. Steiner (1972). *Economics.* 3rd ed. New York, Harper & Row.

Lipsey, R. G. and P. O. Steiner (1981). *Economics.* 6th ed. New York, Harper & Row.

oewenstein, G. (1992). The Fall and Rise of Psychological Explanations in the Economics of Intertemporal Choice. *Choice over Time.* G. Loewenstein and J. Elster. New York, Russell Sage Foundation: 3–34.

Loewenstein, G. (1999a). "Because It Is There: The Challenge of Mountaineering... for Utility Theory." *Kyklos* 52: 315–344.

Loewenstein, G. (1999b). "Experimental Economics from the vantage-point of Behavioural Economics." *The Economic Journal* 109: F25–F34.

Loewenstein, G. and J. Elster, Eds. (1992). *Choice over Time.* New York, Russell Sage Foundation.

Loewenstein, G. and E. Haisley (2008). The Economist as Therapist: Methodological Ramifications of "Light" Paternalism. *Perspectives on the Future of Economics: Positive and Normative Foundations.* A. Caplin and A. Schotter. Oxford, Oxford University Press: 210–245.

Loewenstein, G. and D. Prelec (1991). "Negative Time Preference." *The American Economic Review* 81(2): 347–352.

Loewenstein, G. and D. Prelec (1992). Anomalies in Intertemporal Choice: Evidence and an Interpretation. *The Quarterly Journal of Economics,* 107(2): 573–597.

Loewenstein, G. and R. Thaler (1989). "Anomalies: Intertemporal Choice." *Journal of Economic Perspectives* 3: 181–193.

Loewenstein, G., et al. (2001). "Risk as Feelings." *Psychological Bulletin* 127: 267–286.

Lopes, L. L. (1991). "The Rhetoric of Irrationality." *Theory and Psychology* 1: 65–82.

Luce, R. D., et al., Eds. (1963a). *The Handbook of Mathematical Psychology I.* New York, John Wiley and Sons.

Luce, R. D., et al., Eds. (1963b). *The Handbook of Mathematical Psychology II.* New York, John Wiley and Sons.

Luce, R. D., et al., Eds. (1965). *The Handbook of Mathematical Psychology III.* New York, John Wiley and Sons.

Luce, R. D., et al. (1990). *Foundations of Measurement 3. Representation, Axiomatization, and Invariance.* San Diego, Academic Press.

Luce, R. D. and H. Raiffa (1957). *Games and Decisions, Introduction and Critical Survey.* New York, Dover Publications.

Luce, R. D. and J. W. Tukey (1964). "Simultaneous Conjoint Measurement: A New Type of Fundamental Measurement." *Journal of Mathematical Psychology* 1(1): 1–27.

Maas, H. (2005a). "Mill and Jevons on the Private Laboratory of the Mind." *The Manchester School:* 620–649.

Maas, H. (2005b). *William Stanley Jevons and the Making of Modern Economics.* Cambridge, Cambridge University Press.

MacHale, D. (1985). *George Boole: His Life and Work.* Dublin, Boole.

Machina, M. J. (1982). "'Expected Utility' Analysis without the Independent Axiom." *Econometrica* 50(2): 277–323.

Machina, M. J. (1989). "Dynamic Consistency and Non-Expected Utility Models of Choice under Uncertainty." *Journal of Economic Literature* 27(1622–1668).

MacKenzie, D. A. (2006). *An Engine, Not a Camera, How Financial Models Shape Markets.* London, MIT Press.

Mäki, U., Ed. (2009). *The Methodology of Positive Economics. Reflections on the Milton Friedman Legacy.* Cambridge, Cambridge University Press.

Mandelbrot, B. and R. L. Hudson (2004). *The (Mis)behavior of Markets, A Fractal View of Financial Turbulence.* New York, Basic Books.

Mandler, M. (1999). *Dilemmas in Economic Theory.* New York, Oxford University Press.

Marschak, J. (1946). "Neumann's and Morgenstern's New Approach to Static Economics." *The Journal of Political Economy* 44(2): 97–115.

Marschak, J. (1950). "Rational Behavior, Uncertain Prospects, and Measurable Utility." *Econometrica* 18: 111–141.

Mas-Colell, A., et al. (1995). *Microeconomic Theory.* New York, Oxford University Press.

McClure, S. M., et al. (2004). "Separate Neural Systems Value Immediate and Delayed Monetary Rewards." *Science* 306: 503–507.

McConnell, C. R. (1960). *Economics, Pirnciples, Porblems, and Policies.* New York, McGraw-Hill.

McConnell, C. R. (1975). *Economics.* New York, McGraw-Hill.

Mehrling, P. G. (2005). *Fischer Black and the Revolutionary Idea of Finance.* Hoboken, NJ, Wiley.

Mehrling, P. G. (2011). *The New Lombard Street, How the Fed Became the Dealer of Last Resort.* Princeton, NJ, Princeton University Press.

Mendelsohn, E. (1989). "Robert K. Merton: The Celebration and Defense of Science." *Science in Context* 3(1): 269–289.

Michell, J. (1999). *Measurement in Psychology.* Cambridge, Cambridge University Press.

Michell, J. (2007). Representational Theory of Measurement. *Measurement in Economics: a handbook.* M. Boumans. Amsterdam, Elsevier: 19–39.

Mill, J. S. (1844). On the Definition of Political Economy; and on the Method of Investigation Proper to it. *Essays on Some Unsettled Questions of Political Economy.* J. S. Mill. London, Longmans: 86–118.

Mindell, D. A. (2002). *Between Human and Machine: Feedback, Control and Computing before Cybernetics.* Baltimore, Johns Hopkins University Press.

Mirowski, P. (1989). "'Tis a Pity Econometrics Isn't an Empirical Endeavor: Mandelbrot, Chaos, and the Noah and Joseph Effects." *Recherche Economiche* 43: 76–99.

Mirowski, P. (1990). "From Mandelbrot to Chaos in Economic Theory." *Southern Economic Journal* 57(2): 289–307.

Mirowski, P. (2002). *Machine Dreams, Economics Becomes a Cyborg Science.* Cambridge, Cambridge University Press.

Mirowski, P. and D. W. Hands (1998). A Paradox of Budgets: The Postwar Stabilization of American Neoclassical Demand Theory. *From Interwar Pluralism to Postwar Neoclassicism.* M. S. Morgan and M. Rutherford. London, Duke University Press: 260–289.

Mongin, P. (2009). Duhemian Themes in Expected Utility Theory. *French Studies in the Philosophy of Science.* A. Brenner and J. Gayon. Berlin, Springer: 303–357.

Morawski, J. G. (1986). "Organizing Knowledge and Behavior at Yale's Institute of Human Relations." *Isis* 77: 219–242.

Morgan, M. S. (1990). *The History of Econometric Ideas.* Cambridge, Cambridge University Press.

Morgenstern, O. (1972). "Descriptive, Predictive and Normative Theory." *Kyklos* 25(4): 699–714.

Morgenstern, O. (1973). Some Reflections on Utility. *Expected Uility Hypotheses and the Allais Paradox.* M. Allais and O. Hagen. London, D. Reidel Publishing Company: 175–183.

Moscati, I. (2007a). "Early Experiments in Consumer Demand Theory: 1930–1970." *History of Political Economy* 39(3): 359–401.

Moscati, I. (2007b). "History of Cosumer Demand Theory, 1871–1971: A Neo-Kantian Rational Reconstruction." *European Journal of the History of Economic Thought* 14: 119–156.

Moscati, I. (2010). Were Jevons, Menger and Walras Really Cardinalists? On the Notion of Measurement in Utility Theory, Psychology, Mathematics and other Disciplines, ca. 1870–1910. *University of Turin Working Paper Series.*

Mosteller, F. and P. Nogee (1951). "An Experimental Measurement of Utility." *Journal of Political Economy* 50: 371–404.

Mullainathan, S. (2007). Development Economics through the Lens of Psychology. Working Paper, Harvard University.

Murchison, C., Ed. (1929). *The Psychological Register*. Worecester, MA, Clark University Press.

Nagel, E. (1963). "Assumptions in Economic Theory." *American Economic Review* 53(2): 211–219.

National Research Council (1943). *Psychology for the Fighting Man: Prepared for the Fighting Man Himself*. Washington D.C., Infantry Journal.

Nozick, R. (1993). *The Nature of Rationality*. Princeton, NJ, Princeton University Press.

Ortmann, A. and R. Hertwig (2002). "The Costs of Deception: Evidence from Psychology." *Experimental Economics* 5(2): 111–131.

Peckham, H. H. (2005). *The Making of the University of Michigan 1917–1992, Edited and Updated by M. L. Steneck and N.H. Steneck*. Ann Arbor, University of Michigan Press.

Phillips, L. D. and D. Von Winterfeldt (2006). Reflections on the Contributions of Ward Edwards to Decision Analysis and Behavioral Research. *LSEOR*. London, LSE.

Pindyck, R. S. and D. L. Rubenfield (1995). *Microeconomics*. Englewood Cliffs, NJ, Prentice Hall.

Plott, C. R. and V. L. Smith, Eds. (2008). *Handbook of Experimental Economics Results, Volume 1*. Amsterdam, Elsevier.

Poitras, G. and F. Jovanovic, Ed. (2007). *Pioneers of Financial Economics, Volume 2: Twentieth-Century Contributions*. Cheltenham, UK, Edward Elgar.

Pooley, J. (forthcoming). A "Not Particularly Felicitous" Phrase: A History of the "Behavioral Sciences" Label.

Pooley, J. and M. Solovey (2010). "Marginal to the Revolution: The Curious Relationship between Economics and the Behavioral Sciences Movement in Mid-Twentieth-Century America." *History of Political Economy* 42 (annual supplement): 199–233.

Porter, T. M. (1986). *The Rise of Statistical Thinking 1820–1900*. Princeton, NJ, Princeton University Press.

Prelec, D. and G. Loewenstein (1997). "Beyond Time Discounting." *Marketing Letters* 8(1): 97–108.

Rabin, M. (1993). "Incorporating Fairness into Game theory and Economics." *American Economic Review* 83(5): 1281–1302.

Rabin, M. (1994). "Cognitive Dissonance and Social Change." *Journal of Economic Behavior and Organization* 23: 177–194.

Rabin, M. (1998). "Psychology and Economics." *Journal of Economic Literature* 36(1): 11–46.

Ramsey, F. (1931). *The Foundations of Mathematics and other Logical Essays*. London, Routledge.

Raphelson, A. C. (1980). "Psychology at Michigan: The Pillsbury Year, 1987–1947." *Journal of the History of the Behavioral Sciences* 16: 301–312.

Rapoport, A. (1989). *The Origins of Violence: Approaches to the Study of Conflict*. New York, Paragan House.

Rapoport, A. and A. Tversky (1970). "Choice Behavior in an Optimal Stopping Task." *Organizational Behavior and Human Performance* 5: 105–120.

Roll, R. (1970). *The Behavior of Interest Rates*. New York, Basic Books.

Roll, R. (1981). "A Possible Explanation of the Small Firm Effect." *The Journal of Finance* 36(4): 879–888.

Roll, R. (1983). "The Turn-of-the-Year Effect and the Return Premia of Small Firms." *Journal of Portfolio Management* 9: 18–28.

Ross, D. (2003). Changing Contours of the Social Science Disciplines. *The Modern Social Sciences.* T. Porter and D. Ross. Cambridge Cambridge University Press: 7: 205–237.

Ross, D. (2008). "Two Styles of Neuroeconomics." *Economics and Philosophy* 24(373–383).

Samuelson, F. (1985). "Organizing for the Kingdom of Behavior: Academic Battles and Organizational Policies in the Twenties." *Journal of the History of the Behavioral Sciences* 21(1): 33–47.

Samuelson, P. A. (1947). *Foundations of Economic Analysis.* Cambridge, MA, Harvard University Press.

Samuelson, P. A. (1950). "Probability and the Attempts to Measure Utility." *The Economic Review* 1: 167–173.

Samuelson, P. A. (1952). *Economics.* London, McGraw-Hill.

Samuelson, P. A. (1966 [1952]). Utility, Preference and Probability (reprint from French). *The Collected Scientific Papers of Paul A. Samuelson.* J. Stiglitz. Cambridge, MIT Press: 127–136.

Samuelson, P. A. and W. D. Nordhaus (1985). *Economics.* New York, McGraw-Hill.

Savage, L. J. (1951). "The Theory of Statistical Decision." *Journal of the American Statistical Association* 46: 55–67.

Savage, L. J. (1954). *The Foundations of Statistics.* New York, John Wiley & Sons.

Schelling, T. C. (1960). *The Strategy of Conflict.* Cambridge, MA, Harvard University Press.

Schelling, T. C. (1969). "Models of Segregation." *American Economic Review* 59(2): 488–493.

Schultz, H. (1928). "Rational Economics." *The American Economic Review* 18(4): 643–648.

Schultz, H. (1928). *Statistical Laws of Demand and Supply with Special Application to Sugar.* Chicago, University of Chicago Press.

Schultz, H. (1938). *The Theory and Measurement of Demand.* Chicago, University of Chicago Press.

Sears, R. R. (1973). "Donald George Marquis: 1908–1973." *American Journal of Psychology* 86: 661–663.

Sedlmeier, P. and G. Gigerenzer (1997). "Intuitions about Sample Size: The Empirical Law of Large Numbers." *Journal of Behavioral Decision Making* 10: 33–51.

Sedlmeier, P. and G. Gigerenzer (2000). "Was Bernoulli Wrong? On Intuitions about Sample Size." *Journal of Behavioral Decision Making* 13: 133–139.

Selcer, P. (2009). "The View From Everywhere: Disciplining Diversity in Post-World War II International Social Science." *Journal of the History of the Behavioral Sciences* 45(4): 309–329.

Senn, P. R. (1966). "'What Is "Behavioral Science?' – Notes toward a History." *Journal of the History of the Behavioral Sciences* 2(2): 107–122.

Sent, E.-M. (1998). *The Evolving Rationality of Rational Expectations.* Cambridge, Cambridge University Press.

Sent, E.-M. (2001). "Sent Simulating Simon Simulating Scientists." *Studies in History and Philosophy of Science* 32(3): 479–500.

Sent, E.-M. (2004). "Behavioral Economics: How Psychology Made its (Limited) Way Back into Economics." *History of Political Economy* 36(4): 735–760.

Sent, E.-M. (2005). "Simplifying Herbert Simon." *History of Political Economy* 37(2): 227–232.

Shackle, G. L. S. (1949). *Expectations in Economics*. New York, Wiley.

Shackle, G. L. S. (1961). *Decision, Order and Time in Human Affairs*. Cambridge, Cambridge University Press.

Shefrin, H. M. and R. Thaler (1988). "The Behavioral Life-Cycle Hypothesis." *Economic Inquiry* 26(609–641).

Shiller, R. J. (1979). "The Volatility of Long-Term Interest Rates and Expectations Models of the Term Structure." *Journal of Political Economy* 87: 1190–1219.

Shiller, R. J. (1981). "Do Stock Prices Move too Much to be Justified by Subsequent Changes in Dividends?" *American Economic Review* 71(3): 421–436.

Shiller, R. J. (1989). *Market Volatility*. Cambridge, The MIT Press.

Shiller, R. J. (2000). *Irrational Exuberance*. Princeton, NJ, Princeton University Press.

Shleifer, A. (2000). *Inefficient Markets, an Introduction to Behavioral Finance*. Oxford, Oxford University Press.

Simon, H. A. (1955). "A Behavioral Model of Rational Choice." *Quarterly Journal of Economics* 69(1): 99–118.

Simon, H. A. (1957). *Models of Man, Social and Rational – Mathematical Essays on Rational Human Behavior in a Social Setting*. New York, John Wiley & Sons.

Simon, H. A. (1959). "Theories of Decision-Making in Economics and Behavioral Sciences." *American Economic Review* 49(1): 253–283.

Simon, H. A. (1962). "New Developments in the Theory of the Firm." *American Economic Review* 52(3): 1–15.

Simon, H. A. (1963). Economics and Psychology *Psychology: A Study of a Science*. S. Koch. New York, McGraw-Hill.

Simon, H. A. (1978). "Rationality as Process and as Product of Thought." *The American Economic Review* 68(2, Papers and Proceedings of the Ninetieth Annual Meeting of the American Economic Association): 1–16.

Simon, H. A. (1986). "Interview: The Failure of Armchair Economics." *Challenger* November–December: 18–25.

Simon, H. A. (1987). Behavioural Economics. *The New Palgrave Dictionary of Economics*. J. Eatwell, M. Milgate, and O. Newman. London, Macmillan: 221–224.

Skidelsky, R. (2003). *John Maynard Keynes, 1883–1946: Economist, Philosopher, Statesman*. London, Macmillan.

Slovic, P. and S. Lichtenstein (1971). "Reversal of Preferences Between Bids and Choices in Gambling Decisions." *Journal of Experimental Psychology* 89: 46–55.

Slovic, P. and S. Lichtenstein (1973). "Response-Induced Reversals of Preferences in Gambling: An Extended Replication in Las Vegas." *Journal of Experimental Psychology* 101: 16–20.

Slovic, P. and S. Lichtenstein (1983). "Preference reversals: A broader perspective." *American Economic Review* 73(4): 596–605.

Slovic, P. and A. Tversky (1974). "Who Accepts Savage's Axiom?" *Behavioral Science* 19(6): 368–373.

Smith, V. L. (1959). "The Theory of Investment and Production." *The Quarterly Journal of Economics* 73(1): 61–87.

Smith, V. L. (1960). "Problems in Production-Investment Planning over Time." *International Economic Review* 1(3): 198–216.

Smith, V. L. (1962). "An Experimental Study of Competitive Market Behavior." *The Journal of Political Economy* 70(2): 111–137.

Smith, V. L. (1965). "Experimental Auction Markets and the Walrasian Hypothesis." *The Journal of Political Economy* 73(4): 387–393.

Smith, V. L. (1967). "Experimental Studies of Discrimination Versus Competition in Sealed-Bid Auction Markets." *The Journal of Business* 40(1): 56–84.

Smith, V. L. (1968). "Economics of Production from Natural Resources." *The American Economic Review* 58(3): 409–431.

Smith, V. L. (1969). "Measuring Nonmonetary Utilities in Uncertain Choices: The Ellsberg Urn." *The Quarterly Journal of Economics* 83(2): 324–329.

Smith, V. L. (1974). "Economic Theory and Its Discontents." *The American Economic Review* 64(2): 320–322.

Smith, V. L. (1982). "Markets as Economizers of Information: Experimental Examination of the 'Hayek Hypothesis.'" *Economic Inquiry* 2: 165–179.

Smith, V. L. (1989). "Theory, Experiment and Economics." *The Journal of Economic Perspectives* 3(1): 151–169.

Smith, V. L. (1994). "Economics in the Laboratory." *Journal of Economic Perspectives* 8(1): 113–131.

Smith, V. L. (2008). *Rationality in Economics, Constructivist and Ecological Forms.* Cambridge, Cambridge University Press.

Stapleford, T. A. (2011). Positive Economics for Democratic Policy: Friedman, Institutionalism, and the Science of History. *Building Chicago Economics: New Perspectives on the History of America's Most Powerful Economics Program.* R. van Horn, P. Mirowski and T. A. Stapleford, Cambridge University Press: 3–35.

Stevens, S. S. (1939). "Psychology and the Science of Science." *Psychological Bulletin* 36(4): 221–263.

Stevens, S. S., Ed. (1951). *Handbook of Experimental Psychology.* New York, John Wiley & Sons.

Stevens, S. S. (1951). Mathematics, Measurement, and Psychophysics. *Handbook of Experimental Psychology.* S. S. Stevens. New York, John Wiley & Sons: 1–50.

Stigler, G. (1988). *Memoirs of an Unregulated Economist.* New York, Basic Books.

Summers, L. H. (1986). "Does the Stock Market Rationally Reflect Fundamental Values?" *The Journal of Finance* 41(3): 591–601.

Suppes, P., et al. (1989). *Foundations of Measurement 2. Geometrical, treshold and probabilistic representations.* San Diego, Academic Press.

Teira, D. (2006). "On the Normative Dimension of the St. Petersburg Paradox." *Studies in History and Philosophy of Science* 37: 210–223.

Thaler, R. (1985). "Mental Accounting and Consumer Choice." *Marketing Science* 4(3): 199–214.

Thaler, R. (1987). The Psychology of Choice and the Assumptions of Economics. *Laboratory Experiments in Economics: Six Points of View.* A. Roth. Cambridge, Cambridge University Press: 99–130.

Thaler, R., Ed. (1992). *The Winners Curse: Paradoxes and Anomalies of Economic Life.* New York, Free Press.

Thaler, R., Ed. (1993). *Advances in Behavioral Finance.* New York, Russell Sage Foundation.

Thaler, R., Ed. (2005). *Advances in Behavioral Finance.* Princeton, NJ, Princeton University Press.

Thaler, R. H. (1980). "Toward a Positive Theory of Consumer Choice." *Journal of Economic Behavior and Organization* 1: 39–60.

Thaler, R. H. (1991). *Quasi Rational Economics.* New York, Russell Sage Foundation.

Thaler, R. H. (2000). "From Homo Economicus to Homo Sapiens." *Journal of Economic Perspectives* 14(1): 133–141.

Thaler, R. H. and S. Benartzi (2004). "Save More Tomorrow: Using Behavioral Economics to Increase Employee Saving." *Journal of Political Economy* 112: S164–187.

Thaler, R. H. and C. R. Sunstein (2003). "Libertarian Paternalism." *The American Economic Review* 93(2): 175–179.

Thaler, R. H. and C. R. Sunstein (2008). *Nudge, Improving Decisions About Health, Wealth, and Happiness.* New Haven, CT, Yale University Press.

Thomas, W. (2007). "The Heuristics of War: Scientific Method and the Founders of Operations Research." *British Journal for the History of Science* 40(2): 251–274.

Thurstone, L. L. (1927a). "Psychophysical Analysis." *American Journal of Psychology* 38: 368–389.

Thurstone, L. L. (1927b). "A Law of Comparative Judgment." *Psychological Review* 34: 273–286.

Thurstone, L. L. (1927c). "A Mental Unit of Measurement." *Psychological Review* 34: 415–423.

Thurstone, L. L. (1931). "The Indifference Function." *Journal of Social Psychology* 2(2): 139–167.

Thurstone, L. L. (1947). *Multiple-factor Analysis: A Development and Expansion of the Vectors of Mind.* Chicago, University of Chicago Press.

Thurstone, L. L. (1959). *The Measurement of Values.* Chicago, University of Chicago.

Thurstone, L. L. and E. J. Chave (1929). *The Measurement of Attitude, a Psychophysical Method and Some Experiments with a Scale for Measuring Attitude toward the Church.* Chicago, The University of Chicago Press.

Thurstone, L. L. and L. V. Jones (1957). "The Rational Origin for Measuring Subjective Values." *Journal of the American Statistical Association* 52: 458–471.

Todd, P. M., et al. (2011). *Ecological Rationality: Intelligence in the World.* New York, Oxford University Press.

Tversky, A. (1967a). "Additivity, Utility and Subjective Probability." *Journal of Mathematical Psychology* 4: 175–202.

Tversky, A. (1967b). "A General Theory of Polynomial Conjoint Measurement." *Journal of Mathematical Psychology* 4: 1–20.

Tversky, A. (1967c). "Utility Theory and Additivity Analysis of Risky Choices." *Journal of Experimental Psychology* 75(1): 27–36.

Tversky, A. (1969). "The Intransitivity of Preferences." *Psychological Review* 76: 31–48.

Tversky, A. (1971). *Elimination by Aspects: A Probabilistic Theory of Choice.* Ann Arbor, Michigan, University of Michigan. Department of psychology.

Tversky, A. (1972). "Elimination by Aspects: A Theory of Choice." *Psychological Review* 79: 218–299.

Tversky, A. (1991). Introduction. *Frontiers of Mathematical Psychology, Essays in Honor of Clyde Coombs*. D. R. Brown and J. E. K. Smith. New York, Springer-Verlag: xiii–xxvi.

Tverksy, A. and W. Edwards (1966). "Information versus reward in binary choices." *Journal of Experimental Psychology* 71(5): 680–683.

Tversky, A. and D. Kahneman (1971). "Belief in the Law of Small Numbers." *Psychological Bulletin* 76: 105–110.

Tversky, A. and D. Kahneman (1974). "Judgment under Uncertainty: Heuristics and Biases." *Science* 185: 1124–1131.

Tversky, T. and D. Kahneman (1981). "The Framing of Decisions and the Psychology of Choice." *Science* 211: 453–458.

Tversky, A. and D. Kahneman (1992). "Advances in Prospect Theory: Cumulative Representation of Uncertainty." *Journal of Risk and Uncertainty* 5: 297–323.

Tversky, A. and D. H. Krantz (1970). "The Dimensional Representation and the Metric Structure of Similarity Data." *Journal of Mathematical Psychology* 7: 572–596.

van Winden, F. (2007). "Affect and Fairness in Economics." *Social Justice Research* 20(1): 32–52.

von Neumann, J. (1988). The Mathematician. *The World of Mathematics: A Small Library of the Literature of Mathematics from A'h-mosé the Scribe to Albert Einstein*. J. R. Newman. New York, Simon and Schluster: 2029–2039.

von Neumann, J. and O. Morgenstern (2004 [1944]). *Theory of Games and Economic Behavior*. Princeton, NJ, Princeton University Press.

von Plato, J. (1994). *Creating Modern Probability*. Cambridge, Cambridge University Press.

Vromen, J. (2007). "Neuroeconomics as a Natural Extension of Bioeconomics: The Shifting Scope of Standard Economic Theory." *Journal of Bioeconomics* 9(145–167).

Wald, A. (1950). *Statistical Decision Functions*. New York, Wiley.

Wallis, W. A. and M. Friedman (1942). The Empirical Derivation of Indifference Functions. *Studies in Mathematical Economics and Econometrics, In Memory of Henry Schultz*. O. Lange, F. McIntyre, and T. O. Yntema. New York, Books for Libraries Press: 175–189.

Wanner, E. (1973). "Do We Understand Sentences from the Outside-in or from the Inside-out." *Daedalus* 102((3) Language as a Human Problem): 163–183.

Wanner, E., et al. (1975). *Garden Paths in Relative Clauses*. S.L., S.N.

Wanner, E. and S. Shiner (1976). "Measuring Transient Memory Load." *Journal of Verbal Learning and Verbal Behavior* 15: 159–167.

Weaver, W. (1967). *U.S. Philanthropic Foundations: Their History, Structure, Management, and Record*. New York, Harper & Row.

Weintraub, E. R. (1991). *Stabilizing Dynamics, Constructing Economic Knowledge*. Cambridge, Cambridge University Press.

Weintraub, E. R., Ed. (1992). *Toward a History of Game Theory*. London, Duke University Press.

Weintraub, E. R. and P. Mirowski (1994). "The Pure and the Applied: Bourbakism Comes to Mathematical Economics." *Science in Context* 7(2): 245–272.

Wong, S. (1978). *The Foundations of Paul Samuelson's Revealed Preferences Theory, a Study by the Method of Rational Reconstruction*. London, Routledge.

Wright, P. and D. Kahneman (1971). "Evidence for Alternative Strategies of Sentence Retention." *Quarterly Journal of Experimental Psychology* 23: 197–213.

Yerkes, R. M. (1941). "Psychology and Defense." *Proceedings of the American Philosophical Society* 84: 527–542.

Zappia, C. (2008). "Non-Bayesian Decision Theory Ante Litteram: The Case of G.L.S. Shackle." Depeid Working Papers 4/2008.

Index

Other Books in the Series (continued from page iii)

Harro Maas, *William Stanley Jevons and the Making of Modern Economics*

Philip Mirowski, *More Heat Than Light: Economics as Social Physics, Physics as Nature's Economics*

Philip Mirowski (ed.), *Nature Images in Economic Thought: "Markets Read in Tooth and Claw"*

Donald Moggridge, *Harry Johnson: A Life in Economics*

Mary S. Morgan, *The History of Econometric Ideas*

Takashi Negishi, *Economic Theories in a Non-Walrasian Tradition*

Heath Pearson, *Origins of Law and Economics: The Economists' New Science of Law, 1830–1930*

Malcolm Rutherford, *The Institutionalist Movement in American Economics, 1918–1947: Science and Social Control*

Malcolm Rutherford, *Institutions in Economics: The Old and the New Institutionalism*

Esther-Mirjam Sent, *The Evolving Rationality of Rational Expectations: An Assessment of Thomas Sargent's Achievements*

Yuichi Shionoya, *Schumpeter and the Idea of Social Science*

Juan Gabriel Valdes, *Pinochet's Economists: The Chicago School of Economics in Chile*

Robert Van Horn, Philip Mirowski, and Thomas A. Stapleford (eds.), *Building Chicago Economics*

Karen I. Vaughn, *Austrian Economics in America: The Migration of a Tradition*

E. Roy Weintraub, *Stabilizing Dynamics: Constructing Economic Knowledge*